MIND WARRIOR

S0-AKK-206

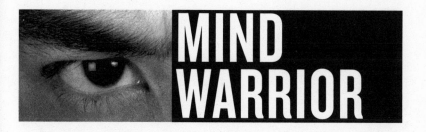

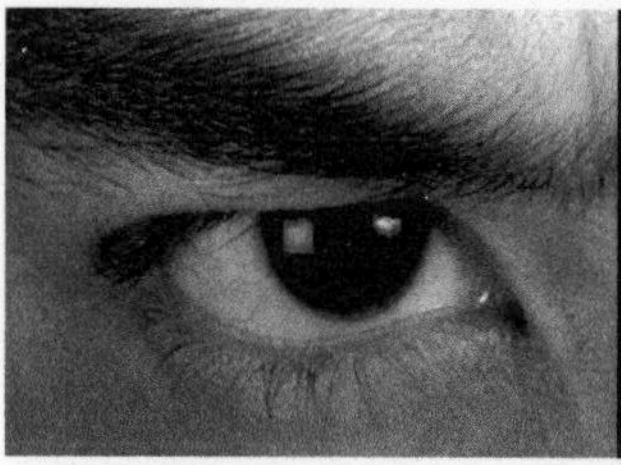

MIND WARRIOR

Strategies for Total Mind Domination

DR. HAHA LUNG

with Christopher B. Prowant

CITADEL PRESS
Kensington Publishing Corp.
www.kensingtonbooks.com

CITADEL PRESS BOOKS are published by

Kensington Publishing Corp.
119 West 40th Street
New York, NY 10018

Copyright © 2010 Haha Lung

All rights reserved. No part of this book may be reproduced in any form or by any means without the prior written consent of the publisher, excepting brief quotes used in reviews.

All Kensington titles, imprints, and distributed lines are available at special quantity discounts for bulk purchases for sales promotions, premiums, fund-raising, educational, or institutional use. Special book excerpts or customized printings can also be created to fit specific needs. For details, write or phone the office of the Kensington special sales manager: Kensington Publishing Corp., 119 West 40th Street, New York, NY 10018, attn: Special Sales Department; phone 1-800-221-2647.

CITADEL PRESS and the Citadel logo are Reg. U.S. Pat. & TM Off.

First printing: October 2010

10 9 8 7 6 5 4 3 2 1

Printed in the United States of America

Library of Congress Control Number: 2010925002

ISBN-13: 978-0-8065-3200-4
ISBN-10: 0-8065-3200-9

Shihan Peter Gilbert, Sensei Lenox Cramer,

Eddie Harris, Eric Tucker, and the warriors of the Zendokan.

Black science: Generic: any strategy, tactic, or technique used to undermine a person's ability to reason and respond for themselves. Synonym for mind control and manipulation. Term originally coined by C. B. Black.

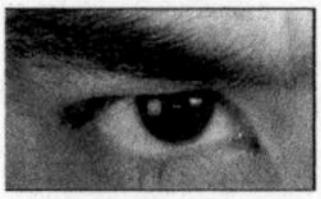

CONTENTS

DISCLAIMER

The information contained herein is meant for historical and informational purposes only. Kids, don't try this at home!

Heaven forbid you should ever find yourself in such dire, needful straits—or in just a really, really pissed-off mood!—that you should feel tempted or otherwise justified in using the information contained herein for ruthless personal gain and/or personal vengeance against your enemies. Heaven *forbid* . . .

And then Heaven *help* your enemies!

MIND WARRIOR

Part I

GETTING YOUR OWN ACT TOGETHER

INTRODUCTION:

"Winning on the *Only* Battlefield"

You must do your damndest and win. Remember that is what you live for. Oh you must! You have got to do something! Never stop until you have gained the top or the grave.

—General George S. Patton

SOMEONE ONCE SAID of Mark Twain . . . or was it a comment on Oscar Wilde . . . "That man is more dangerous with a typewriter than Wyatt Earp ever was with a gun!" Certainly the pen can be mightier than the sword, especially when Twain and Wilde and others like them knew so well how to wield barb of the tongue and rapier of wit as adroitly—and as telling—as does an accomplished warrior his blade.

Indeed, there is little doubt these writers, these ruthless wielders of the pen, knew the secret, the same secret known by commanders of the sword, from Sun Tzu, Alexander, Hannibal, Caesar through Napoleon, Grant, Sherman, and Lee and down to Rommel and Patton.

"All battles are first fought in the mind."

It matters not whether you're being attacked by a mugger or by another nation, faced with such crisis, the mind reacts or fails to react and we, correspondingly, rise and roar to the occasion or fall flaccid in the dust. So empires rise, so they fall. As with empires, so with individuals. So it behooves us to study such things.

And should we choose the prudent course, to *study to survive*, what should we, what will we, learn about our enemy—and about ourselves?

First, we will seek to discover our enemy's weakness. Ah, but by doing so, we may discover our own glitches and gaps in our synapse. We'll diligently dig to uncover the secrets he thinks are safely buried. And in the process perhaps learn to better—deeper!—bury our own dark secrets.

Ultimately, any such quest of this sort means we must dare to face "The Beast," that beats within us all—the beast licking its lips in anticipation, screaming "Fight!" or else, wisely, bidding us to "Flight!" to live to "Fight!" another day. This Beast denied, that beats within the breast of all of us.

And so we must study others who have quested and, ultimately, bested the Beast, some good, some bad, some *enfant terrible* indeed—but *Mind Slayers* all! Those hardy few who came before who have dared uncover and then diligently master topics, tactics, and techniques both fraught with danger and heretofore forbidden.

And in the end—provided, of course, we *survive* to that end!—what can we expect as our ultimate prize of learning, of having studied to survive? What will we have learned?

We will have learned as all brave and bold men and women—*Mind Slayers* all!—who have treaded this path before us learned:

> *"We needn't resort to the knife when reason will suffice."*

We needn't swing the bludgeon when bargaining is still on the table. We needn't beat our plowshares into swords[1] so long as we can browbeat or otherwise befuddle our enemy into believing our way is the best way—the only way.

Thus, we needn't bloodily and bodily slay a foe when we can startle, stifle, and, when need be, snuff out any flame of resistance to our will.

---

1. "Beat your plowshares into swords." Book of Joel, 3:10. Compare with Isaiah, 2:4.

We needn't slay our enemy on the field of physical battle when we can defeat him—slay him!—where he is most vulnerable—*his mind!*

No man can harm you near as much as your own thoughts unguarded.
—The Buddha

I.

The Beast Within (Who Doesn't Like to Do Without!)

HOW MANY TIMES growing up were you told to "Stop acting like an animal"? That's hardly fair since, unlike so many humans, animals all seem to have admirable qualities:

- Wolves mate for life.
- Elephants create memorials out of the bones of their dead.
- Dog is man's best friend—since loyalty is the first and final measure of a friend.
- Even from the octopus we can learn to be more pliable and versatile. Indeed, our eight-armed cousin can easily wiggle his way into the tiniest of crevices in pursuit of prey, and hide inside empty clamshells, leaving one of his tentacles wiggling like a worm outside the shell to lure in unsuspecting fish. When threatened, he emits a cloud of dark ink that not only acts like a jet to propel it away from a predator, but also hides the octopus's escape route and/or blinds any enemy close enough to get "inked." And, speaking of camouflage, special skin cells allow the octopus to change color, chameleon-like, helping him blend in with his background and to hide unnoticed on the sea floor.

Of course, we can also learn from animals' short-comings. For example, drop a bumblebee into an open water glass and instead of simply escaping out the top, the bee will buzz around inside the glass, literally bouncing off the walls, until it dies. There's a lesson in there for us—maybe that we should practice thinking outside the box—or glass, as the case may be. And don't forget that aerodynamically it's impossible for the bumblebee to fly—although, evidently someone forgot to tell the bumblebee.

Perhaps it's just Western culture that finds little to admire in our lesser—or should we say differently—evolved finny, furry, and feathered brethren? In Asia, Eastern astrology assigns each newborn a birth sign "beast," thought to control a person's attitudes and influence their activities. These beasts are: rat, ox, tiger, rabbit, dragon, snake, horse, sheep, monkey, cock, dog, and pig.[2]

Still in Asia, for the indigenous Caucasian Ainu of Japan, the bear is a sacred totem. Across the Pacific, Native Americans often embraced personal protective animal guardians called "totems." Often such totems watched over the whole tribe.

Curiously, during our development in the womb, we pass through every stage of animal—from fins to fur to, literally, upstanding citizen—as we grow from gamete to zygote to fetus, almost as if Mother Nature is reminding us—literally—where we come from. Would it so pain us then to be as loyal as the dog? As adaptable as the chameleon and the octopus? As faithful to our mate as the wolf? As filial and fane to our brethren as the elephant?

In his *Discourses*, Machiavelli (1469–1527) advises the aspiring Prince that he must cultivate the fierceness of the lion while tempering it with the cunning of the fox.

Conversely, in Japan the fox is considered an ill omen—analogous to a black cat crossing your path. Still, for good or ill, the cunning of the fox is renowned, at least in myth and metaphor. The following story is told to novice martial arts students desirous of constantly learning new techniques, mistaking quantity for quality:

---

2. For a complete study course on using Junishi-do-jutsu astrology to better your life (and unbetter your enemy's life!) see *Black Science* (Paladin, 2001), *Mind Manipulation* (Citadel, 2002), *Mental Domination* (Citadel, 2009), and *Mind Assassins!* (Citadel, 2010) by Dr. Haha Lung and Christopher Prowant.

Fox and Cat meet in a clearing. Fox asks Cat what kind of self-defense moves she knows.

Cat shrugs. "I have only one trick. When confronted by danger, I quickly climb a tree."

Fox laughs. "I, on the other paw, have studied hundreds of techniques, both my own species and those of other animals. I have hundreds of techniques to choose from!"

Just then the two are attacked by a pack of ravenous wolves! Using the single trick she has mastered, Cat instantly scurries up a nearby tree, out of reach of the pack. Uncertain which of his hundreds of techniques to use, unable to decide which would serve him best, the fox ends up being served for dinner.

If there's a moral in all this, it's that we should *listen* to the advice of our "animal" brain all the time . . . but not necessarily *follow* the advice of our animal brain all the time.

OUR "ANIMAL" BRAIN

Every human being is a problem in search of a solution.
—Ashley Montagu

You can't trust your brain. It lies to you constantly. Your brain lies to you because situated literally smack dab in the middle of your head is your midbrain's *limbic system*. It's here that most of our emotional processing takes place. Author Vance Packard wryly observed that this limbic system controls what he called "The 4 F's":

- Fighting
- Feeding
- Fleeing
- *and Sex*[3]

This limbic system is the older, earlier part of your brain, having evolved earlier than the physically and philosophically "higher" areas of the brain—the

3. *The People Shapers* by Vance Packard (Little Brown, 1977).

cerebrum and the cerebellum. Our midbrain is thus both literally and figuratively "closer" to the body, as it is connected to the spinal cord by way of the medulla oblongata—the mass of nerve tissue at the base of the brain that controls bodily functions such as blood circulation and breathing.

The limbic system is our "$E = Mc^2$" area of the brain where "energy" (thoughts, feelings) is transformed into physical action and symptoms—making us blush when embarrassed, cry when we're sad, and shake, sweat, and feel butterflies in the stomach when we're scared.[4]

With good cause, this midbrain has been referred to as our "reptile brain," since the limbic system is where most of our—more basic, that is, *primitive*—emotional processing takes place. This is where Freud's "I want it all and I want it now!" *id* lives—the seat of all our instinctual—socially inconvenient—drives and desires.

Truth be known, our "gut"—as in "gut feeling"—isn't in our gut; it's in our midbrain. So the next time you get a gut feeling . . . *listen to it!* It may be your older, wiser limbic system "animal" trying to warn you of danger.

Our limbic system is composed of five major structures in the brain: the basal ganglia, hippocampus, hypothalamus, thalamus, and amygdala (see Figure 1).

- ***The basal ganglia*** controls well-learned activities, like walking. (Not specifically connected to the subject at hand but fascinating none the less: the basal ganglia contains the pigment *melanin*—responsible for skin color, eye color, and hair color. Melanin is the end product of the brain pleasure chemical dopamine, after it has gone through several chemical reactions.
- ***The hippocampus***[5] helps us learn and remember, storing sensory information.
- ***The hypothalamus*** regulates body systems, aggression, rage, pleasure, and pain.
- ***The thalamus*** acts as "gatekeeper," sorting, sifting through, and censoring messages coming from the senses and heading to the cerebrum—the "higher" part of the brain that controls thinking and

4. Right, your "fight or flight" response.
5. *Not* a small college in Africa.

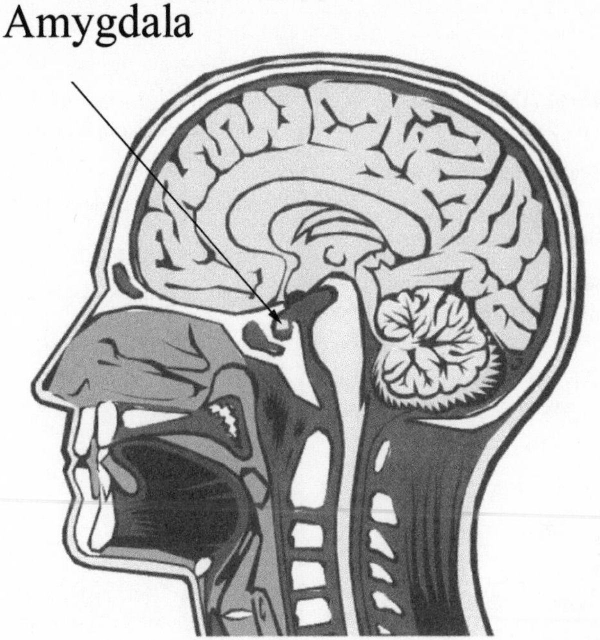

Figure 1.

complex tasks. Think of this as "parental control-blocking" for your brain instead of your TV.

By the way, the cerebrum is divided into two hemispheres (see Figure 2):

The left side is our "inner politician," responsible for language, logic, and sequential thought.

The right side is our "inner artist" controlling visual and spatial abilities, and overseeing our creativity and emotions. This right side is more "abstract," while the left side is more "concrete" and takes things literally. People dominated by the left side are therefore concrete thinkers—practical, no-nonsense, on-time types of people. Right side "abstract thinkers," on the other hand, deal with life on a more ephemeral basis, are less time constrained, but are also less predictable.

In order to better craft their approach strategy, adept Mind Slayers know to listen to the types of sentence phrasing people use—reflecting either right

TRAITS

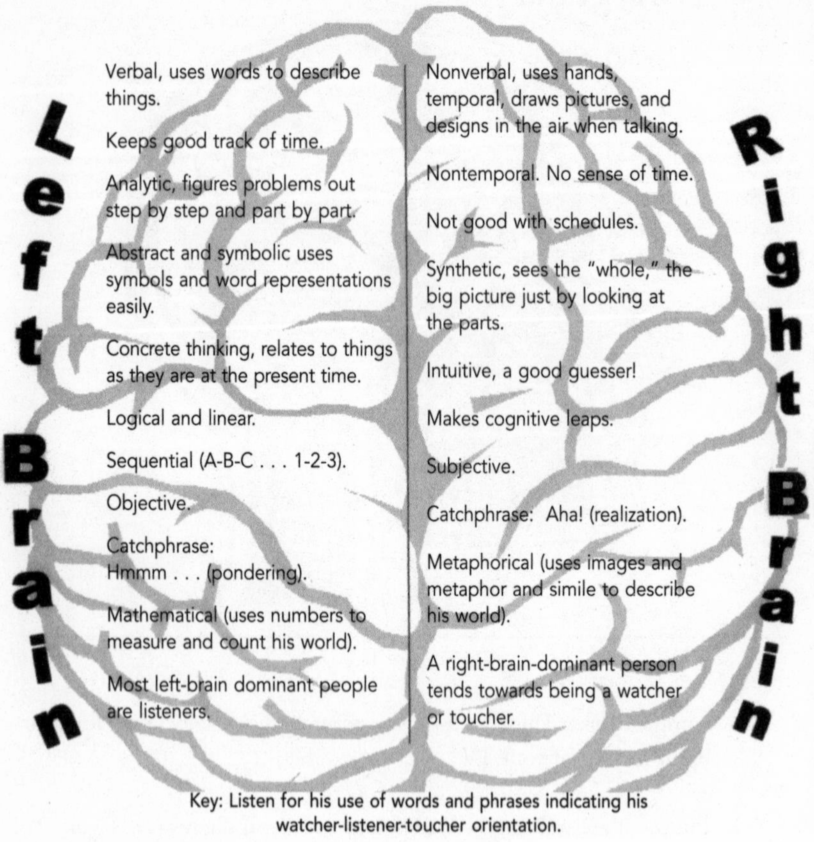

Left Brain
Verbal, uses words to describe things.
Keeps good track of time.
Analytic, figures problems out step by step and part by part.
Abstract and symbolic uses symbols and word representations easily.
Concrete thinking, relates to things as they are at the present time.
Logical and linear.
Sequential (A-B-C . . . 1-2-3).
Objective.
Catchphrase: Hmmm . . . (pondering).
Mathematical (uses numbers to measure and count his world).
Most left-brain dominant people are listeners.
Right Brain
Nonverbal, uses hands, temporal, draws pictures, and designs in the air when talking.
Nontemporal. No sense of time.
Not good with schedules.
Synthetic, sees the "whole," the big picture just by looking at the parts.
Intuitive, a good guesser!
Makes cognitive leaps.
Subjective.
Catchphrase: Aha! (realization).
Metaphorical (uses images and metaphor and simile to describe his world).
A right-brain-dominant person tends towards being a watcher or toucher.
Key: Listen for his use of words and phrases indicating his watcher-listener-toucher orientation.

Figure 2.

brain "abstracts" or left brain literal words and sentences—to determine whether a person is right side–dominant, or left side–dominant, and to craft our strategy.

But most of this is moot since so much of our senses intake gets filtered out or otherwise distorted (think rose-colored glasses) by the thalamus long before it ever makes it to the cerebrum.

- ***The amygdala***, Latin for "almond" (after its shape and size), is actually *two* amygdala, one in each hemisphere. These regulate mood and control emotion and are especially adept at registering and reacting to the emotion of fear.[6]

The amygdala is the "alarm center" of the brain, triggering our flight-or-fight reaction. In times of great stress, the amygdala floods the brain with two powerful stress hormones: adrenaline and noradrenaline. The amygdala's job is simply vigilance. It watches out for anything it *thinks* might be a danger and then acts on that perception of danger lickety-split. The only thing wrong with this is that, despite being situated in the middle of the brain, the amygdala isn't that great a "thinker" and often goes off "half-cocked."

According to author and researcher Mario Bunge, using modern brain-imaging techniques (PET and MRI), it is now possible to tell whether someone "feels" something or "knows" something even though he or she doesn't know that he feels or know it. For example, using a PET scanner, researchers can now detect a subject's emotions and even locate them on either side of the amygdala.[7] But, as previously alluded to, just because a sensation is passed from the senses to the amygdala doesn't automatically mean that information is going to be passed along to the higher, conscious level of the brain.

By examining brain scans, scientists have proven that the amygdala can be triggered by any stimulus that is initially perceived as "threatening"—for example, the image of an angry face or a loud noise. However, in many instances, our higher brain remains blissfully unaware that something has triggered a response in the more primitive parts of the brain, affecting us on a *subliminal* level.

> In short, the amygdala "knows" something that the organ of consciousness (whichever and whatever it is) does not.
>
> —Mario Bunge

---

6. See "The Seven Basic Emotions" and "The Five Warning F.L.A.G.S." sections that follow (pp. 13–15).

7. "The Philosophy Behind Pseudoscience" by Mario Bunge. *Skeptical Inquirer*, July/August 2006: 29–37. See also "Consciousness and Unconscious Emotional Learning in Human Amygdala," *Nature*, 1998.

The validity of this sort of "subliminal suggestion" has been further proven by experiments conducted at the University of California, San Diego, where researchers increased subjects' thirst by secretly flashing them *happy* faces, which the subjects were consciously unaware of.[8] After being exposed to the subliminal pictures, volunteer subjects were willing to pay triple the price for the drink than another group that had secretly been shown *grimacing* faces. Since thirst is controlled by the midbrain, here is further proof that human beings can be affected by *subliminal suggestion* (or one might say "amygdala suggestion") provided the incoming message is (1) emotionally charged and/or (2) aimed to stimulate the person's most basic needs—thirst, hunger . . . sex? And fear.

During one of those notorious 1950s subliminal suggestion experiments that were carried out on moviegoers without their knowledge, the word "blood" was inserted between flashing frames of a horror movie. Result? Exiting patrons—those who stayed through the whole movie—reported the movie to be one of the "scariest" movies they'd ever seen (even though the actual movie was no more graphic and blood-splattered than other horror movies of the time). Though their higher brain kept telling itself, "It's only a movie! It's only a movie!" their amygdala kept seeing—and processing—the threatening word "blood" over and over again.

Time and again, research has shown that subliminal suggestions work best when they carry (1) simple and (2) emotionally charged messages. For example, rather than repeatedly flash "Drink Zap Cola"—since our amygdala *is* still a stupid reptile that can't spell "Zap Cola," it would be more effective—subliminal suggestion-wise—to instead send the simple message "thirsty" and/or "dry"—simplistic, emotional concepts our dumbass amygdala can grasp.[9]

Inserting subliminal messages into movies is portrayed in Brad Pitt's *Fight Club* (1999), where, at the end of the movie, if you watch real close, they allow you to "catch" them inserting their "playful" subliminal suggestion.

Still on the subject of the amygdala, the news isn't all bad. While, true, the amygdala embarrasses us just as many times as it saves us ("Snake! Oh, sorry, just another garden hose."), the amygdala is also where such helpful things as hypnosis and meditation take place.

8. "About Face" by Charles Q. Choi. *Scientific American*, August 2006:26.

9. It also helps if the theater sells only Zap-brand cola!

So, whereas the amygdala "stresses" us out ("flight or fight") on the one hand, it can just as easily help us relax, on the other. We learn to do this by learning self-hypnosis and meditation.

Recall that the amygdala responds (sans thought) to sensory information. Therefore, in the same way a "garden hose snake" (sensation from the eyes) or a loud explosion (sensation gathered by the ear) can both cause a startle response in the amygdala, so too if you sit back in a quiet place with eyes closed, concentrating on your breathing—without help (meditation) or with someone's guidance (hypnosis)—the sense information then coming into the amygdala:

- Slow, deep breathing, hence . . .
- Slower heart rate, causing . . .
- Release of tension in the muscles, aided by . . .
- No alarming or otherwise distracting sights or sounds will cause the amygdala to relax. And when the amygdala's relaxed, the body and mind are both relaxed.

THE SEVEN BASIC EMOTIONS

The specific part of your midbrain where emotions are processed in a primitive structure is called the "periaqueductal gray." (Okay, let's agree to call it PAG for short.) This PAG is found in all mammals, not just humans, and produces our basic emotional impulses, like grief and love.[10] Yes, your dog and/or cat *do* feel lonely and sad when you're not around.

So far, seven basic emotions have been isolated in the PAG, emotions common to all humans and to other mammals as well. The first four of these are associated with basic survival:

- **Fear:** The most basic of all survival emotions, first of "The Five Warning F.L.A.G.S."[11]
- **Lust-desire:** This is the source of our strong attraction of any sort, including and especially our desire for food, shelter, and sex. Desire can also give way to "greed." Lust and greed, two more of the Five Warning F.L.A.G.S.

---

10. "Animal Passions" by Douglas Starr. *Psychology Today*, March/April, 2006.

11. Fear, lust, anger, greed, sympathy. See next section, the Five Warning F.L.A.G.S.

- **Anger-rage:** Still another of the Five Warning F.L.A.G.S. Anger-rage can galvanize us to fight back tooth and nail.
- **Separation anxiety:** This is our fear of loss.

The remaining three consist of more subtle emotions:

- **Nurturance:** Our desire to be nurtured matures into a need to nurture in return. This causes us to bond and to actively seek bonding with others.
- **Empathy-sympathy:** We identify (empathize) with others' pain, from helpless little animals to fellow human beings, resulting in the desire to offer care. Sympathy, the final of the Five Warning F.L.A.G.S. This emotion sometimes registers as "regret" and "guilt."
- **Achievement-play:** Our urge to compete and complete.[12] This gives us the thrill of winning, of achieving, of outfoxing the other guy. This should remind you of Abraham Maslow's "self-actualization" needs.[13]

While all healthy individuals are capable of expressing any and all of these emotions,[14] for one cause or another—mama, trauma, or drama!—we tend to favor and thus express certain emotions more than others. This is called our "personality."

For example, someone who's chronically pissed-off at the world (your boss or mother-in-law, for instance) is dominated by the emotion *anger.* But perceiving this doesn't necessarily tell you *why* he or she is all pissed-off at the world—that's where $70 an hour shrink bills come in!

So, while recognizing *what* emotion is dominating a person at any given time is pretty easy, the *why* (i.e., "Where the hell is all this Jerry Springer drama coming from?!?") isn't as easy to decipher.

Whereas someone's "personality" might be "Mr. Angry Man," all that anger may really be coming from his fear emotion or from his separation

---

12. Basis of the Gestalt school of psychology. See "Three Types of Shit, Three Types of Insight" in *Ultimate Control* by Dr. Haha Lung and Christopher B. Prowant (Citadel, 2010).

13. See Figure 4, page 39.

14. Research has shown that serial killers (and possibly politicians!) lack the ability to express empathy-sympathy.

anxiety emotion.[15] That's why it behooves us to hone our ability to dig a little deeper, under the façade of overtly expressed emotions—what a person is "saying"—to "hear" what they're not saying—often inadvertently revealed by speech faux pas[16] and body language.[17]

THE FIVE WARNING F.L.A.G.S.

Forewarned is forearmed. And to be "four-armed" is to become The Destroyer of Worlds!
—Duke Falthor Metalstorm[18]

Long ago, Japanese Mind Slayers[19] succeeded in isolating the Gojo-goyoku, literally "The Five Weaknesses": fear, lust, anger, greed, and sympathy. The mnemonic "Warning F.L.A.G.S." is not only a handy way for remembering your enemy's five potentially fatal flaws; in addition, it invokes an image of "storm warning" flags flapping against the wind, warning of the potential of our own dangerous emotional storm (see Figure 3, p. 16).

Though arrived at intuitively by ancient Asian masters, you'll notice how well Gojo-goyoku stacks up alongside the seven basic emotions so far verified by recent scientific studies, like the one just mentioned.

If you've already read *Mind Manipulation* (2002) and *Mind Control* (2006), then you've probably already realized the advantages and mastered the art of factoring the Five Warning F.L.A.G.S. into all your daily dealings—whether dealing from the bottom of the deck or dealing your enemies out a world of woe!

Keep in mind how information and data come into our heads via the senses. Then, what's left after being picked over by our id-dominated mid-brain is passed along to our "higher reasoning" centers where, in theory at

---

15. Yeah, that's why you gotta go to college for beaucoup years to get you one of *them thar* psychology degrees!

16. "Shadow-talk."

17. "Shadow-walk."

18. An obvious play on words invoking the Hindu god of destruction *Shiva*, always depicted as having four arms. Upon watching the first atomic explosion, which he was instrumental in creating, scientist Robert Oppenheimer quoted from the Hindu holy book Bhagavad-gita. "I have become Shiva, destroyer of worlds!"

19. With a little help from the Chinese *wu-hsing* Five Elements theory.

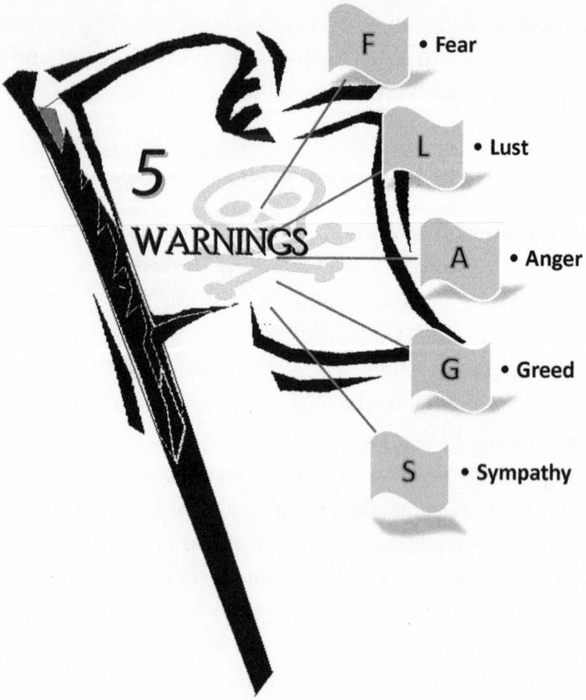

Figure 3.

least, they will be further processed, filtered, censored, minimized, or magnified. Thus, between our amygdala shooting first and asking questions later, and our "higher reasoning" abilities *overthinking* an experience to death, what we ultimately end up with—thoughtwise and realitywise!—often bears little or no resemblance to what we actually saw or heard that first engaged our senses.

We'd all like to think that, despite the best efforts of the reptilian midbrain, the fact that incoming sensory information eventually finds its way to the "higher reasoning" areas of the brain would somehow ensure we'd at least have a fighting chance of coming up with rational decisions and reasonable responses.

What you have to remember is that our "higher reasoning" centers can make their final decisions based on the *best available information* they have on hand—information that has already been chewed over, spit out, and, in all likelihood, pissed on by our high-strung, emotionally distraught reptile of a midbrain.

Big surprise then:

> The brain's wiring emphatically relies on emotion over intellect in decision making. —Dan Vergano[20]

Time and again, studies have found that none of us can ever be completely free from our emotional biases. As a result, we now see the merging of advertising and economics with neuroscience to create a whole new field of psychology dubbed "neuroeconomics," the study of how the brain makes buying and selling decisions and how irrational, emotional biases influence consumer decision making as much as, if not more so than, facts and rational thought.

Once we realize—*admit* to ourselves—how completely our emotions—particularly these Gojo-goyoku five "weaknesses"—tint and taint the decisions we make, we can (1) discipline ourselves, better guarding ourselves against making impulsive decisions, and (2) encouraging our enemy to do quite the opposite!

How to Master Fear

What worries you, masters you.
—John Locke

Did you know you can literally be scared *to death*, this according to cardiologist Dr. Ilan S. Wittstein of the Johns Hopkins University School of Medicine.[21]

But fear isn't necessarily a bad thing and fear isn't always your enemy. Truth be known, we're probably all alive today only because some time in the past fear made us run like hell! According to Hannah Arendt: "Fear is an emotion indispensable for survival."

---

20. "Study: Ask with care/Emotions rule the brain's decisions" by Dan Vergano. *USA Today*, 8.7.06:6D.

21. *Maxim*, July 2009:22. See also *Mind Manipulation* by Dr. Haha Lung and Christopher Prowant (Citadel, 2002).

First off, we need to learn to distinguish between *real* fear, and F.E.A.R.—False Evidence Appearing Real.

F.E.A.R. is when we misperceive a situation, when we go off half-cocked and crazy with fear because of false impressions and faulty information. Such uncalled for behavior is called "awfulizing"—making fearful mountains out of what should be all too manageable molehills. As already alluded to, this happens primarily when incoming information from the five senses is acted upon by the more primitive midbrain *before* our higher reasoning part of the brain has a chance to look the new information over. Of course, to make matters worse, sometimes "filters" (e.g., prejudices, phobias, fetishes) in our higher brain also distort incoming information—by (falsely) associating fresh information with our past failures.

We can avoid this kind of distortion by practicing Sun Tzu's ideal of dealing with small problems long before they become big problems. This works when dealing with fear as well. Consider the three types of fears:

- **Physical fears:** Things that can actually harm us physically
- **Mental fears:** Anxieties about not measuring up, about what others think about us, etc.
- **Spiritual fears:** Usually just called "superstitions"

In turn, there are varying—deepening—degrees of fear:

Vague dis-*ease:* Based on an immediately perceived—real or imagined—threat.

Anxiety: Fancy name for chronic worry. Fear that comes to visit for a reason (real event/threat) and decides to stay for no reason (fear that event/threat will reappear).

Dread: Debilitating fear that literally paralyzes you, preventing you from doing something. Phobias qualify for this category.

Now, to simplify our understanding of fear, first realize that all fear falls into two categories: external fear and internal fear.

External fear: Understandable fear arising from actual threats to life and limb and livelihood, to ourselves, and also to our loved ones.

These "outside fears" generally have more actual meat to them. In other words, there's some things you *should* run away from . . . and *you will!* When your survival-oriented midbrain perceives a threat—real or imagined—and sends an instant message directly to your muscles—"Feet don't fail me now!"—like the time *without "thinking" about* (i.e., without our higher brain having a chance to think about it because our midbrain was already reacting!) we jumped back from that "snake!" laying on the ground in front of us, only to later realize, much to our embarrassment (only our *higher* brain gets embarrassed, by the way) that it was just a piece of harmless garden hose.

Timeline: We see (sense) what we perceive to be a snake (a threat, until proven otherwise). This sensory information goes straight to our midbrain for initial processing. However, since our midbrain "sees" *something* that could be a snake—an immediate threat!—it sends a *priority* signal to the body (i.e., basal ganglia and spinal cord) to "Jump away!" A slightly slower—secondary—signal is sent to the "higher" brain for processing. And it is here (in the higher reasoning part of the brain) that we finally "realize" it's only a piece of garden hose. Our higher brain then sends a signal back to the midbrain to please tell the rest of the body to relax.

Such automatic physical reactions—reactions you have little control over—can be expected to occur anytime you (actually your midbrain) feel threatened. Say you're getting ready to physically fight another person. If you're like most *untrained* fighters, your mouth gets dry, you turn pale, you break out in a sweat (even though your skin feels cool to the touch), your body begins to tremble, and you get that sickly warm feeling in your gut most people refer to as "butterflies in the stomach." The average Joe (or Jane), untrained in combat, often castigates themselves for being "afraid" or even for being "a coward"—never realizing that all these are *natural body reactions* for a person to have when faced with fear.

Faced with a physical threat, knowing we're going to need our arms and legs for running and/or fighting, our midbrain reroutes energy (blood flow) to our extremities, temporarily shutting down superfluous systems like digestion (that explains those butterflies) and paling of the face. As almighty adrenaline[22] floods directly into our bloodstream in preparation for action, we sweat (keeping us from overheating, making our flesh slipperier and harder for an enemy to grasp hold of). And we tremble—not because we are cowards—but as a sign of the excess *power*, power available to us for "flight or fight."

Internal fear: This fear, or "Inside Fears," arises from thoughts and anx-

---

22. Yeah, the stuff that helped that little woman lift the car off her trapped kid . . . the stuff that turns the Hulk green.

ieties usually lacking any actual external threat. Inside fears are more subtle, more concerned with fighting the "ghosts" and "demons" in your head than any actual fire-breathing dragons or Darth Vaders stalking you in the physical world. These fears range from nagging feelings of self-doubt to obsessive-compulsive disorder (OCD) rituals.

For example, OCD isn't the *problem*, per se, it's the *solution*—or rather, *a* solution, a "superstitious" counter designed to deal with the fear the sufferer has that, unless they perform the OCD ritual flawlessly, some potential "awfulized" catastrophe (existing only in the afflicted person's mind) will come true. As often debilitating as some demandingly repetitive OCD rituals are (e.g., repeated hand washings, having to open and close doors and drawers incessantly), what the ritual is designed to *prevent* is even more frightening—at least in the sufferer's *fear-filled* mind.

Phobias & superstitions both possess the potential to paralyze us, both mentally and physically causing us to overreact to harmless stimuli or else paralyzing us from acting at all.

Phobias are defined as persistent, illogical fears of a person, situation, or object.

Experts tell us there are literally *hundreds* of different kinds of phobias. Worse yet, every person has one or two of them.[23]

On the positive side, our ol' buddy the amygdala helps us vividly recall emotionally charged events from our past, often helping us stay safe by reacting to a threat "instinctively." On the other hand, sometimes, during times of extreme stress and trauma, the body floods the brain with hormones that "carve" especially "deep" sensory impression memories into the brain—creating phobias. Phobias are often created in this way, especially when we are younger and our gray matter is, literally, more impressionable. Research is currently being done to determine whether or not phobias could be deliberately created using hypnosis.[24]

According to David Icke, in his 2002 *Alice in Wonderland and the World Trade Center Disaster,*[25] there is a process known as "Trauma-based Mind Con-

---

23. *20/20 Thinking* by Maggie Greenwood-Robinson, Ph.D. (Avery/Penguin Putnam Inc., 2003:334). For a complete list and examination of the most common phobias, see *Mind Control* by Dr. Haha Lung and Christopher Prowant (Citadel, 2006).

24. See *666 Devilish Secrets of Hypnosis* by Dr. Haha Lung (publication pending).

25. Bridge & Love Publishing/MO, 2002.

trol" by which individuals, especially children, can be brainwashed or imprinted with a specific memory—or *phobia*.

Icke explains it thus:

> The mind has a defense mechanism that shuts out, or "compartmentalizes," the memory of extreme trauma. This is why people cannot remember the moment of impact in a serious road accident. Their mind creates an amnesiac barrier around the event so they don't have to keep reliving that horrible memory . . . If you could systematically traumatize someone through torturing others as they watched, you could shatter a person's mind into a honeycomb of self-contained compartments or amnesiac barriers.

Theoretically, this kind of "compartmentalization" could be used for good to help us understand such trauma-induced problems as repressed memory; PTSD in veterans and first-responders; MPD (multiple personality disorder); and the unreliability of eyewitness testimony coming out of highly traumatic events.

Perfection of this technique could be used to inflict test subjects with myriad symptoms, ranging from embarrassing but relatively harmless fetishes (designed to undermine a person's credibility) to potentially paralyzing phobias that could then be used to control those individuals. FYI: In *Mind Penetration* (Citadel, 2007), in the chapter "Oswald & the Sleeping Tigers," we discussed how Lee Harvey Oswald's Japanese mentor, Dr. Fujisawa, helped pioneer and perfect such "compartmentalizing" (i.e., mind control) techniques.

The good news:

> Fears are educated into us, and can, if we wish, be educated out. —Karl A. Menninger

Superstition: According to Voltaire, "We worship, we invoke, we try to appease only what we fear." The French satirist and cynic went on to warn us "the most superstitious times have always been those of the most horrible crimes."

The *American Heritage Dictionary*[26] defines superstition as "a belief, practice or rite resulting from ignorance of the laws of nature or from faith in magic

26. Second College Edition, 1991.

or chance; A fearful or abject state of mind resulting from such ignorance or irrationality . . . From the Latin *Superstitio*, literally '*To Stand Over*' someone." *Webster's II New Riverside Dictionary*[27] pretty much agrees, defining superstition as "belief that is maintained, despite evidence that is unfounded or irrational; a belief, practice, or rite resulting from faith in chance, magic . . . or dogma."

In this modern age of computer information and Internet "enlightenment," we like to think the human race has grown up, that we've evolved beyond the fear of—and irrational attempts to placate—things that go bump in the night. However, a recently completed, long-term study done by the Allensbach Institute in Germany concluded that superstitions—such as the irrational belief in good and bad omens—persist and are in fact more popular today than a quarter century ago, that today only one adult in three (33⅓ percent) rejects all forms of superstition, with twice that many (66⅔ percent) still clinging to their superstitions.[28]

More than 150 years ago, in his *The Ego and Its Own,* German, philosopher Johann Kasper Schmidt, better known as Max Stirner, warned that they remain even when we believe we've successfully exorcised all our irrational and prejudicial "demons" out of our head, declaring, "Man, your head is still haunted!"

Neither time nor distance seems to have dulled Stirner's sad but astute observation.

Today, not only is superstition alive and well, but it's still being used by ruthless Mind Slayers to inspire terrorism and to enslave.

Recently, authorities in Benin City, Nigeria, broke up a slavery ring specializing in shipping young Nigerian girls to Italy as prostitutes. In order to keep these sex slaves docile, the young girls were first brought before a juju (a traditional tribal witch doctor) who mixed locks of the girls' hair with chicken, dove, and lizard blood to craft talismans meant to mystically "bind" the young girls to their new owners. The terrified girls were told that if they dared disobey their new masters by trying to escape, they would first go insane and then die!

Only after Nigerian police proved to the girls that they had raided the juju shrine and burned these blood-soaked binding talismans, thereby

27. Revised Edition, 1996.

28. "Superstition on the Rise!" in *Awake!* magazine, January 2006.

"breaking the spell," were any of the superstitious slave girls willing to testify against their kidnappers.[29]

However, evidently frightening young Nigerian girls into prostitution remains a lucrative business.

May 2009: Madrid police arrested twenty-three suspects, including those identified as the ringleaders, in a nationwide prostitution smuggling operation that Spanish officials called a "voodoo extortion gang" using the threat of voodoo "curses" to control the victims.[30]

How about the eighty-year-old Indian holy man who claimed his right leg had magical powers, always insisting the leg could grant wishes to anyone who touched it? One night, the "magic" limb was amputated and stolen by two strangers to his village who first plied him with liquor before hacking off the leg with a sickle and making off with it.[31]

And what about the Taiwanese gambler suing the Venetian casino in Las Vegas, claiming the establishment used ancient feng shui[32] techniques to break his winning streak? Reportedly, after winning $400,000 in the casino, the man returned to his room only to a find black cloth hanging on the wall in his room and two white cloths strategically placed—feng shui-wise—in the hallway outside his room. Returning to the casino, the man subsequently lost all his winnings as well as an additional $2,000,000. According to the lawsuit, whoever placed the white-and-black cloths in his path there knew the feng shui "taboo" to gamblers.[33]

For those of you whose first impulse is to believe[34] superstitions are "harmless," consider how many cults have been founded, how many witches burned, and other tortures, abominations, and acts of terrorism committed

---

29. "Human traffickers conjure 'magic' to control victims" by Katherine Houreld. Associated Press/*Cleveland Plain Dealer*, 10.1.06:A14.

30. "Voodoo extortion gang arrested." *Cleveland Plain Dealer*, 5.24.09.

31. Reported in *The Week*, 12.28.07:16.

32. The ancient Asian art of feng shui attempts to regulate the flow of *chi* (life force) through the proper placement and juxtaposition of objects and materials intended to influence yin (negative attraction) and yang (positive attraction). For a complete course in understanding feng shui, see *Mental Domination After Winning $400,000* by Dr. Haha Lung and Christopher Prowant (Citadel, 2009).

33. *The Week*, 6.12.09:16.

34. Remember, you can't write "believe" without sticking "Lie" in the middle.

down through the centuries all because of belief in one superstition or the other.

In the same way "cult" is what the big church calls the little church, so too one man's *superstition* is another man's *religion*. And, need you be reminded that, especially in this day and age, you can get killed for insulting another man's religion by referring to it as a "superstition," no matter how well their dogma fits Mr. Webster's definition? Or as Schopenhauer advised: "It's safer trusting fear than faith."[35]

Using fear as a weapon

> Fear is our most useful tool for fouling up our foes: Intimidation—motivation through fear—is an ever-present head game played in a myriad of ways. If you give it some thought, you might be shocked to find that a large percentage of your actions are motivated by fear. You may be motivated by the fear of physical harm, the fear of losing someone's love, or the fear of being embarrassed, to name a few. Some of these fears are valid, but most are not. It's the preponderance of unfounded fears which unnecessarily disrupts your life. —Robert J. Ringer[36]

There's a witty Parker and Hart *Wizard of ID* cartoon where the King's castle is surrounded and barbarian attackers are yelling up at the King for him to "Throw down your arms and surrender!" To which the King nonchalantly calls back, "Ok! You win! We can't fight you *and The Plague* at the same time!" The following panel shows the residents of the castle looking over the parapet, dumbfounded by *sudden silence*, nary an enemy in sight!

It just goes to show that, no matter how big and scary an enemy is, there's always something he's afraid of. Just hope you can find that "something" before he figures out what it is *you're* afraid of!

When searching for that glitch in your enemy's program, keep in mind that some people really are literally scared of their own shadow. By "shadow,"

---

35. Ever the optimist, Arthur Schopenhauer (1788–1860) also advised his students to eat a toad each morning, reasoning that it would then be unlikely they'd encounter anything more bitter the rest of the day!

36. "*Looking Out for #1*" by Robert J. Ringer. (Fawsett Crest, 1977:73). See also "Looking Out for Number One: Bring in the Ringer!" in *Ultimate Control!* by Dr. Haha Lung and Christopher B. Prowant (Citadel, 2010).

we mean the stuff we keep hidden away from polite, prudish society. This is our "nightside" face, full of desire—and possibly spite—that we keep to ourselves, the inconvenient—possibly *illegal*!—shadow we're afraid will somehow, someday show itself to the world. This is our "I know what you did last summer" stumble, our "What happens in Vegas . . . *just followed your drunk ass home!*" secret. Can you say blackmail waiting to happen?

Speaking of things you don't want the neighbors to find out about, did you hear about the crafty erotic videos distributor who instead of sending the XXX videos ordered by his customers sent them all full refund checks . . . But, strangely, none of the checks ever got cashed. Why? The company name boldly emblazoned on the checks read: "Bestiality & Other Perversions Video." Yeah, that's a check you want to be caught cashing down at your local bank![37]

Fear and the killer "B"s: Having first mastered their own fear—or at least having buried those fears deep enough that their enemy—you—won't be able to dig them up and use them against them, Mind Slayers are then free to employ the Six Killer "B"s: blind, bribery and blackmail, bloodties, brainwashing, bullying, and bury. These six tried-and-true techniques for infiltrating an enemy's mind all contain elements of fear:

- **Blind** an enemy to your plans. Cut off his means of communication, his ways of gathering intelligence. Leave him in the dark—the dark is always scary! Make him fear what is to come—hopefully he has an overactive imagination. Keep him guessing. Lack of information is always frightening—not to mention *deadly*!
- **Bribery and blackmail** both rely on (un)healthy doses of fear. Using the former, the victim worries he'll lose out if he doesn't take the proffered bribe. As for the latter, fear is literally its calling card.
- **Bloodties** are those initiation rites and indiscretions supposed friends, gang brothers, and other cult members hold over your head to ensure your loyalty.[38] Fear of betrayal and exposure keeps you toeing the party line.

37. From *Urban Legends* by Thomas J. Craughwell. (Black Dog & Leventhal, 2000).

38. In August 2009, the London *Daily Mail* reported that actor John Travolta, longtime member of the Church of Scientology, was thinking of leaving the "cult" but that, according to his friends, he might be afraid to leave Scientology because it keeps files on members' personal lives. (*The Week*, 8.7.09:10)

- **Brainwashing** finds numerous uses for fear, from making the captured POW fear he has been forgotten to driving "wedges" between comrades by making them fear they have been betrayed.[39]
- **Bullying** is all about fear, whether the threat of physical violence or fear of losing your job if you don't do "a little favor" for the boss.
- **Bury,** our final Killer "B," relies simply on reminding people about their inborn fear of dying . . . the sudden, "accidental," undoubtedly horrible demise of you, your loved ones, or even your favorite pet . . . all *preventable*, if you're smart enough to play ball.

Future fear alert: Scientists have recently figured out a way to create "fearless" mice by knocking out the stathmin gene, which is believed to be responsible for regulating our reaction to fear. The good news is that this breakthrough could open the way for the creation of anti-anxiety drugs designed to help people suffering with paralyzing anxieties and phobias. It has also been speculated that such a drug could be used to suppress fear in soldiers.

On the "way too much potential for abuse" side, how about instead of turning *off* this "fear gene" you deliberately turn it *on*? Voilà! You've now got a way to "infect"—and control—people with debilitating—permanent!—fear.

For more on controlling fear—your own and your enemy's—review the Buddhist "Five Primary Fears," and the "Seven Tibetan Fears" in *Mind Control* (Citadel, 2006).

Fear is a four-letter word.
—Joshua Only

How to Master Lust

The emotion lust includes strong attraction of any kind, sexual or not. We all have lusts, things we covet badly enough to get "stuck on stupid," compromise our integrity, and occasionally look the other way while someone else does all the dirty work.

---

39. See *Theatre of Hell: Dr. Lung's Complete Guide to Torture* by Dr. Haha Lung and Christopher Prowant (Loompanics Unlimited, 2003).

But, like fear, lust isn't always a bad thing. Our lusts motivate us. Take this away from a man and he becomes easier to manage.

We live for the things we can't get. We strive for those things just out of reach, and by such reaching—testing limits, pushing against our walls—we evolve into better hunters, or else we become better at avoiding the hunters, or both. Evolving = surviving.

The worst thing that can happen to us in life is that we finally get everything we want. Game over. No more challenge, and we die a fat-man's death.

For a Mind Slayer, the goal then is to help the enemy get his heart's desire, to achieve his every lust, to the point where he'll no longer be a threat or competition. For more ways to master lust, your own as well as the lust of others, see "The Art of Seduction" in *Mind Control* (Citadel, 2006) as well as "Seduction and Strategy" and "The Zen of Seduction" in *Mental Dominance* (Citadel, 2008).

How to Master Anger

There is debate within the American Psychological Association (APA) as to exactly how the emotion anger should be classified. Some noted psychology researchers believe that anger should have a classification all its own in the manual of mental disorders since its been documented that anger (1) destroys interpersonal relationships, (2) impedes sexual functioning, (3) makes it more likely we'll earn less, (4) makes it more likely we'll end up in the criminal justice system, and (5) overall, makes it less likely we'll achieve our life goals.[40]

There are two types of anger—let's hope our enemy suffers from both. Better yet, let's *help* our enemy suffer from both!

Acute anger is the kind of anger that comes and goes, usually quickly, leaving few permanent affects. Something that instantly pisses you off—like stubbing your toe or misplacing your car keys.

Chronic anger, on the other hand, is the kind of smoldering resentment we feel against another person (for real or imagined slights). Others are just angry at the universe, God, fate, karma, and kismet in general for not recognizing

---

40. See "APA meeting: Being gay isn't a mental illness" by Sharon Jayson. *USA Today*, 8.10.09:5D.

their oh-so-apparent genius. Beware: people with this kind of seething, simmering anger inside of them often end up "going postal." Cowards at heart, they end up expending their anger—and ammunition—on innocents.

Sun Tzu, Chapter XIII: such disgruntled people are easy to "turn" as spies to your cause. Turnabout's fair play. It might be a good idea to "weed your own garden," making sure none of your employees, Iago-like "friends," and even estranged family members harbor any hidden anger toward you—anger an alert Mind Slayer can turn against you.

When aimed against ourselves, psychiatrists call this kind of anger "self-loathing." We often feel this way when we "ca-*bitch*-ulate," when we give up and give in, when we start hating ourselves for being cowards, for *not* standing up and speaking out.

Halfway between acute and chronic anger is a new type of anger you have to watch out for. It's called intermittent explosive disorder (IED).

Somewhat akin to road rage, IED is defined (and diagnosed) as "a usually calm and responsible person who 'snaps' and commits a violent act." To qualify, you have to show "a pattern in which tension builds up until an explosion brings relief, followed eventually by regret, embarrassment, or guilt." These attacks of impulsive rage "seem to be out of proportion to the immediate provocation" and "have serious consequences."[41]

Neither of these types of anger, acute or chronic, are the problem. *Inappropriate* anger—anger disproportionate to the situation—is the problem.

For example, you come home from work and immediately step in dog doo on your front lawn and you explode into a killer rage. Well, chances are you'd been collecting components for that explosive outburst all day at work: Caught in gridlock, arriving late, you spill coffee on your pants while getting reamed out by your boss, add to that the day's miscellaneous paper cuts, a lost stapler, that damned copier again . . . and again . . . and again, not to mention one hundred and one computer glitches and that A-hole in the next cubicle over snapping his chewing gum all afternoon like a sixteen-year-old cheerleader with a retainer.

Bad when it happens to you. Great when we can make it happen to our enemies. This kind of situation plays right into Musashi's "Cutting at the Edges" strategy—attacking an enemy in a roundabout way, that is, if you can't openly oppose him face to face, force for force, snipe at him from the

---

41. *Harvard Mental Health Letter*, Vol. 23. No.3, September 2006:5.

tree line (Colonial Minuteman style!), attack his flanks, nip at his heels, letting the air out of his tires (figuratively and literally—if it will make him late for that important meeting!). As his world begins to crumble around the edges, he'll become more desperate—more strident—to hold the center together. And thus more willing to listen to what you have to say.

It has been said a quick-to-anger opponent is a godsend. We all know from experience that the angrier we are, the more we "see red," and the less likely we are to see thing clearly. Quick to anger, quick to the grave.

Mind Slayers deliberately place stumbling blocks in their enemy's path—irritating stumbling blocks to delay his progress and drain his resources (of which *time* is always the most precious).

Three seems to be the magic number—or the breaking point! Three "little" missteps or mishaps, first irritating him, then pissing him off, and finally leading him to one really good—most inappropriate—explosive angry outburst at the wrong time, wrong place. Good-bye rival. Of course, you may have to give him just a little "encouragement," since only ten percent of anger is actually followed up by acted-out aggression.[42]

Perhaps you recall the oft told Japanese story of the forty-seven ronin whose master was goaded into angrily drawing his sword on the Imperial grounds, winning him an automatic death penalty.[43] And while we're jerking our enemy around, we also need to jealousy guard ourselves against someone "pulling our chain," causing us to lash out in (self-destructive) anger. Once the root of anger is identified, it's possible for a person to learn to control their anger, primarily by becoming less responsive to petty frustrations. It's better if you figure this out before your foe does!

By the way, some people *like* getting angry since it gives them a "rush," an actual neuro-chemical jolt to their brain as the amygdala triggers flight-or-fight chemicals to flood their system. Back in olden (or rather *Odin*) times, Norse Vikings called such people "berserkers," and they were much prized for their ferocity in battle. Not so much so in modern times, where such numbnuts are known as "anger junkies."

And, like fear and lust, all anger isn't bad. Sometimes anger *is* an appropriate response. When you or a loved one is the victim of an injustice, or

42. "The Lion Tamer" by Cecilia Capuzzi Simon. *Psychology Today*, July/August 2001:54.

43. For the full story of the forty-seven ronin see *Ultimate Control* by Dr. Haha Lung and Christopher Prowant (Citadel 2010).

when you witness a child or a dumb animal being abused, it's not only okay to get angry . . . it's *time* to get angry!

How to Master Greed

Greed is just another form of lust, but instead of chasing lingerie, you're chasing Lincolns!

Buddha's second noble truth is that "Suffering is caused by Desire"—we want things we either can't get or don't need. Thus, we define greed as "the universal desire to have more than we *need*."

The first thing we "need" to do is learn the difference between a "want" and a "need":

> Distinguish between gain and loss. Nothing you can hold in your hand can ever truly be held for long. Distinguish between need and desire. I desire many things. I need few. My enemy can entice me with both of these—drawing me here, sending me running there. All I truly need beats within my breast. All I desire can all too easily fall into my enemy's coarse hand. The more a man possesses, the more easily he can be possessed. —Hannibal the Conqueror, Truth V[44]

Usually, we justify wanting more than we need by convincing ourselves (and whomever we're trying to get more from) that we're "putting something away for a rainy day." But, come on, how many pairs of Nikes can you really wear at one time?

Signs of obsessive collecting and/or hording by your enemy can be (1) a window into his personality and (2) a way to weasel your way into his confidence. His collecting habits and hobbies could reveal a hidden greedy streak in him, a flaw that could be turned to your advantage. Recall Poe's *The Cask of Amontillado* (1846) where the revenge-minded narrator uses his knowledge of his arrogant nemesis's habit and hobby of fine wines to trap him.

Dictators and cult leaders all seem to have this flaw of "collecting" works of art and other valuables, perhaps subconsciously planning for the day when

---

44. For the rest of Hannibal's "99 Truths," see *Ultimate Control* by Dr. Haha Lung and Christopher B. Prowant (Citadel, 2010). See also *The 99 Truths: Hannibal's Black Art of War* by Dr. Haha Lung (publication pending).

they'll have to get out of Dodge in a hurry—or out of Baghdad, as the case may be.

Control freaks often collect people, surrounding themselves with sycophants, while others collect wives and mistresses like trinkets.

The formula for getting your own house in order, so far as exorcising greed is concerned, is:

"Feed your need. Starve your greed."

Of course, for Mind Slayers setting their sights on an enemy, it's just the opposite:

"Feed their greed. Starve their need."

In other words, encourage an enemy's greed; help him indulge in his wanton desires until he tires and then have your way with him. In the same vein, starve his need by seizing every opportunity to deprive your enemy of needed supplies—men and materiel:

> War does not feed my sons. But at least it will keep my enemy's sons from eating as well!
>
> —Hannibal the Conqueror, Truth XXXVI

It's been said that the more things you have, the more things have you. This is especially true when an enemy tries to get at you by first destroying your possessions—undermining you psychologically as well as financially in one fell swoop. Imagine both the mental and fiscal impact that losing your home would have on you—and on your loved ones, their pain being just more impact on you as well.[45]

Always be aware—paranoid!—that your enemy might be smart enough (or scared enough) not to make a direct attack against you personally. Always remember: an enemy doesn't have to get at *you* . . . to get at you.

What would happen if the business where you work suddenly burned to the ground? Or if something happened to its owner—your boss? What if your boss was suddenly indicted and the company went belly-up? Could you survive financially?

Of course we're not saying wanting a nice, comfortable life, a place for you and your family to lay their heads, is being "greedy." We're just remind-

45. Musashi's "Cutting at the Edges" again.

ing you, you could be vulnerable from attack from that direction. He could hurt you by hurting the thing(s) and people you care about. *The Godfather* ring a bell? Hello: your champion horse's head in your bed? Or as Hannibal so succinctly put it in the first of his "Truths":

> Enemy! When you look at me don't see something you hate . . . see the very thing you love the most. For that is what I will surely rip from you if you ever rise against me!

Don't let your greed make you bleed.

How to Master Sympathy

> ***We are fascinated, troubled, and desperate to know how human behavior can go so wrong, fearful that we, too, might behave badly in a similar situation.***
>
> **—Ethan Watters**[46]

In his fascinating 1857 autobiography, *Memoirs of Vidocq: Master of Crime*, Francois Eugene Vidocq (1775–1857) makes mention of a master thief named Jossas, better known by the grandiose nom de guerre the Marquis de Saint-Amand de Faral. Nicknamed "Passkey" by his fellow felons, Jossas's specialty was to first use his charm and "title" to ingratiate himself with wealthy targets, and then—when their backs were turned—to make impressions of their locks so as to make duplicate keys and return to rob them. One such nut, however, proved especially hard for the wily Jossas to crack.

Jossas had targeted a bank in Lyons holding an especially tempting vault. Step one was Jossas arranging to be properly introduced to the banker on the pretext of doing business profitable to the bank.[47] In this way, Jossas succeeded in his usual modus operandi, taking impressions and making duplicate keys of all the locks standing between him and his goal. But, despite his best maneuvering, he kept failing to get an impression of the key for the actual vault since the cashier in charge never parted with the key. Finally, on one

46. "Why Do People Behave Badly?" by Ethan Watters. *Discover*, December 2005.

47. Recall a similar exchange between Edmund Dantes and the crooked banker in *The Count of Monte Cristo*, the book Vidocq's exploits are said to have helped inspire.

pretext or the other, Jossas convinced his new "best friend" the cashier to accompany him on a coach ride to the next town over. Nearing their destination,[48] they were suddenly confronted by a man desperately trying to get help for a woman lying on the bank apparently dying, bleeding from her mouth and nose! Leaping from their carriage, Jossas and the cashier desperately tried to help the lady's companion stem the bleeding. Nothing seemed to help until Jossas, a well-traveled man, remembered hearing that such hemorrhaging could be stopped by pressing a metal object—for example, a key—against the back of the bleeding person's neck. Both the woman's companion and Jossas quickly searched their pockets and found they carried no such key. Reaching into his own pocket, the cashier first offered his door key . . . which didn't work. Finally, the cashier offered the sacred vault key he carried. Accepting the vault key, Jossas quickly pressed it to the back of the woman's neck and—Voilà!—the woman's bleeding stopped. Jossas then handed the vault key back to the cashier. Turning aside any offer of recompense from the grateful man and woman, Jossas and the cashier continued on their way.

Three nights later the bank's vault was robbed, opened by the perfect duplicate key Jossas had made from the perfect impression pressed into the wax on the back of the "bleeding woman's" neck!

The perfect use of a "sympathy" ploy.

By the way, Vidocq's life itself is required reading for any student of the Black Science.

Former criminal-turned-police-spy-turned founder of the Surete (the French secret police after which both Scotland Yard and the FBI were modeled), Vidocq's youthful exploits—including frequent sword duels and daring prison escapes, many of which resulted from his use of disguises—became the inspiration for the character Edmund Dantes in *The Count of Monte Cristo* (1845), written by Vidocq's close friend Alexander Dumas. Likewise, Vidocq's escapades while a frequent fugitive from the law are credited with helping inspire the character of Jean Valjean in *Les Miserables* (1862), written by Victor Hugo (1802–1885), yet another friend of Vidocq's.[49] Many believe Vidocq to

48. FYI: People are more relaxed near the end of a journey than when starting out. That's why most automobile accidents happen within a few miles of home.

49. Vidocq's early adventures while traveling with bands of Gypsies and rogues may have also helped inspire Hugo's novel *The Man Who Laughs*, which was, in turn, the inspiration for the popular Batman arch-nemesis the Joker.

have also been the real-life template for Arthur Conan Doyle's Professor Moriarty, perennial nemesis of Sherlock Holmes.

Many of the crime detection and law enforcement innovations pioneered by Vidocq while head of the Surete are still in use today by law enforcement personnel worldwide.

As disturbing as this fact might be to you, and contrary to what we'd all like to believe about ourselves, we're *not* born with an altruistic—sympathetic—urge to help our fellow man. In fact, our decidedly *nonaltruistic instinct*—actually, a survival mechanism—has been proven time and again since an initial 1960s Princeton University study that revealed that people were *less* likely to aid a stranger if they thought they were just one among several witnesses.

So ingrained in us is our "If I don't get involved then I might not get shot or, worse yet sued!" survival mechanism that some cities and states went so far as to pass Good Samaritan laws, making it a crime *not* to help someone you know is in trouble (e.g., a victim of an accident or crime).

As much as we'd like to think the best about our fellow man (and about ourselves) there are two psychological facts that fight against this.

First: *Xenophobia*[50] is natural. Nature *made* us afraid—or at least cautious—of strangers for our own good. A stranger approaches and, if only for the sake of our loved ones, we *should* be cautious, at least until we can discern whether he's up to no good. If he does turn out to be a danger, then we're already on the alert, already halfway to protecting ourselves—vigilance being job one when it comes to self-defense.

If, on the other hand, that stranger turns out to be our newest BFF just waiting to happen, then no harm done. We can all laugh about our paranoia over a cold brewski.

In psychology, this is called "implicit social cognition," the deep-rooted assumptions we all carry around and often act on without ever realizing it.[51]

We used to have instincts like that, instincts designed to keep us alive. But, as Nietzsche lamented (okay bitched!), society has pretty much bred such things out of us.

And would it really come as all that big a surprise if you were to discover—*gasp!*—that we're *naturally* more suspicious of people who don't

---

50. The fear of strangers.

51. cf. "*Birth of a Notion*" by Steve Mirsky. *Scientific American*, October 2009.

look like us? *Omega!* Isn't that something like racial profiling? Yeah, exactly like racial profiling . . . and it's kept the human race alive all these millennium.

Think about it. Isn't this opposite exactly what professional con men, politicians, and cult leaders do to get close to their victims? Rather than excluding us out of "prejudice," they instead mold themselves and their message to perfectly suit us.

Remember: we like (and therefore tend to listen to) people who are like us. The more a con man or politician (redundant?) can convince us he's "just like us"—therefore he understands us, has the same needs as us—the more likely we are to buy a big steaming pile off of him.

Don't let "political correctness" get you killed. And please Mr. Airport Security Checkpoint Officer, don't let *your* political correctness get *me* killed!

What's that you protest: "I never judge people based on superficial characteristics!" Right, you mean you never notice a stranger's:

- ***Height*:** Are they tall or short? Women like taller men and men are just as shallow when it comes to women. On sight, men view taller women as more intelligent, assertive, and ambitious. Conversely, men view shorter women as more nurturing and considerate. (*Psychology Today*, Sept./Oct. 2005:32) And didn't Randy Newman write a song about how irritating short people are?
- ***Age*:** Old people are senile. Young people are brain dead and irresponsible.
- ***Size and shape*:** Everyone "knows" fat people lack self-control, are lazy, and have more health problems. Do I really need that "weight" added to my company's health care premiums? Didn't Shakespeare mention something about lean-skinny people having a "hungry look" about them, like they can't be trusted?
- ***Race and apparent ethnicity*:** Will "that" kind of person get along with my other workers? Aren't those people all terrorists? (Damn! There goes all my *really* good ethnic jokes out the window!)
- ***How they're dressed*:** Dress can also be an indication of overall attitude: formal, casual, slovenly. If a young "sagger" can't be depended on to keep his own trousers pulled up, what makes you think he can be dependable in other areas? How a person dresses can also be another clue to ethnicity. "Better not hire this guy 'cause, first time

my ol' buddy Bob comes in the store and makes a crack about this guy's 'funny' hat, I'll get my ass sued off!"

- ***How they stand or sit*:** This is where the time we took to study such things as body language starts to pay for itself:

> ***For what the mind shows in the face by maintaining in it the expression of intelligence and propriety that ought to be required also in the whole body.***
> **—Marcus Aurelius**

Standing or sitting by themselves? Antisocial, thinks he's better than the rest of us. In the mix, laughing, telling jokes? He's a suck-up. Leaning against the wall? Drunk or just lazy. Arms and legs crossed—closed off—another indication the new guy's antisocial.

- **Itchin', twitchin', and bitchin':** Or what nowadays is called "body language." For more on body language, see the chapter that follows: "Who Lies . . . and How to Catch Them Doing It!" and "The Moves They Make" section therein.
- ***The company they keep*:** Like your family, your friends are a reflection of you, or at least of what you're willing to put up with. Beer buddies or the martini crowd? Hanging around the watercooler with your coworkers shooting the breeze or huddled down in your cubicle shooting the boss a memo snitching out all your coworkers who are hanging around the watercooler shooting the breeze? This is where "cutting-at-the-edges" comes into play—whether you're the one using it, or whether your enemy is using it against you.
- ***Introvert versus extrovert:*** Extroverts work the crowd, gossiping with coworkers, moving from clique to clique at a party. They talk a lot. And when they talk, they put their whole body into the conversation—leaning in close to people, touching others. They use their hands to enliven their many tales of adventure. Hint: practice this.

Extroverts also get bored quickly, moving on to their next conquest or performance.

Extroverts fall into the "doer-feeler" category. They act on their emotions (e.g., their initial enthusiasm for a project) without thinking things completely through—"We'll cross that bridge when we come to it!"

Extroverts *need* to keep moving; they need to be doing something at all times. If your ally is an extrovert—keep him busy. If your enemy is an extrovert—keep him busy, too, but keep him busy chasing after shadows. Or you can frustrate him by making him spin his wheels, stifling his forward momentum.

Introverts, on the other hand, are quieter. They're in the "thinker-planner" category. They listen more. They watch—and they see—*everything*.

They like to hold a drink or something in their hand (masking their nervousness). And, besides, they don't need their hands free to tell stories like the extrovert. Introverts don't tell stories—they relate facts, they recite statistics, they crunch numbers.

Introverts speak slower because they think about their answers before answering.

Because they take longer to answer, introverts are often misjudged as being less of a threat when, in actuality, introverts can be *more* of a threat since—as listeners—they hear and see things an extrovert might miss.

Also, while all eyes are on the extrovert's antics (literally and figuratively), the introvert can be working diligently—behind the scenes, under the radar—accomplishing his agenda—or the goal you've given him.

While the extrovert is busy entertaining the crowd, including his and the introvert's boss, the introvert is standing next to the boss. The boss is laughing *at* the extrovert. But he's laughing *with* the introvert, *sharing* a pleasurable experience with the boss. It's called "bonding."

When the introvert is your ally or worker, use this unassuming personality to accomplish projects and negotiations behind the scene, where a more flamboyant extrovert might draw undue or untimely attention.

If your enemy is an introvert *don't underestimate* him. Still waters run deep.

Pull the enemy introvert out of his shell by forcing him into the limelight, where he'll sputter and stumble.

Are we ever wrong in our first impressions? Sure. But we're also *right* often enough to keep us doing this. Yeah, kinda like the lottery and/or scoring with really hot chicks! This strategy undoubtedly has its roots in that xenophobic survival instinct.

Second: There's no such thing as altruism. Everybody gets paid. Where one person might get paid in stacks of cold, hard Benjamins, another person's "pay off" may simply be they're leaving the scene feeling good about themselves, having reaffirmed their self-identity that they did "what a good person/Christian/Good Samaritan would do." Therefore:

1. Don't expect someone to come to your rescue—if they do, great! There are really are good people in the world, but that doesn't means they're not getting paid (if only in good feeling). In life, before you can help others, you first have to help yourself. Count on being your own "rescuer" and then, should others rush to help, all the better your chances of surviving.
2. Since you know that—one way or another—everybody gets paid, whenever you want someone to do something for *you*, show them what's in it for *them*.
3. Become aware of your own "sympathy urge," the urge (often subconscious) to identify (empathize) with, and therefore want to help, others. There's nothing wrong with wanting to help others—whether out of sympathy or because you see a buck in it for you somewhere. The important thing is to examine your own motivations for helping, and for doing anything else for that matter, *before* your enemies do.

Penetrate inwards into men's leading principles, and thou will see what judges thou art afraid of, and what kind of judges they are themselves.
—Marcus Aurelius

"NEEDS" VERSUS "WANTS"

To move mountains, to move castle walls,
both can easily be done by machines.
Ah, but to move the hearts of men . . . that can only be done by other men!
—Vlad Tepes, Dracula's Art of War

There's a big difference between what human beings *want* and what they *need*. Denying an enemy what he needs stifles his advance. Planting unreasonable wants (desires) in his mind ensures your victory.

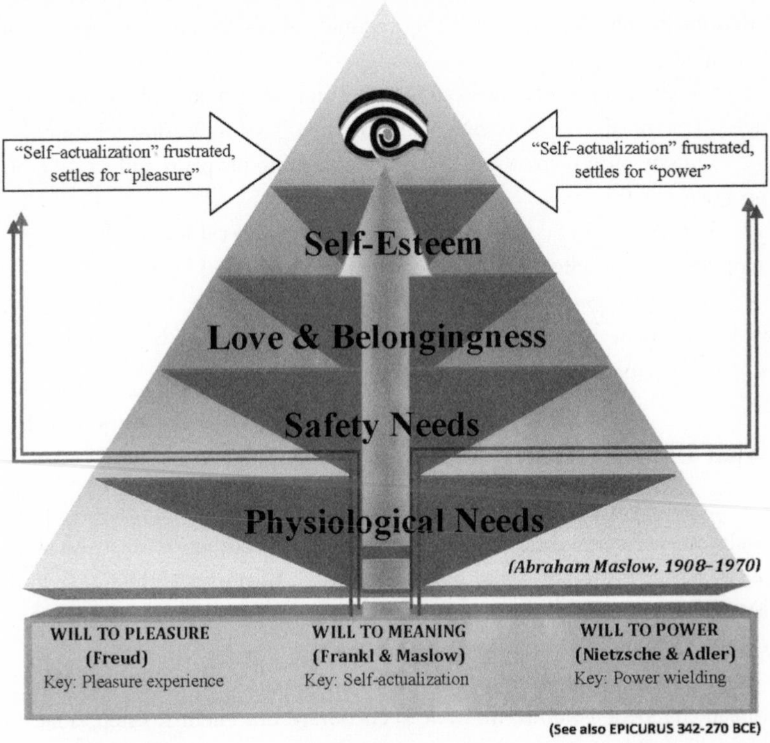

Figure 4.

What Do They Need?

Buddha taught that "Suffering begins with desire," that wanting things we don't need is the beginning of all our problems. Yet all of us have things we *need* in order to survive.

Psychologist Abraham Maslow (1908–1970) is famous for summing up a basic list of human needs and priorities in what has become known simply as Maslow's Pyramid.

At the most basic level, all of us have physical needs (food, sleep, sex) and safety needs (protection, freedom from fear, a need for familiar and reassuring structure in our lives).

Once these basic physical and safety needs are satisfied, we turn our attention to the second tier of the pyramid, needs for love and a sense of belonging.

Self-esteem needs (a need to feel vital and valued) and self-actualization needs (the need to explore one's full potential) top off Maslow's Pyramid.

To deny our enemy these needs is to frustrate his plans and to stifle his progress.

At the most basic level, your enemy's needs are all logistical: he needs supplies (food, shelter, health concerns) for himself and his men.

For many, sex is also a need—horny, they lose focus, become irritable, which, in turn, distorts their perspective and interferes with their interpersonal relationships and their command decisions.

What Do They Want?

Beyond what a person needs, there's the things they want. Some of our wants are realistic, others not. For example, there's nothing wrong with *wanting* to win the lottery—who doesn't! However, to start spending money we haven't yet won from the lottery isn't very realistic and benefits no one—except possibly Lenny the loan shark!

Of course, while keeping our own wants securely in the "It could realistically happen" column, we want to encourage our enemy to step as far off base as possible. In addition to encouraging him to run through Hell in gasoline underwear, we also want to pay close attention to his agenda—his long-range wants and how he plans to get them—in other words, his agenda.

Often, his goals will be crystal clear, other times obscured. Sometimes, he does this deliberately to hide his true intentions—his true agenda—from us; other times, he may not be fully aware of what his true agenda actually is. (Yeah, more of that "subconscious psychology" that always seems to be popping up!) Don't panic. You—still—don't need a psychology degree to understand what makes your enemy tick.

Just pay attention. One thing comes out his mouth, but—just for an instant—you think you see something different twinkling in your enemy's eye. Trust your gut feeling—or, to be more precise, your ol' buddy the amygdala's *sixth sense* paranoia. If you suspect someone has a hidden agenda, they probably do. And odds are their hidden agenda falls into one (or more) of six basic categories (see Figure 5):

WHAT'S YOUR F'N AGENDA?

What They Want	How They Talk	Key Words	Type	Your Approach
Fame	Talks about famous people. Drops names.Complains about how famous people are always complaining.	Success. Paparazzi, Los Angeles, Hollywood, and TV.	Needs strokes and praise. Craves recognition.	Give him a way to "show 'em all." Appreciate his "genius" and talent. Compare him favorably to other famous people.
Fortune (Financial Gain)	Talks about money. Brags about things he has. Complains about taxes.	Capital gains. Production. Stocks and Bonds. Investments. New York and Tokyo.	He's in it for the money. A gun for hire. Trust him only as you're paying him better than your competition.	Hire him. Pay him well but never trust him. Others of his type tempt with "too good to be true" offer.
Faith	Talks about the future (with veiled hints he knows something you don't). Religious references.	Conservative. Family values. Judgment, law. Punishment.	Authoritarian. Born again. Taliban.	Assure him the world is going to change to fit his needs. There's a place of honor reserved for him in the kingdom to come.
Followers	Talks about organizing. How to move people and resources from place. Bringing people together. Need for strong leadership.	Community. Brotherhood. Faith. Patriotism. God-speak.	Needs validation from outside, insecure. Paranoid. Looking for love.	Give him your loyalty and love. Help him form his own cult (security blanket) or give him a trusted position in your own.
Future (Gain)	They talk about religion and/or political changes that will change everything. They are up on the latest innovations and movers and shakers.	Change. Economy. Restructuring. Rush Limbaugh. Projections. Trends.	Wallows in "elephant shit" (i.e., grandiose plans of what will happen "when/if").	Show him his place in the new world, show him how to (literally) invest in your future.
Frustration	Talks in generalities. About how people let them down. Has grandiose ideas but everyone's too stupid to see his genius. Cynical.	Stupid. Short-sighted. Fair (injustice). "Old boys' network"; "system's fixed"; "You gotta know someone."	Needs to get his grudge on. Lives for "the big payback." Wants revenge but he calls it justice.	Show him how to get even and then some.

Figure 5.

- ***Fame agenda:*** He wants to be famous and, the next best thing to being famous himself, wants to *have* famous friends. He's a name-dropper and knows the names of "up-'n'-coming" stars you've never heard of. Casually tossing their names out and seeing your lack of recognition reinforces his fantasy that he's an "insider." He knows the names of streets in Los Angeles although he's never been there. He uses words like "exposure" and "talent." Always up on the latest gossip, he drops names of people he wishes he knew. This is true whether he's seeking fame on the silver screen or just in the office. This agenda type is always secretly bitter (frustration agenda). For a man, it's that the world in general hasn't discovered his genius. For women, the world hasn't acknowledged her talent and beauty.

  He complains how famous people "just don't appreciate what they've got" (more frustration agenda); still, he wants to be one of them. Offer to help him be discovered and you'll have his undivided attention. I'm ready for my close-up, Mr. DeMille.
- ***Fortune agenda*:** It's all about the money. This type of person is both a gold digger and grave robber, always trying to dig up those dead presidents. Usually a Watcher (more on this in a minute), he likes to see and likes other people to look at and admire his "stuff."

  When he talks, it's always about money. He brags about the things he has and admires (*lusts* after) the possessions of others. All his relationships turn to crap since whoever—whatever—is hanging off his arm is for show like a Rolex knock-off.

  Uses words like "capital gains," "production costs," and worries about "taxes," especially how "bad" it'll be when he's "forced" to move into a higher tax bracket. Likes talking about New York and Tokyo.

  Despite all his (or her) wheelin' and dealin', he's still a sucker for "Get rich quick!" schemes and—beware—he keeps a couple of Ponzi schemes in his own back pocket in case of emergencies. Trap him with something shiny.
- ***Faith agenda*:** He's convinced himself he's a true believer—even though this kind always has a few skeletons in his closet that he's deathly afraid are going to be resurrected one day. At the least, he's a hypocrite. Worst-case scenario: he's "born again" *Taliban*! (Read Margaret Atwood's *The Handmaid's Tale,* 1985.)

Listen for words like "conservative," "traditional," and "family values."

Like all "cultists," he harbors a secret spite and dreams of "The Big Payback"—Judgment Day—when he'll be sitting on a golden throne in glory looking down on the rest of us poor—heathens!—rotating on the spit. This part of his faith agenda overlaps into a frustration agenda.

- ***Followers agenda*:** He's collecting a "posse," a "crew," starting his own "clique" or cult. Sometimes he also has a faith agenda and is a vigorous recruiter for his cause—although, you can bet he's keeping a running score—notches on his Bible or Koran—of all the souls he saved.

He loves to organize things and talk about organizing things: the office Christmas party, Little League, church events. He's already seen to the seating arrangements—a very important post by the way, office politics feng shui.

His "volunteer spirit" often "guilts" others into volunteering. He's always the one running the show. So when you arrive, you find he's volunteered to be in charge and he's already got *your* whole schedule planned out.

His kind is secretly insecure and is looking for validation outside himself. By assuming the "badge of leadership" (from Scoutmaster to Master of Ceremonies) he's assured the run of things and the recognition he craves. (A little fame agenda mixed in.)

He's always talking about past organizational successes and/or trying to involve you in his future plans.

"Community," "brotherhood," "civil participation," and "fellowship" are the kind of words he likes and the kind of words you'll hear coming out of his mouth.

If he can't put together a decent following outside his family, his family becomes his cult. He'll brag about how well behaved his kids are, of how his wife is always attentive to his every need. (See *Sleeping with the Enemy,* 1994.)

In extremis, he's a cult leader waiting to happen.

- ***Future agenda*:** In his mind, he has a vision of the future that he's trying to make happen *in the present*. Sometimes, he's a true believer who really expects that his version of the future will come about. (In this respect, he shares a lot in common with faith agenda.)

Other times, he's just talking elephant shit[52] that doesn't have a snowball's chance in Hell of ever coming about. He always talks in the future tense. Stays away from present-reality questions like "How much money have you collected so far?" and "How many people have actually signed up for this project?"

He can be political and/or religious but, unlike the faith agenda, all his aspirations are abstract.

Words like "potential" and "prospective" and "possible" give him a woody.

- ***Frustration agenda*:** He's out to get his grudge on. He's mad at something, maybe mad at everything. This type can borrow elements from the first five agenda categories: he can be mad because the universe doesn't recognize his greatness (fame), because he's living in a degenerate world (faith) where no one will listen to him (followers), because if he could only get a loan (fortune) or win the lottery (future) he could accomplish his dream.

  He's a complainer and a blamer. Every word that comes out of his mouth is cynical. He's the type of guy who complains when the word "Free!" isn't spelled right.

They're called "hidden" agendas because people striving after fame and fortune, faith and followers, or those harboring resentful frustrations aren't always so easy to spot.

People get good at hiding their secret hates and hubris and horrors. It's even possible for a person to have an agenda hidden from themselves—subconscious motivations and desires that push or pull them in one direction or another without their even realizing it.

---

52. Fritz Perls, one of the founders of the Gestalt school of psychology says there's three types of *shit* a therapist encounters from patients: *chickenshit*: small talk, meant to avoid talking about weightier, more troubling issues; *bullshit:* lies people tell about themselves and often to themselves; and finally, *elephant shit:* those grandiose plans and unrealistic expectations we have for the future, another way of avoiding a bothersome, powerless present.

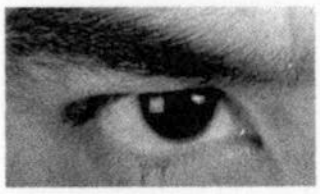

2.

Twenty Ways to See What They Don't Want You to See

Self-importance is our greatest enemy. Think about it—what weakens us is feeling offended by the deeds and misdeeds of our fellowmen. Our self-importance requires that we spend most of our lives offended by someone.
—Carlos Castaneda

OUR BRAIN is who we are. And who we are is composed of two basic brain things: sense impressions and memory. Tibetan monks (lamas) have a belief called "The Six Aggregates,"[53] according to which there is no "Us," no "You," no "I"—there are only our five senses (i.e., aggregates) constantly bombarding our brain with information.

It works like this: as our brain jumps back and forth at blinding speed, first from this sensation to that sensation, it gives the *illusion* that there is somebody in there in charge—a separate "mind" keeping track of all incoming information. Think of the five senses as separate blades on a fan. When the fan is turned off, we can easily see the five *separate* blades. But, turn the fan on, and suddenly the five spinning blades give *the illusion of being a single solid object*.

---

53. For a more complete discussion of "The Six Aggregates" see *Mind Control* by Dr. Haha Lung and Christopher Prowant (Citadel, 2006).

Sorting through all incoming information, putting it away into neat, perfect little files for later (perfect) recall, is our false "mind," our "identity"—aggregate number six, seemingly a separate "entity" but in actuality made up of (1) reactions to our five sense impressions and (2) our "memory" of past reactions to *similar* sense impressions.

So when you say "I," "me," and "mine," Tibetans say, "Bull!" (or whatever the word for bull is in Tibetan). According to those Tibetan lamas, there are just the five senses (aggregates) dancing around, giving the illusion of a sixth "aggregate," our mind—"us."

Keeping that . . . "in mind," win, lose, or draw, we are ruled by our senses sending information to the midbrain amygdala and (hopefully) on to some higher reasoning area of the brain.

It's not surprising then to discover that, while each of us uses all five of our senses at various times to various degrees to gather information, each of us has a preferred way of gathering sense information, favoring one over another.

THE THREE SENSORY MODES: WATCHERS, LISTENERS, AND TOUCHERS

Mind Slayers classify people into three types, depending on their primary mode of gathering information:

- **Watchers:** Dominated by what they see
- **Listeners:** Ruled by what they hear
- **Touchers:** Processing information primarily through their sense of touch, but this mode can also include the sense of smell and taste.[54]

We all use these three senses of sight, hearing, and making actual physical contact with objects—but still each of us tends to favor one style of information gathering more and this becomes a vital component to our personality. Why we favor one sense over another is still a topic of debate with, as with most things involved in the psychology of human beings, half coming down

54. When we smell something, scent molecules actually touch our nose. Likewise, when we taste something, the taste buds on our tongue are actually touched.

on the side of nature—genes and jungle scenes—while the remainder favor nurture—"mama, drama, and trauma."

How we gather information, in turn, has a lot to do with how we then regurgitate that information back out into the world.

Watchers will concentrate on how they appear when presenting their spiel; whereas listeners will practice their speech over and over and over again. Touchers, on the other hand, will keep reminding themselves to "Sit up straight!," "Work your way inside that crowd talking over there," and "Pump some flesh!" (i.e., shake as many hands as possible).

How to Spot 'Em

Don't worry, you won't have to guess whether people are Watchers, Listeners, or Touchers. Even when they don't want to, people will still tell you their sensory mode preference in a half dozen ways. For example, check out what they choose for:

- **Careers?** A toucher (taste-oriented) would be right at home as a chef (though *not* on *Hell's Kitchen*!). They will also like working with their hands (dah, *touching*) which is also used a lot in cooking.

Though we usually associate teachers with talking, listeners actually make the best teachers since they can better determine a student's individual needs by *really* listening. And what about martial arts teachers? Very hands-on, and yet they must be both visually acute (a little Watcher) and have a certain amount of kinesthetic body awareness (a little Toucher) as demanded of most athletes.

How about a cop? We pay them to be Watchers, true, but shouldn't they also be good Listeners—if only to pick out a suspect's lies during interrogation?

In the same vein, say you're interviewing applicants for the job of night watchman. What kind of sensory mode do you hire? The name "night *watchman*" pretty much tells the tale. Of course, a Listener might also work out, until you put him on a job with a lot of background noise guaranteed to distract him. Likewise, a Toucher will get bored to death if you have him sitting around too much of his shift.

Artists are mostly Watchers: drawing, painting, photographing what they see. Ah, but what about sculptors, wood-carvers, quilt makers? Right, Touchers. What about musicians? They're artists, too, and undoubtedly Listeners.

- **Entertainment?** Going to a see movie (Watcher) versus going to a music concert (Listener) versus participating in a dance (body contact—watch him ladies, he's a Toucher!).
- **Hobbies?** A man who enjoys working on his lawn or takes up the hobby of gardening would definitely possess elements of a hands-on Toucher, but he might also be Watcher-oriented since it's the sight of the finished product (immaculate lawn, brightly flowering garden) that makes his day.

Someone who collects vintage records would definitely be a Listener, but what are we to make of ballroom dancers whose hobby (or livelihood) centers around music? Right, Touchers.

Watchers collect paintings, baseball cards, and comic books. Watchers like to read (because it involves using their eyes). They tend to have good (looking) handwriting, to doodle[55] while thinking, and are good spellers—you'll often catch them closing their eyes to recall what words *look* like and/or catch them actually hand-writing the word out; again, so they can *see* whether or not it's spelled correctly.

"Trekkies" and other sci-fi hobbyists are overwhelmingly Watchers, with a fair number of Listeners (those guys who can recite every friggin' line Mr. Spock ever uttered!) sprinkled in.

It's no surprise that comic book collectors are Watchers, comic books being a visual medium, but don't be surprised to also find a few Touch-oriented collectors.

Listeners enjoy talking so they also enjoy wordplay and verbal riddles. They are easily captivated by a good talker. Like Watchers, Listeners remember faces well and enjoy listening activities, from music to reading poetry aloud. Listeners like music and often collect records.

Reward a Listener with concert tickets or a new CD.

---

55. Doodling involves doing something with the hands, seeming to indicate a Toucher, but, like many artists, the end product—scribbling and scratchings—intrigue the Watcher's eye.

- **Sex?** A Toucher and a Listener (which usually means they're a "talker" as well!) aren't going to last together for long. Likewise, a Watcher can't hook up with a partner who's shy about leaving the lights on![56]
- **Words and phrases?** It's been noted that Barack Obama's favorite, most oft-repeated phrase is "Let me be clear." This marks him as a visually dominated person. Detractors will *quickly point* out that this quite possibly also marks him as a person more concerned with how something looks than how it actually performs, in other words, the show must go on!

Recently two University of Vermont scientists found a unique, Internet-based approach to measuring the rise and fall of the American public's "sense of well-being." They gathered data from several sources: downloading 230,000 songs from Hotlyrics.net, noting the mood of each song—melancholy, upbeat, angry—and correlating that information with when the particular types of songs were downloaded. They then added to their database hundreds of millions of sentences from Wefeelfine.org, which scans 2.4 million blogs for the phrases "I feel" and "I am feeling." Finally, these texts were searched for key words, which were then given a negative to positive rating (1 to 9) on a "happiness" scale. For example, positive words like "triumphant" and "love" received a rating of 8.7, while a decidedly negative word like "hostage" rated a lowly 2.2. From this raw data, the scientists were able to calculate the average "societal happiness" each day, going back decades. Predictably, overall mood rises during vacations and national holidays, and it tends to drop during 9/11 and its anniversaries. Scientists plan on analyzing Twitter messages next.[57]

You may have heard of the supersecret NSA[58] using its massive global satellite array known as *Echelon* to monitor radio and cell phone transmissions worldwide, looking for increased transmissions traffic, key words, and phrases, all of which might help it identify terrorist operations.

The good news is that you don't need to pore over millions of bits of

56. For everything you ever wanted to know about sex and the art of seduction but were afraid to ask, read *Mental Domination* by Dr. Haha Lung and Christopher Prowant (Citadel, 2009).

57. See *The Week* 9.21.09:19.

58. National Security Agency, founded 1948, the same year as the CIA.

information on the words and phrases people—particularly your enemies—use; instead, you can often figure out a person's dominating sensory mode just by listening to the words and phrases they use on a regular basis. The verbal imagery we choose to describe how we see and interact with the world betrays us as Watchers, Listeners, or Touchers:

Where a Watcher will tell you "I *see* where you're coming from," a Listener reveals himself with "I *hear* what you're *saying*," and a Toucher might phrase it "I am *solidly behind you* on that" or "I'm sure I can *support you* on that." The same newspaper headline that "screams" for the Listener, "jumps out" at the Toucher and "blindsides" or "dazzles" the Watcher.

Rather than making a decision based on only one or two descriptive words used by a person, look for *patterns* of speech that reveal a person favoring one form of verbal imagery over the others.

Watchers process the world through their eyes and their choice of words will be easy to "see": "He was *short* with me" or "That's certainly a *tall* order." For Watchers, a person is "positively glowing," "radiant," or a "shining" example to others. Words are "beautiful," the boss in an "ugly" mood.

Watchers might tell you "I *see* what you're trying to *show me*. Could you *see* your way *clear* to send a *presentation* I could take a *gander* at? We *see eye-to-eye*. He is a bit of a *shady* character. He tried to *blindside* me, but I *saw* right through him—he's transparent as *glass*!"

Key: Watchers are a shining example of people who like to be dazzled. Make sure your hand is quicker than their eye.

Listeners hear an office "buzzing" with gossip, a room "humming" with excitement. A name often "rings" a bell. They use lines like "I *hear* what you're *saying*, *loud and clear!* That's *music* to my *ears*. *Cha-ching!*" and ask questions like "What did so-and-so *say* about this idea?" or "What's the *word* around the office?" or "What's the *scuttlebutt* on *the grapevine*?"

Key: Listeners like (1) the sound of their own voice and (2) sound effects. Tell them what they like to hear and keep their attention with plenty of bells and whistles.

Touchers use direction (describing their mood as "up," "down," or "feeling low") and temperature (describing people as "cold," receptions as "chilly," and babes as "hot"). They use tactile-oriented words describing others as "a hard nut to crack" or "a smooth operator."

In dealing with others, Touchers chide themselves for being too "soft," other times too "rough." Using movement imagery, Touchers describe atti-

VERBAL PHRASES THAT BETRAYS US

WATCHERS	LISTENERS	TOUCHERS

Clear (cut)	Pay attention to . . .	Hits the nail on the head
Vague	Silence	A feel (for business, etc.)
Flash (of inspiration)	Attuned to . . .	Slip this by you
Imaginative	Question	Run this by you
Enlighten	Afterthought	Make contact with
Photographic memory	Give an earful	Fits the bill
"It just dawned on me . . ."	"Sounds good to me."	Turn (around/over)
"It appears to me . . ."	"Music to my ears."	Sway the jury
Beyond a shadow of a doubt	Clear as a bell	Smooth operator
	Hold your tongue	Fast-paced
Bird's eye view	Rings a bell	Shaky
Eye-to-eye	"To tell the truth . . ."	Topsy-turvy
Face-to-face	Make music together	Underhanded
Paint a picture	Word-for-word	Get the upper hand
"See to it that . . ."	"My ears are burning."	Up/down
"Look into . . ."	Voice (an objection)	"Hot under the collar"
Drawing a blank	Voice (an opinion)	Dirty (evil)
"I see through you."	Buzzing (gossip)	Chilly (reception)
Patterns emerging	Screaming headlines	Foot in the door
Bright future	Give me your ear . . .	Get a handle on
Up front (easily seen)	"That clicks for me."	Get a load of this
"Behind the eight ball"	In a manner of speaking	"Touch base with you"
Well-defined	"Can we talk?"	Boils down to . . .
Tall order	"Let me hear your opinion."	All washed up
Glowing report		Come to grips with . . .
In person	"I hear what you're saying."	Calm, cool, collected
One-on-one		Walking on thin ice
Vision (ary)		Treading water
"I see what you're saying."		Pain in the ass
Get a little insight		Cool under pressure
		Pull some strings
		"Hold your horses."
		"I feel you."

Figure 6.

tudes ("keeping one's head above water"), intent ("trying to sway the jury" or "waiting for the other shoe to drop"), and actions ("give him the brush-off"). A dead giveaway is when Touchers get "vibes" and actually interject the word "feel" into their speech: "It just *feels* wrong to me," "We don't *feel* as *close* as we used to," and "I have a *feel* for business a *feel* for the game." And a savvy Toucher businessman always has his "fingers on the pulse" of the market.

Touchers shake your hand vigorously and pat you on the back while assuring you "I *feel where you're coming from*! You're a *sharp* fellow. I *applaud* the way you *handle* yourself. I'm *looking*[59] *forward* to *touching base* with you on that, maybe *kick around* a few numbers, as soon as we can arrange a *get-together*. It's a bit of a *sticky mess*, but I can *smell* a *sweet* [taste] deal *a mile away*. I *feel* confident we can *bulldoze* our way *through* to *the finish line* if we *press* them on the *small details*."

Key: Touchers often express themselves using time, place, and distance references and like people who do the same.

Body Language?

Watchers' eyes are always watching, moving from side to side, perhaps squinting. They're always adjusting their glasses in order to see better. They are often easily distracted. To test this, let them see you drop a small, innocuous object—a paperclip, for example—and observe if their eyes follow the object to the floor. Like bird dogs born and bred to spot small movement, Watchers are unable to resist moving objects.

Watchers are good at remembering faces (but not names) and are excellent at noticing details (your lodge pin, college ring, tattoos, scars). Give it up: that fine-looking babe at the bar is not only a looker but also a "Watcher,"[60] and she's already zeroed in on the tan line from that wedding ring you just slipped off and slipped into your pocket.

Watchers tend to keep their chins up, trying to see as much as possible (as opposed to Listeners, who keep their heads balanced or leaning toward one ear or the other, and Touchers with head down, neck muscles relaxed).

While on the subject of looking and seeing, the direction a person's eyes move when asked a question can also be a giveaway to that person's sensory mode preference:

---

59. Don't let the word "looking" make you mistake him for a Watcher! He's "looking forward," invoking *distance*.

60. Breathing high in the chest.

Watchers' eyes glance upward a lot, as if reading from the computer screen or blackboard in their mind's eye.

Listeners tend to glance sideways, actually looking toward their ears, as if to adjust volume or mic check: "Is this thing on?"

Touchers tend to look down, often studying their hands as if noticing them for the first time.

Keep in mind that, for most people, the right side is their "imagination side" while the left side is their "memory recall" side. Add this piece of knowledge to your growing knowledge of sensory modes and—Shazam!—instant *lie detector*.[61]

Listeners are leaners. If you think he's a Listener, test him by starting a sentence at normal sound level and then deliberately drop the sound level. Watch to see if he *leans in closer and/or tilts his head* in order to hear better. Also, during normal conversations, keep an eye out for him leaning his head first to one side and then to the other, as if trying to pick up the least sound.

Listeners breathe evenly from midchest. And if you're a Listener yourself, you can practice spotting others' sensory mode by listening to how they breathe: deeper for Touchers, shallower for Watchers.

Listeners often talk, sing, and hum to themselves (listening to the music in their head), often tapping their foot (don't mistake this tapping for Toucher activity).

Touchers are, perhaps predictably, the easiest of the three sensory modes to spot via their body language.

A dead giveaway for spotting Touchers is their tendency to touch others when talking and to physically handle objects when working. They also use their hands when talking and unconsciously tap their pencils and bounce their feet while studying.[62] They enjoy physically challenging—hands-on—work (e.g., taking engines apart, putting puzzles together). Touchers are poor spellers and tend to breathe from their bellies.

A Toucher might ask to "look" your proposal over to the point where

---

61. More on how to spot a liar in the following chapter, "Who Lies . . . and How to Catch Them Doing It!"

62. Toucher foot tapping usually involves *both feet*, often with back and forth tapping. This is especially true when a Toucher is being interrogated and forced to "Sit still!" On the other hand (or foot, as the case may be), Listener foot tapping to music (if only the music in their head) tends to involve only one foot.

you initially mistake him for a Watcher. But study him carefully and you might notice him literally fondling the folder, rubbing his hands over the cover,[63] perhaps even bouncing the folder up and down in his hands, literally weighing your proposal—all signs he's a Toucher. In the same vein, while he's mulling over your proposal, you may catch a Toucher licking or smacking his lips or massaging his gums with his tongue, perhaps grinding his teeth.[64] Licking his lips (Toucher taste behavior) is a sign you've caught his attention—literally whetting and wetting his appetite. Grinding his teeth means he's bored[65] and you're losing him. For more on body language see the chapter that follows: "Who Lies . . . and How to Catch Them Doing It!" and "The Moves They Make," section therein.

How to Trap 'Em

Once Mind Slayers determine whether the enemy is a Watcher, Listener, or Toucher, they can then take steps to craft both speech and actions to better ensnare him—either by enticing him through the use of sensory input he naturally responds favorably to, or else by deliberately stifling him via strategically placing sensory information at odds to his favored mode as a stumbling block in his path. Pegging a person's sensory mode to whether your potential victim (uh, subject) is a Watcher, Listener, or a Toucher is vitally important in order to tailor an effective approach designed specifically to (1) catch their attention or (2) sway their opinion in your direction. For example:

- Force Watchers and Touchers to sit and *listen* to lengthy, boring audiotapes.
- Increase a Watcher's discomfort by meeting him in a windowless room, void of decoration. Watchers' minds tend to wander when forced to *listen* to others talk.

---

63. Realizing he's a Toucher beforehand, you'd make sure you placed your proposal in a well-textured binder pleasing to the touch (authentic leather, for instance).

64. Key: look to see if his jaw-line muscles are alternately tensing and relaxing.

65. Grinding teeth is "self-stimulation" for a bored Toucher, as is rubbing clothing and other forms of "self-grooming." Touchers under interrogation often groom themselves, often more a sign of nervousness (thus, reassuring themselves), not necessarily a sign of lying. (See *The Truth About Lying* by Dr. Haha Lung, publication pending).

- Listeners like to talk, so if you want to raise their stress level, don't give them a chance to get a word in edgewise.
- Increase a Toucher's anxiety by making sure he has nothing to do with his hands.[66]

When doing business with a Toucher, let him handle the cold, hard cash or else physically examine the product. For example, if you're trying to sell him a car, get him seated behind the wheel, let him feel the leather seats.[67] When dealing with a Toucher, don't *talk* a mile a minute and don't waste your time describing how something *looks*. Instead, let the Toucher feel, smell, or taste the product. Even if you're trying to sell him a piece of land three states away, bring him a sample of the soil or a pinecone from the site to touch and smell.

Police interrogators offered Toucher a deal in return for his "cooperation." When rewarding a Watcher, give him a big wall plaque or a degree, something he can hang across from his desk and look at every day.

When debating, arguing, or negotiating, in order to fluster and frustrate your opponent, deliberately choose opposing sensory modes. If he's a Toucher, blind him with vivid visual descriptions, wall charts, and descriptive metaphors.

When confronted by two individuals with differing information gathering styles, drive a wedge of contention between them by choosing a style favored by one but not the other, killing two birds with one stone by freezing one of them out of the conversation, while stroking the other for being "perceptive," "savvy," and just plain "smart enough" to understand what you're saying.

THE EIGHT MASKS

I spy your face, dare you spy mine?
Tho' masks be different,
Manners be kind!
—*Finder's* ditty, circa 1776

---

66. An old interrogator's trick. See *Theatre of Hell: Dr. Lung's Complete Guide to Torture* by Dr. Haha Lung and Christopher Prowant (Loompanics Unlimited 2003).

67. More on the tricks of the trade the car salesman uses in the following section, "What to Study: A Master Persuader's Guide/Study the "Mini-Masters."

Our personal preferences, including but not limited to our sensory mode preference, make up our "persona," our personality—who we are, how we think, and how that thinking in turn influences whether or not we play well with others.

Fittingly, the word "persona" comes from the Latin word for "mask" and originally simply meant a mask worn by an actor in a play. And, in many respects, this is indeed the mask we wear in public, the face we show the world. But, as with all masks, beneath the one the world knows, there's the one that never shows, another face the world might be shocked to see, and you even more chagrined to have it revealed—that true face, beneath the mask you wear each day, perhaps the mask that wears you down each day.

In their must-read *A Sociology of the Absurd* (1989), sociologists Stanford M. Lyman and Marvin B. Scott reveal the importance of "social contracts," the "I'm okay, you're okay" glue (some would say bullshit!) holding civilization together. These are the mores, courtesies, condemnations, and traditions that keep us from each others' throats—some carved in stone, some unspoken—all agreements that "I'll validate your mask, you validate my mask" and "We'll both agree to play fair and not pull the mask off one another (especially during an election year!)." In other words, "I'm full of it and you're full of it but I won't blow your cover if you don't blow my cover!"

There are eight of these persona masks[68] we all wear from time to time, to varying degrees and with varying degrees of success, depending on circumstances. Some of these masks are necessary for keeping up social appearances; others grow out of social obligations that Lyman and Scott call "agreed upon social scripts," again: "I validate you, you validate me."

While we're all capable of assuming any of these eight masks and at any given time, not too surprising for getting-stuck-in-a-rut-prone human beings is the fact that some of us wear the mask so long our "true face" comes to resemble it.[69]

Master Mind Slayers, accomplished shape-shifters all, never content nor confine themselves to sporting only one of these eight personas; instead, they master the art and ability of slipping into and out of any and all needed persona as suits their agenda du jour.

---

68. A quick mnemonic for remembering these eight persona masks is that together their first letters spell "CASH LIES," which, in many ways, they are, indeed, *lies* we *cash* in on.

69. Yes, there was a creepy 1960s *Twilight Zone* episode based on just this premise.

Mask of the Chameleon

Ephemeral, a true shapeshifter, mood and manner always changeable, amorphous, hard to pin down. Some chameleons are deliberately "shifty," others simply because they can't help themselves—it's their nature, blending into the background, following the path of least resistance.

This type of person makes the perfect enemy since he has little ambition and no inspiration. He has no purpose in life. When placed in charge of others, his orders are vague and hard to follow on the one hand, and ever-changing to the point of confusion on the other.

With the Chameleon as your enemy, all you have to do to defeat him is encourage his lack of commitment. Encourage him to try out for "Couch-Potato of the Year," advising him to "sit on" his idea a while, wait and see what develops. No need to get in a hurry: "Haste makes waste."

Conversely, give the Chameleon personality a dose of the aggressive Hero personality below, and a Chameleon becomes the most unpredictable of enemies, one constantly changing shape and tactics, a clay face capable of confounding you at every turn by his lack of consistency and predictability.

If a predictable enemy is a godsend, then an unpredictable enemy must surely come straight from the bowels of Hell! Thus, being unpredictable was Sun Tzu's bread and butter (or, rice and butter if you prefer). Other Asian master strategists also took this principle to heart:

> Nothing is constant in war save deception and cunning. Herein lies the true Way. —T'sao T'sao

> Dodge left, strike right. Dodge right, strike left. Fake an attack forward to cover your retreat. Pretend retreat . . . before springing forward with ferocity! —Li Chung[70]

One obvious Westerner who spent plenty of time learning the ways of Asian Mind Slayers was espionage phenom Sidney Reilly. An obvious Chameleon-Hero hybrid, he was also the real-life prototype for the fictional James Bond.[71]

Hannibal the Conqueror (247–183 B.C.)—called "The Sun Tzu of the

70. Eighth century Chinese strategist.

71. See "Sidney Reilly: Rules of the White Dragon," in Part II.

West"—was another such Chameleon-Hero hybrid, a man of practiced inconsistency, always keeping his enemies guessing:

> I stagger left and my enemy laughs at "The Drunken Man." Suddenly, I strike right! And all laughter ceases! I stumble back, my enemy falls headlong onto my sword as he tries clinging to me. —Truth XXXI[72]

Always beware lest, while you're busy trying to spy out the Chameleon-Hero's "pattern," he attacks! Do not allow yourself to be distracted and/or to siphon off your valuable resources trying to discern his pattern—*he doesn't have one*. He's flying by the seat of his pants, reckless, making it up as he goes along, rolling with the punches while looking for his opportunity to deliver the knockout blow.

However, when taken to the other extreme, you encounter a foe who changes his mind and his strategies so often, even his own men are confused by his orders. As already mentioned, this is a great kind of enemy to have—one who confuses his own men, saving *you* the trouble of having to do so!

Since he lacks any clear direction, any commitment to a cause, the Chameleon can easily be "turned," that is, convinced to join your cause and/or easily recruited as a spy or double-agent.[73]

If you do succeed in recruiting him to your cause, keep a close eye on him. Don't assume that because of his ability to blend into any background that the Chameleon automatically makes a *trustworthy* spy. Because of his lack of commitment, he can all too easily be turned (again) by the enemy—a triple agent!

Mask of the Accountant

Sanguine, practical, no nonsense, and utilitarian, the Accountant can also be cheerful and appear confident—but only within his own field of expertise, his comfort zone.

A good and loyal worker bee, he secretly dreams of "the good life," but he lacks the originality and depth to make it happen on his own. Get his

---

72. See *The 99 Truths: Hannibal's Black Art of War* by Dr. Haha Lung (publication pending). See also *Ultimate Control* by Dr. Haha Lung and Christopher B. Prowant (Citadel 2010).

73. See *Sun Tzu* Chapter XIII.

attention by offering to help him accomplish this. Tempt his opportunistic streak with a "Too good to be true" offer. But make sure you dot all the *I*s and cross all the *T*s before showing him your proposal. No matter how enthusiastic he is about a project, he'll still read every word of the fine print—with a heavy sigh—before he signs on the dotted line.

Mask of the Shy

Sensitive and sentimental, in the extreme the Shy is introverted and timid, resulting in his often being indecisive. He'd fit in perfectly with those guys on *The Big Bang Theory*.[74] A nerd, yes, but often a master in his field (e.g., the stereotypical computer whiz).

His flaw—and your gaping gateway into his world—is that he's lonely and repressed from keeping his secret (often taboo) desires hidden.

Once you uncover his secrets, rather than betray his secrets, encourage and reinforce them, binding him closer to your cause. Assure him that, "back in the day," "a long time ago," "back in the Middle Ages" it was okay to do such-and-such (whatever his secret sin is). Thus, the savvy Mind Slayer enters his world through his fascination for the nostalgic.

He is in love with the way he *believes* the past was. Feed that belief and you can have him eating out of your hand. Idealize the past with him and you will be his friend. Use phrases like "traditional values" and "respect for the past." In extremis, he sometimes "loses" himself in things past, like collecting. Inside, he's playing historical video avatar/role-playing games. Outside: Civil War or knightly Renaissance re-enacting.

Mask of the Hero

He adapts well, he's sociable. Unlike the Accountant, the Hero lives in the present. He's action-oriented, impulsive, and easily excitable—any of which can work either for or against him.

Quick to anger, he's just as quick to be distracted by his next cause and forget his initial anger.

If he is your ally, beware of his ADD.[75] Out of boredom, he may jump

74. CBS TV.

75. Attention deficit disorder—short attention span.

the gun and attack your mutual enemies too soon. In his enthusiasm, he may not pay close enough attention to potentially fatal flaws in his plans. Details bore him.

If he's your subordinate, give him plenty to keep him busy. He's a good soldier and a tireless worker but one easily distracted and bored. To counter this, always have novel assignments waiting for him, missions that won't give his mind time to shift, drift, or get miffed.

Give him his marching orders and then turn him loose. He becomes passionate in action, and tends toward being authoritarian in attitude, but generally accomplishes anything he sets his mind to—or anything *you* set his mind to!

If the Hero is your enemy, distract his attention with plenty of bells and whistles. Send one of your lieutenants out to openly challenge him (i.e., distract him, capture his attention, probe for weakness) while your main force seizes your true objective.

Taking offense at a personal insult gives him an excuse to "go off the reservation," to (literally) strike out on his own. If he's your enemy, insult him in order to draw him out, whether to draw him out from the safety of some actual physical fortress to unwisely do battle with you on open ground, or else egging him on into raising the bet on a pair of threes.

Best-case scenario, he's the unconventional maverick who saves the day in his own way: think Patton. Worst-case scenario, he's an out-of-control rogue element you can ill-afford: think Oliver North.

The Hero makes a good spy except for his flaw of becoming passionate about a cause-within-a-cause (i.e., his zeroing in on a single person or aspect of the overall assignment), losing sight of the big picture. Utilize his talents best by *not* filling him in on the big picture. Deploy him only on a "need to know" basis, feeding him a series of immediate, individual assignments to accomplish—all of which culminate in your accomplishing the big picture.

Mask of the Lover

Only slightly less impulsive than the Hero, the Lover is sociable and adapts well to any environment, instantly passionate and committed—perhaps even fanatical—about any project he takes on. Always calculating, he can become an authoritarian when he (inevitably) becomes worried that the project is going to go wrong unless he personally sees to every minute detail of the operation. He's a micro-manager, and thus better suited to working alone lest he infuriates coworkers and causes dissension within the ranks.

As a commander, he keeps his soldiers on too short a leash, not utilizing their full potential.

As a ruler, he violates Sun Tzu's proscription against trying to run a battlefield while sitting on a throne a thousand miles away.

He may suffer from obsessive-compulsive disorder (OCD) or he may just be anal as all get out!.

Mask of the Indifferent

Unmotivated, lacking interest, if the Indifferent is your enemy, keep him unmotivated by not (overtly) disturbing him with your plans and preparations. With any luck, he'll sleep right through your invasion!

On the other hand, if he's your ally, make him your "front man," literally putting him out front where:

1. You can keep an eye on him.
2. You can give him a motivational kick in the ass as needed.
3. His *laissez faire demeanor,* laid-back attitude, and just generally lazy appearance will alleviate your enemy's suspicion you are up to something, lulling your enemy into either a false sense of security (extrapolating that all your men are likewise slackers) and/or a false sense of superiority ("We're better than those slackers").

Mask of the Edge

He lives in the moment, often impulsive, always watchful. An uneven and nervous temperament, he's often given to extremes of mood swings. Possibly bipolar,[76] some perceive him as a "flip-artist," as being wishy-washy, always switching horses in midstream.

He's the original cat on a hot tin roof, restless, suspicious. Loud noises (and opportunities) make him jump, but you never know *which way* he'll jump. Still waters will be the death of him, because he too often leaps before

76. Given to fluctuating wildly between extremes of energetic euphoria and paralyzing depression.

he looks—not out of reckless bravado (like the Hero) but out of fear of losing out, being left out, or being late to take advantage of an opportunity.

His tarot card is "the fool," a man literally perched on *the edge* of a great precipice, oblivious to the danger. If he's your ally, business partner, or lover, don't let him take you down with him.

If the Edge is your enemy, give him a hand . . . in the small of his back!

Mask of the Skeptic

This kind questions everything. Good in the long run for efficiency, but slow to start. However, he has a proven track record of persevering once you point him in the right direction and set him in motion. Capable of operating on his own, capable of making good, unemotional, and methodical—but slow—decisions. Put the Skeptic on your team to balances out the Hero personalities on your staff so eager to leap without looking. The Skeptic always looks and—given enough time—usually sees what needs seeing and what needs doing.

He likes things orderly, so show him a better way to organize his world and he'll be loyal (customer) for life. "New World Order" doesn't sound all that bad to him.

Attract him to you and impress him into your cause with your personal orderliness.

TEN GOOD EXCUSES . . . BUT NOT ONE GOOD EXPLANATION!

Sometimes you have to look reality in the eye, and deny it.
—Garrison Keillor

Along with the eight different faces—persona—a person can sport to help make things go their way, there's also nine kinds of excuses people tend to give when things *don't* go their way. This is not the same thing as lying per se, or at least that's what most people (1) want to believe themselves or (2) try to make the rest of us believe.

First off, an excuse is *not* an explanation.

An explanation carries within it the idea that you're actually going to explain your questionable actions. An explanation is therefore *an answer to a question*, an answer we can reasonably expect to contain a modicum of factual information—who, what, when, where, how, and, most important, why. That last part, why, is usually where most people—trapped, desperately looking for a way out!—come up short in the explanation department and instead settle for spitting out the most readily available excuse.

So, nine times out of ten—that's right, a whopping ninety percent of the time—when most people get caught with their hand in the cookie jar, when backed into a corner and being pressed for an explanation . . . what they end up reaching for is an excuse.

Knowing then that it's in our nature, when trapped, to look for a way out, *before the next time* you're caught with chocolate chips on your breath, when the shade of lipstick on your collar *isn't* your wife's, or when you just can't seem to nail down a single darn one of those "weapons of mass destruction," you might want to take a few minutes to commit the following tried-and-true types of excuses—*not* explanations—to memory.

The "Where's the Body?" Excuse

You protest that no one was harmed by your actions; it was a "victimless crime": stuff like gambling, insider trading, prostitution, that "medicinal" herb you're growing in your backyard. Not worth getting local law enforcement out of bed. No harm, no foul. No offense meant, none taken . . .

But, on the darker side, you'll hear this excuse from child molesters who use it to justify their behavior: "No one got hurt," they'll say, while time and again claiming that the three-year-old "wanted it," or even that they were doing the kid "a favor" by "introducing" them to sex. Or you'll hear it from serial killers: "They were only prostitutes. Who's gonna miss 'em?"

This kind of twisted thinking bleeds over into the next excuse and drips all the way down to excuse number seven, where they can argue that they were somehow doing the kid—and the world—a favor.

The "It's in the Bible" Excuse

This excuse *is* similar to the Where's the Body? excuse, except that, in this instance, there really *is* a body, or at least a victim everybody agrees is a victim. Except that, in the perpetrator's mind, the victim *deserved* what they got because "You reap what you sow"—you know, like it warns about in the Bible.[77] This one's also sometimes known as The Reaper's Excuse. In other words, your "bad karma" or "God's wrath" finally catches up with you.

At first glance, "You reap what you sow" sounds good, even logical. But this excuse is often reasoned *in reverse*.

If cause produces effect, isn't it logical that any effect must have a cause? Of course. But some use this kind of reverse logic to indict others. Such ass-backward reasoning says that if "everybody reaps what they sow," then *victims* must have done something in their past to deserve what happens to them. It's called "victim blaming." "And since they had it coming, God must have picked me to administer it to them," thinks the rapist or serial killer with *delusions of grandeur.*

It has been theorized that one of the reasons convicted sexual predators are so quick to embrace religion when they enter prison is because, in their twisted minds, the Biblical declaration "You reap what you sow" sounds like "My victims got what they deserved!" and "I was only doing God's will."[78]

Taken to the extreme, this "It's in the Bible" Excuse is used to justify—or ignore—both actions and inactions taken for and against minorities and other marginalized segments of society:

- Black neighborhoods are "crime ridden" because they refuse to police themselves
- If gays didn't act so "queer," drawing attention to themselves, they wouldn't be getting bashed all the time
- And "Just look at the way she was dressed. She was askin' for it. No wonder she got raped!"

Knowing perverts and predators think this way, police interrogators often get them to confess by "complimenting" the suspects for being so "perceptive" as to spot a victim who (because of their behavior) "*deserved* to be taught a lesson."

Conversely, speaking of law enforcement personnel, there's a psychological diagnosis called "The Wyatt Earp Syndrome," where those professionals

77. Or Koran, if you prefer.

78. Yeah, same as those brainwashed sickos who hijacked those planes on 9/11.

involved in law enforcement and in the judicial system feel they have a right and a duty to do "whatever it takes" to get criminals off the street.

Thus, we find instances of police and prosecutors manufacturing evidence and false testimony (e.g., from "questionable" jailhouse informers) when they fear a serious criminal might go free, either because they don't have enough (real) evidence to hold them or else because they don't believe the evidence they do have will be enough to convince a jury beyond a reasonable doubt.

Named for the controversial Western lawman often accused of bending the law in order to enforce it, The Wyatt Earp Syndrome[79] can affect not just police and prosecutors but anyone in a position of authority (e.g., prison guards) who believe the end justifies the means when it comes to punishing criminals, believing that they've been given power "for a reason" (almost by *divine* authority) and therefore have the right to put criminals away by any means necessary: planting evidence, torturing "confessions" out of prisoners, even murder.

Police and prosecutors know that even if a convicted criminal gets his conviction overturned by a higher court of appeals, the appeals process is likely to take years—years that the dangerous criminal is off the street. Even when discovered manufacturing evidence, prosecutors rarely receive more than a slap on the wrist.

During the "liberation" of Iraq, we saw how easily even the best trained soldiers on earth, when faced with an implacable and fanatical foe, often feel justified in resorting to torture and sometimes summary execution in an effort to break the enemy's will.

Fanatical religious fundamentalists[80] savor vicarious satisfaction when something bad happens to those who do not immediately heed their "message of hope and salvation."

It's a little hard to dispute an excuse when you got God Almighty cosigning for you.

This kind of vigilante thinking carries over into our sixth excuse of "Manifest Destiny," below.

---

79. For more on The Wyatt Earp Syndrome and other psychological justifications (i.e., excuses) used to condone abuse and torture, see *Theatre of Hell: Dr. Lung's Complete Guide to Torture* by Dr. Haha Lung and Christopher B. Prowant (Loompanics Unlimited, 2003).

80. Thrice redundant!

Psychology calls this schadenfreude sadism, and it seems we're all just a little guilty of it—applauding just as loudly as the next fellow when we finally sell Osama's bloody head on eBay. Say you won't.

The "What's Good for the Goose Is Good for the Gander" Excuse

If some rich CEO on Wall Street can Ponzi scheme investors out of millions . . . why do I gotta go to jail for boostin' a pack o' smokes from my local 7-Eleven? What's good for the goose is good for the gander.

Caught red-handed, criminals so often whine, "But the cops are crooked *too*!" as if the trespass of the one somehow alleviates the culpability of the other. Everybody's doing it, so why can't I?

This excuse is a retarded rendition of the rule of *lex talionis*: "An eye for an eye." Though often quoted as justification and explanation—*excuse*—for our retaliating in kind, the original intent of this Hebrew law was "Not *more* than an eye for an eye"—meaning punishment should not be excessively harsh, but rather the punishment should fit—be proportionate to—the crime.

Once a police interrogator recognizes that the criminal he is interrogating functions on this "What's good for the goose is good for the gander" level, the interrogator quickly convinces the suspect to turn on his partners by openly chiding the suspect about how the suspect's so-called partners are already making a deal with the prosecutor to snitch him out for lesser time. Even for a hardened street thug who follows "the code" against becoming an informer, being told that his buddies are getting special treatment for selling him up the river is all the excuse the suspect needs to snitch on them *first*.

The "Running Bull" Excuse

In Pamploma, Spain, where they do that crazy running of the bulls thing every year, those who successfully complete the run (i.e., those who avoid becoming "mad-cow shish kebab"!) become part of an exclusive fraternity whose ceremonial toast motto is "To lying, to cheating, and to stealing!" As explained to the uninitiated (i.e., the as of yet *un*gored!):

> When we lie . . . we lie to save a friend. When we cheat . . . we cheat Death. And when we steal . . . it is a young girl's heart!

Let's go back to that first part, "Lying to save a friend." That's what this particular excuse hinges on: "I did it to help a friend."

Variations of this excuse include "I robbed that store to buy food for my family." And "I crashed that plane into the World Trade Center to please God." In other words, I did it to help someone else.

In other words, whatever wrong I did, I did it for a good reason, for a good cause, maybe even for God himself! Sometimes, like the motto of a slow-running Pamploma (h)ornaments, you do a bad thing to help someone—a loved one, God, Uncle Sam—or Auntie Osama, as the case may be. Anyway you look at it, you did it for a good reason—that's your excuse.

This excuse is another way of saying, "The end justifies the means." Not so bad when used to justify acts as harmless as telling a little white lie to keep a friend out of trouble. Bad thing when you're using it to justify crashing a plane into the World Trade Center and killing three thousand innocent people.

The "Abuse" Excuse

Poor, poor pitiful me. Something happened to me in my childhood that I just can't get over—mama, drama, *and* trauma!—so I'm not responsible for my adult actions. This is the excuse of every child molester who ever lived: "My alcoholic stepmother forced me to model Victoria's Secret while listening to Michael Jackson records—played backward!"

Bull. The numbers just don't show it: For every thousand kids who get molested, only one of them grows up to be a molester. So when you hear some diaper-sniper whining about how he was molested as a child, remind him how those other nine hundred and ninety-nine grown-ups who were molested as children went on to lead productive lives, some even taking jobs in law enforcement or social services especially so they could protect children. No excuses.

Anytime we accept this Abuse Excuse, we act as the enabler to someone.

The "It's Biological" Excuse

Poor, poor pitiful me. I was born into the wrong color skin, into a body without a penis. I can do the job just as well as any man . . . Oh, but I need you to lower the bar a just a little . . . just a little more . . . That's it, just a wee bit more . . . And I need you to throw out that promotion test because nobody but those white guys passed the test . . . Oh, that's right: the United State Supreme Court already decided that was a no-no. Guess you'll just have to study harder next time.

You can either win with the skin you're in, or use it as your excuse for never trying.

A variation of this It's Biological Excuse is claiming what's called "biological imperative," as in "Mother Nature made me do it!" (e.g., "Men just have a greater sex drive, honey. I swear it was *just* sex. That's all it was. She didn't mean a thing to me!").

And let's not forget that, down through the history of mankind, real and imagined biological differences have been used as the excuse for everything from gender bias to genocide.

The "It's Geographical" Excuse

Nobel Prize–winner Bertrand Russell (1872–1970) once noted that "Sin is geographical." So it seems are excuses.

Poor, poor pitiful me. Those greedy Europeans took our land! Yeah . . . but wasn't that only a few years after *you* took the land from that other tribe who didn't learn to ride horses—brought by Europeans by the way—as quickly as your tribe did? Kinda made chasing down them buffalo a whole lot easier too, huh? And remind me again why Custer was so good at finding all those *hidden* Indian camps? Oh, right, those smaller tribes you screwed over got their revenge by selling you out to the white-eyes.

Poor, poor pitiful me. I was raised in a crack-infested neighborhood awash in poverty—My God! Conditions were so bad we could barely afford MTV, PlayStation 3, and season tickets to the Cleveland Cavaliers! Is it any wonder I grew up to mug senior citizens for their Social Security checks?

Poor, poor pitiful me. My family put the "poor" in "poor white trash." I was born in Appalachia and they say we can't leave till we learn how to spell it! And, to make matters worse, there's something in all that trailer park aluminum that not only attracts tornados[81] but's probably what's caused my IQ to be lower than a snake's belly. Sorry, Cletus. If you could spell "DNA" you'd probably know what the problem is. That, and that paint thinner you

81. Remember, you heard it here first.

been huffing all day. Chances are you did it to yourself, Bubba. Stupid is as stupid does, right Forrest?

Poor, poor pitiful me. I'm doomed to go to prison!

It's true that twenty-five percent of all black males will go to prison some time in their lives. But that means three times as many, seventy-five percent, *don't* go to jail—ever. Instead, they go on to lead productive—boring—NBA contract-free lives (just like the rest of us!). No excuses.

And while we're on the subject of crime in general, the majority of convicted felons who do time in prison, get out and stay out. Those who don't probably shouldn't have been let out of prison in the first place. No excuses.

Poor, poor pitiful me. I was born in Beverly Hills with a silver spoon in my mouth (and I've have been sticking it under my nose ever since!). It's such a *burden* being so filthy rich (what with all those taxes, keeping up with the Trumps, and such); so hard being a gazillion-dollars-a-picture movie star, all those paparazzi always wanting to take my picture, Oprah calling me at odd hours; and it's such a diamond-studded yoke around my neck being a "celebrity"—especially one (1) without any real talent and (2) without my own reality series! Oh, but I do so "identify" with all "the little people" (like the ones who do my nails and bring me my bottled water—*imported* only!). Like them, I can barely stand my pitiful existence.

The "Manifest Destiny" Excuse

This is where you use science, God, or Manifest Destiny as your excuse.

In case you haven't been studying your American history lately—or ever!—Manifest Destiny refers to the seventeenth-century political philosophy that the fledgling United States was "destined" to stretch from sea to shining sea. And anybody who just happened to already be occupying the land in between the Atlantic and Pacific, and Great Lakes to the Gulf, had better get the hell out of the way! With this Manifest Destiny idea, which worked so well on the French, Spanish, and Indians occupying the lower forty-eight, we took the show on the road to Alaska, the (once) sovereign kingdom of Hawaii, and, while we're on a roll, the rest of Central and South America!

Used as our personal excuse, Manifest Destiny means whatever we did was "meant to happen." This is similar to the "You reap what you sow" Excuse previously mentioned.

We fully intended to do what we did . . . but *it was meant to be*. It was *destined* to happen that way.

Besides, if *we* didn't do it, someone else would have. It's been argued that Judas Iscariot used this very reasoning when deciding to betray Jesus Christ:

> He's the Son of God and he *has* to be betrayed by someone so he can do that resurrection thing . . . so I must be the one *destined* to betray him, chosen by God Almighty himself to do the dirty deed!

Yeah, Judas probably thought he was doing the world a favor—our next excuse.

Thieves use a variation of this Manifest Destiny Excuse as well: "It was just laying there, out in the open. Someone would have stolen it sooner or later."

Sometimes there might be actual merit to this Manifest Destiny Excuse, as in "The Last Can of Beans" scenario:

> *The Apocalypse*. You're surviving in a barricaded-up basement with your wife and two small children and there's only a single can of beans left. Who eats the beans?
>
> Trained by society that it's noble to sacrifice for others, your first instinct might be to divide the beans equally among your wife and kids and go hungry yourself . . . Wrong answer. *You* eat the beans. Not because you're some kind of heartless bastard but because *you* have to stay strong enough to beat the wolves (both four-legged and the even more treacherous *two-legged* kind) back from the door. *You* have to remain strong enough to go out and hunt for more food.

Other times, the Manifest Destiny excuse is used to justify all kinds of half-baked, half-assed "self-actualization," "search for enlightenment," "the need to find myself" quests that are really just excuses in and of themselves to skip out on your responsibilities.

Everyone marvels at Impressionist painter Paul Gauguin's (1848–1903) priceless topless Tahitian beauties, while ignoring the shameful fact that one day Gauguin just up and abandoned his wife and kids in freezing France to sail off to the South Pacific. We can only guess that in his mind Gauguin justified his dead-beat dadism by seeing his art as a "higher calling."

People hiding behind this kind of excuse often claim to get their marching orders from a higher authority, that their plans are part of "God's plan" or else a "natural" part of evolution.

The "I'm Doing the World a Favor" Excuse

If you've never seen the horror movie series *Saw*[82] run out and rent them right now, we'll wait . . . *Saw*'s antihero is a psychopathic villain dubbed "Jigsaw" who only learns to appreciate life when he finds out he's dying of cancer. So—in typical psychopath fashion—he decides to do people "a favor" by kidnapping and torturing them until they learn to appreciate life as much as he does. You see, Jigsaw truly believes he's doing his victims a favor by forcing them to stop taking being alive for granted.

Timothy McVeigh believed he was doing the world a favor, alerting people to the increasing encroachment of government agencies. The 9/11 hijackers also thought they were doing the world a favor[83] by pointing out "crimes" committed by the United States. Did you ever notice how the people who protest the loudest that they're "doing the world a favor" always seem to be the ones blowing *the biggest chunks* out of it!

Back in the day, religions missionaries—Christian and Muslim alike—were zealous in doing "half-naked savages" everywhere a favor by first slapping clothes over any and all exposed flesh and then doing those savages (or "infidels" if you prefer) an even bigger favor by forcing them to convert to a "real" religion at the point of a sword. Those missionaries believed they were doing those "Godless heathens"—and the world at large—an enormous favor.

Child molesters often try to argue how they're doing the kid a favor.

As already discussed, The Wyatt Earp Syndrome convinces police and prosecutors that they're doing society a favor—so anything goes so long as it ends in a conviction.

---

82. *Saw* (2004), *Saw II* (2005), *Saw III* (2006), *Saw IV* (2007), *Saw V* (2008), and *Saw VI*, which hit the movie theaters in October 2009.

83. In addition to doing God's (Allah's) will.

Cult leaders (and members) also justify any and all actions that serve to promote the cult agenda—for the betterment of the world they will one day *rule*!

To use this "I'm Doing the World a Favor" Excuse, you don't have to be doing the *whole* world a favor trying to save it (or enslave it); you could just be looking out for your particular culture, clique, or cult, or simply helping out a friend—à la The Running Bull Excuse.

The key is you truly *believe* you're doing whatever you're doing—no matter how heinous—to help the world, or at least your particular little piece of it.

At one level, if you believe your actions are somehow benefiting the entire world, you're Mahatma Gandhi, Martin Luther King Jr., and Bono all rolled into one, or else you got a real bad case of that "megalomania"[84] thing psychiatrists are always talking about.

Cornered, pressed for an *explanation* (not an *excuse*) for their actions, people often mix and match these nine types of excuses, trying on one excuse after another until finally finding the excuse that best fits their immediate faux pas, failing, fuck-up, or felony.

Each of us have, on occasion, used one or more—if not all!—of these excuses. But for some people—hopefully, your enemy—making excuses in order to skirt responsibility and avoid involvement becomes first a habit, then a way of life.

When it's our enemy hiding behind an obvious excuse, we can either:

- **Expose him** for the shirker, slacker, and liar he is. Or else . . .
- **Encourage him** in his excuse making, the more extravagant and extrapolated the better—helping him further paint himself into a corner.

No matter how disgusted you might be with an enemy's excuse, acting nonjudgmental of the excuse he thinks is an explanation helps you better bond with him, causing him to drop his guard and draw you closer into his camp and confidence. Of course, you'll want to bank the obvious flaws in his excuse for later exposure if/when necessary.

---

84. A mental disorder marked by feelings of personal omnipotence and delusions of grandeur.

It is not surprising that some people favor, and even become dominated by, certain excuses—perhaps having relied on one particular type of excuse over and over since childhood. Only the particulars of time and place change. Their basic—familiar, tried-and-true—excuse stays the same.

The type of excuses a person favors is a very valuable clue to their overall personality type. Upon close examination, you'll often discover their choice of excuse reflects their overall mind-set and life attitude. Which came first, the mind-set or the excuse? Did the mind-set give birth to the excuse or vice versa? Doesn't matter.

Listening to the type of excuse a person uses over and over tells you a lot about how they see themselves (e.g., "I'm the kind of guy who looks out for my friends, even lying if necessary"—a Running Bull personality. Or, God has chosen me to "Do the world a favor" type of fanatic). Others believe it's their Manifest Destiny to accomplish great and important tasks—and anyone who gets in their way had better watch out!

Maybe they'll use the "I was abused as a child" kind of excuse, so any kind of craziness I do as an adult should be forgiven. And what about all those people who feel they're entitled to a free ride, reparations, and special treatment just because they were born in a certain body ("It's Biological" Excuse) or in a certain underprivileged spot ("It's Geographical" Excuse).

Still others never let pity or compassion or a blind puppy stranded by the road get in the way of accomplishing their agenda because "Everybody gets what they deserve," because "You reap what you sow," because "It's in the Bible." So if you fall for this scam I'm pulling on you, you *deserve* to lose your money, your virginity . . . your life! You're looking at your basic sociopathic-psychopathic criminal thinking here.

On the other hand, when we find out our enemy is dominated by one—or more—of these excuse attitudes, it gives us a perfect opening for penetrating his mind.

The "Best Available Information" Excuse

In any battlefield situation, in any boardroom situation, in any bedroom, *real-time intelligence* is crucial. Lack of current, constantly updated information on the battlefield will get you and those depending on you killed. Lack of timely information in the boardroom can cause you to lose out on millions. And unless you are paying perfect attention to what that person next to you in the bed is saying (moaning-wise and otherwise) . . . the night is not going to come to a . . . ahem . . . good climax.

Anytime a couple has a trial separation period, at least one of them—yeah, yeah, it's usually the guy!—uses this "cooling off" period as an opportunity to try out some new "stuff." Later, after the couple gets back together and the truth of his infidelity inevitably comes out, he'll use a variation of this Best Information Available Excuse by pleading, "But baby, *at the time*, I didn't know if we were getting back together or not!"

On the other hand, say you start a war on the excuse you're going after WMDs, only to later discover no WMDs. You can always shrug your shoulders and claim that, with good intention, you were acting on the best available information at the time.

See the "Mastering Propaganda" section on pages 113–19.

A final word on the subject of excuses: A true Mind Slayer would never allow himself (or herself) to be trapped in a situation where they *have* to explain their actions, where they *have* to make excuses.

A Scientific Explanation—Excuse!—for Lying?

According to a 2006 study done at the University of Southern California, some of us may be born with a *genetic predisposition* to lie. When compared to the brains of honest folk, the brains of "chronic liars, cheaters and malingerers" averaged twenty-two percent more white matter in the prefrontal cortex of their brains, white matter acting as the basic "wiring" of the brain, connecting neurons together. White matter also connects the prefrontal cortex to our old buddy the amygdala/limbic system. This could explain why pathological liars can lie—which takes place in their white-matter-rich prefrontal cortex—without showing signs of nervousness, which is controlled by the limbic system.[85]

So the next time you're caught in a bald-faced lie, tell the judge or your rolling-pin-carrying wife you can't be held responsible . . . because it's *genetic*!

85. *National Geographic*, March 2006:32

THE TEN EXCUSES

Excuse	Attitude	How to Exploit Their Excuse
"Where's the Body?"	Nobody really got hurt. Victimless crime.	Help them "justify" their behavior. Show them "facts" and "statistics" to back up their claims (until they become dependent upon you).
"It's in the Bible"	Eye for an eye. Bad Karma. The victims got what they deserve. Effect follows cause.	Help them "marginalize" their victim by supplying them with "evidence" of the others' malfeasance.
"What's Good for the Goose Is Good for the Gander"	Everybody does it. The cops are crooked, too. Two wrongs don't make it right but it damn sure makes it even!	Convince him it's "natural." It's his "right," his "due." The police (etc.) will look the other way . . . wink-wink.
"Running Bull"	It's okay to lie, cheat, and steal to help others. A good end justifies any means. Machiavellian.	Convince him he's on the side of the angels. He can do no wrong because his heart is pure and his goal is righteous.
"Abuse"	Something happened in my childhood (e.g., molestation, poverty, etc.) that gives me *carte blanche*. Past trauma gives me the right to inflict trauma on others.	Become his enabler. Reinforce and feed his denial. The world owes him a living, his revenge, a trophy for "milking" his defect, deformity, or disease to the max.
"It's Biological"	I'm a victim from birth, either born into the wrong skin or the wrong gender. "People like us never get a break." (This despite all the obvious others of their gender, race, or ethnic group who have succeeded in life ("Sell outs! Uncle Toms!").	Become their enabler, sure you understand how tough it is being a certain race or sex or ethnic minority. And you'd understand how "justified" they'd be in "striking back" against society, etc. for the way they've been screwed over all their lives.
"It's Geographical"	Same as the biological excuse, except your excuse this time is that you were born in "the ghetto" or the trailer park, or some backward country that's always been oppressed by some bigger country.	Same as biological, commiserate with them, give them all the excuse they need to either strike back against real (or mostly imagined) wrongs, or else all the excuse they need to sit on their lazy asses.
"Manifest Destiny"	Nothing happens without a reason. It was meant to be. Excuse #2.	Agree with him that destiny, fate, and fortune are all on his side. Secretly make "windfalls" happen to him to reinforce his belief.
"I'm Doing the World a Favor!"	Extrapolation of excuse #4. Timothy McVeigh. Serial killer excuse for killing prostitutes, etc.	Assure him he'll be a "hero" once he accomplishes his mission. The world will be a better place when he's done and everyone will see him as the genius he is.
The "Best Available Information"	I'm only as good as my information . . . and it's not my fault my information was out of date!	Become their enabler; help them blame others for their lack of "timely" information. Feed them out-of-date information to further confuse them.

Figure 7.

ART OF THE QUICK FIX

For those times you don't have time for, or you've run out of, the Ten Excuses, you need a quick fix to help you exit the scene as quickly as possible with as much grace and self-esteem intact as you can carry. At such times, you need a phrase or two that temporarily confuses your detractor-attacker long enough for you to beat your hasty retreat. The need could come when some smarty-pants know-it-all at a party really does know it all and starts backing you into a corner, basically questioning your credentials (credentials that may fly at a cocktail party but would never get you through security at JFK Airport!). Or how about when the boss confronts you for being late for the umpteenth time, and you need to brush him off (I said *brush* him off!) just to keep your job?

First, look your detractor straight in the eye and with a really "intense" (okay, call it "crazy") look on your face—try for a look somewhere between angry and sad—say one of the following:

- "Do you know *anything* about testicular cancer . . . ?" This works especially well if your detractor is a woman. The instant confusion registers on their face, snap, "Humph! I didn't think so." Exit quickly.
- "It seems *female* problems just won't wait." Emphasize the word "female" and every man on earth will suddenly remember he has a pressing engagement anywhere but going there! If you say this woman-to-woman, the other woman's "co-misery/sympathy" gene will kick in as she remembers her own "problems," again giving you valuable breathing space to vamoose.
- If you're a woman facing down an especially recalcitrant female supervisor, lean in close, lower your voice, and say, "You know, *homosexuality* is a very *touchy* subject in the workplace. . . ." No *straight* woman wants to have *that* conversation with a subordinate. Modern-day reality check: should your female boss take this as you "coming on to her" *and like it*, backtrack immediately with "I was only asking because my sister's boy is gender confused and having trouble at work and . . ." Gay herself, your boss will sympathize. PS: Be ready with follow-up "reports" on your gay nephew's progress when it comes up next time.

"I've been having family problems" is much too vague, leaving much too much opening for you to be further cornered by someone asking for detail. Who in their right mind wants to sit around listening to another person's family problems?

These will only give you a *temporary* respite . . . until you have time to come up with a real excuse!

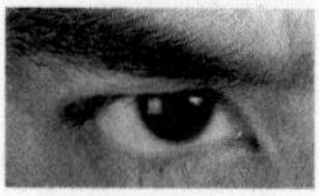

3.

Who Lies . . . and How to Catch Them Doing It!

NO SOONER do people get around to opening their mouths than they start giving themselves away, giving us clues as to what they think is important (like how important they think *they* are!). How did wise Hannibal put it?

> A fool begins by telling you what he knows and ends by telling you what he doesn't know. —Hannibal the Conqueror, Truth XX

You'd think people in general, and career criminals in particular, would just shut up when questioned by the police: "Don't talk to the po-po!" I believe is the current street slang.

Nothing could be further from the truth. Criminals just love to run their mouths. In fact, psychologists have identified this human trait called "duping[86] delight," wherein the person being questioned takes joy in fooling interrogators. Think of the amount of ego involved here when an untrained street punk thinks he can pull one over on professionals—police, psychiatrists, judges—all of whom literally study liars and lying for a living. And you wonder why our prisons continue to fill up.

86. From "dupe," to fool.

Wily Mind Slayers know they cannot only expose an enemy's hidden agenda simply by listening, but can also learn to spot the subconscious "tells" he's giving off, alerting any alert listener to his being deceptive.

Like a cryptographer deciphering a simple "substitution code" (by noting the frequency of certain letters; for example, how the letter *e* shows up in English words more than any other letter), so too by listening carefully—not only to what a person says but also to what he's trying hard *not* to say—to his choice of words, his tone, his mannerisms, and his other body language—we can "hear" what an enemy is saying *and not saying* loud and clear.

THE WORDS THEY SPEAK

"Accustom thyself to attend carefully to what is said by another, and as much as it is possible, be in the speaker's mind."
—Marcus Aurelius

You've undoubtedly heard of "Freudian slips," those words that seem to come out at the worst time, often funny (when we're trying to pick up a date), sometimes career-ending (when we're trying to get re-elected)—*always* embarrassing. The good news is you don't have to hang on your enemy's every word, poring over their every pronoun, listening for their least lisp, waiting for him or her to graciously hand you a juicy Freudian slip you can immediately turn back on them, or else bank for future use.

You've already learned how, by listening to a person's choice of words, you can easily determine their *sensory mode preferences*, which you can then use to craft either your "Get-closer/Getting-to-know-you" approach or your "Get-it-over-with-quick!" attack. (This would be a good time to review the subsection "How to Spot 'em" in Chapter 2's section. "The Three Sensory Modes: Watchers, Listeners, and Touchers.")

According to recent research, when average people are trying to present themselves in a certain way, trying to project a certain image, they choose what they *think* are appropriate nouns (people, places, and things) and verbs (actions), but they often neglect to give as much attention to their use of other articles of speech—a prodigious use of pronouns, for instance.

"Virtually no one in psychology has realized that low-level words can give clues to large-scale behaviors," says psychologist James W. Pennebaker of the University of Texas at Austin, where they've developed a computer program called Linguistic Inquiry and Word Count ("Luke" for short) that analyzes a person's choice of "function words" (e.g., pronouns, articles, numerals and conjunctions).[87]

Luke collects data as to whether a person uses words more associated with "sad" or "happy" emotions, as well as whether the speaker prefers using "I" and "me" versus "us" and "we." At present, Luke collects only raw data (e.g., noting the frequency of words used) that can then be passed on to psychologists whose job it is to figure out what significance a person's choice of words might mean—consciously and subconsciously.

But psychologists aren't the only ones who could use—and, you guessed it, *abuse*!—such information.

Considering that most politicians still get elected for their speaking[88] ability, it's not surprising that the enemy camp, as well as a politician's own camp, has a vested interest in monitoring—and, when need be, manipulating—the manner and meaning of speech of both candidates. For example, when analyzing the 2008 presidential campaign, Pennebaker and his team discovered that John McCain tended to (1) speak directly[89] and (2) speak personally to his constituency, using a vocabulary that was both (3) emotionally loaded and (4) impulsive. Barack Obama, in contrast, (1) made frequent use of casual relationships (indicating more complex thought processes) and also (2) tended to be more vague than John McCain.[90]

In case you don't have a handy Luke computer interface programmed into your handheld tape recorder (don't think they're not working on one!), you can still get a leg up on your enemy just by listening to his word choices and to the frequency of word use:

- ***Insecurity and defensiveness:*** Often indicated by a high use of personal pronouns (e.g., "I," "me," "mine," or referring to yourself in the third person). Curiously, use of personal pronouns has also been associated with recovery in severely ill patients. (Donges, 2009:15)

87. "*You Are What You Say*" by Jan Donges. *Scientific American Mind*, July/August 2009: 14–15.

88. Or, as they say in Ireland, "The slingin' of d'blarney!"

89. That is, say what you mean, mean what you say.

90. Ibid. Also, Pennebaker's team analysis of the presidential candidates is posted at www.worldwatchers. Wordpress.com. See also www.licw.net/liwdescription.php.

- ***Truthfulness (1):*** When telling the truth, people are more likely to use first-person singular pronouns such as "I."
- ***Truthfulness (2):*** Usually indicated by more complex, balanced, and nuanced speech. For example, words such as "but" and "except" are often used when a person is trying to make a distinction between something they did and something they did not do. They may also use conjunctions to balance out information ("and," "or," "but"), for example, weighing both sides of an argument in a single sentence: "I can see how this must look *but* if you'll give me a chance to explain *and/or* at least show you the facts . . ." as opposed to shorter, choppier sentences: "I didn't do it! I have an alibi. I was at Bob's place!"

  It's a no-brainer: complex sentence structures tend to require more complex *thinking* and generally indicate that the person is telling the truth. This could stem from the fact that we tend to put together longer, more complex sentences when we're calm, comfortable, and relaxed (i.e., not guilty) than when we have cause to be tense and nervous (e.g., when lying).
- ***Age:*** As people get older, they typically (1) refer to themselves less, (2) use more "positive" emotion words, and (3) fewer "negative" emotion words. And, contrary to the stereotype of old folks dwelling in the past, *healthy* older people tend to (4) use more future-tense verbs (garden*ing*, golf*ing*, visit*ing*) versus (5) fewer past-tense verbs (garden*ed*, golf*ed*, visit*ed*).
- ***Sensory mode:*** It bears repeating that a person's choice of words will give you insight into their sensory mode.

Use this technique on those occasions when you can't watch a person's eyes to help you establish their "baseline," i.e., his normal manner of speaking when telling the truth, for example, when talking to a suspected liar on the telephone.

Without the additional help (or distraction) of facial clues and body language, you need to first engage that person on a neutral, casual topic, something about which they'd have no reason to lie. Pay close attention to the sound of his *voice* and don't allow yourself to be distracted by his actual *words*. Words are easy to control, but it's a lot harder to control fluctuations in your voice's (1) volume, (2) tone, (3) pitch, and (4) rhythm patterns. *Psychotronics update:* There are now handheld electronic devices as well as computer programs that average people can use in order to sift through a person's voice to determine levels of stress and other factors that indicate lying. These devices have varying degrees of success and are no substitute for mastering the art using your own ears.

The rules for listening to a person's voice in order to establish a baseline are the same as for watching his eyes:

- First, get him talking about neutral, nonthreatening subjects that you know he is telling the truth about.
- Establish what his normal, nonlying voice sounds like.
- Having established what the person talks like when being truthful, you can then switch to more important topics you expect the person might lie about.

THE MOVES THEY MAKE

We sometimes do battle with ourselves and others on a subconscious level. Remember when you *thought* you caught a suspicious gleam in your enemy's eye? You probably did. And hopefully you didn't allow yourself to just shrug it off as only your imagination. If you did, then you either didn't survive to read this book, or else you're reading this from your hospital bed!

Despite the best efforts of civilization and political correctness, your body—your DNA—still wants to survive, and still knows what's best for you. Remember that your "gut" (really our old friend the amygdala) literally evolved millions of years before the "higher reasoning" parts of the brain.

Conversely, lying comes from the higher brain. The amygdala isn't at all good at lying. So, while your higher reasoning center is trying to come up with a plausible explanation as to where that lipstick on your collar came from, your lesser evolved brain is giving the game away by literally sweating its ass off, licking its dry lips, and brushing imaginary lint off your pants.

You have to learn to trust your gut and trust your enemy's gut. Just as your gut will warn you of possible danger, his gut will give him away every time—provided you're paying attention to what his gut is telling you. If there's ever a discrepancy between his words and his body language—trust *your* gut . . . and trust *his* gut.

Your gut—your instincts—will warn you on a *subconscious* level when his words and actions are out of synch. Sometimes, you'll feel the hackles on the back of your neck perk up, or maybe you'll get butterflies in your stomach, or maybe it'll just be a vague feeling of unease . . . *Pay attention to it!*

In the same way as your "gut," *His* gut (body) will give him away.

For more on body language, see the section The "Power Persuader's Guide to Mastery" later in this book.

The Body Language "Rule of Thumb"

Truthfulness requires a certain amount of symmetry and correlation. For example, *both* sides of a person's mouth will turn up equally for a sincere smile. In addition, when a person smiles a sincere, genuine smile, "crow's feet" crinkles appear around the eyes.

Conversely, when a person is being deceptive, their lying eyes (no crow's feet) and smiling mouth don't correlate.

A simple trick to check for this is to surreptitiously obscure part of the person's face you're trying to read with your thumb or with a playing card.[91] For example, when he smiles, cover the lower part of his face to *see* if his eyes are "smiling" as much as his mouth. Or obscure one side of his face to see if the opposite side seems more animated, that is, if one side of his smile is higher than the other (i.e., a "crooked" smile).

TRIED-'N'-TRUE TRICKS OF THE INTERROGATOR'S TRADE

If you're dealing with honorable people, you must be honorable yourself, but if you're fighting implacable enemies, you must not be bound by rules they are preparing to trample on.

—Michael A. Ledeen, *Machiavelli on Modern Leadership*

Long ago, Mind Slayers realized that the tried and true interrogation techniques used by law enforcement professionals, intelligence operatives, and military personnel could easily be adopted and adapted for personal use.

---

91. Old gambler's trick, still very much in use today (see Figure 8, p. 84).

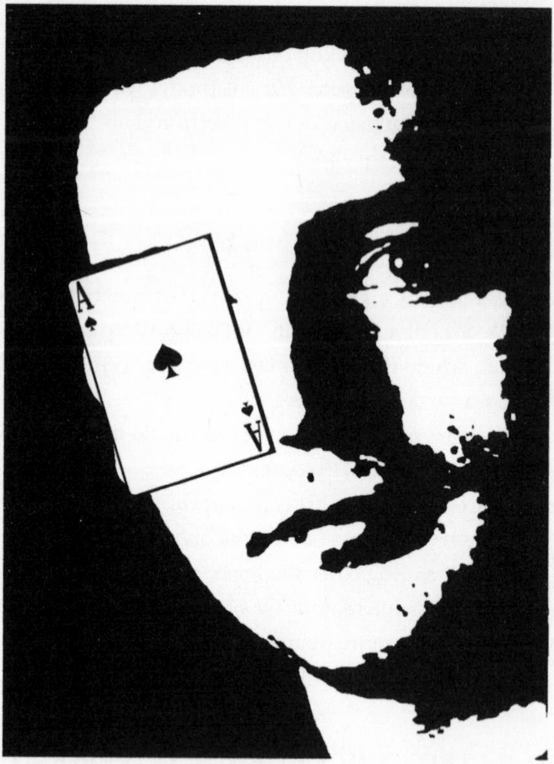

Figure 8.

Learn these if only to protect yourself and your loved ones from being on the receiving end of such interrogation tactics.

On September 6, 2006, the Pentagon issued a new field manual (applicable to all branches of the military) titled *Human Intelligence Collector Operations*. This updated the previous 1992 manual by spelling out new guidelines for interrogating prisoners, especially terrorism suspects. These updated procedures grew out of a recent Supreme Court ruling that even terror suspects are covered by the Geneva Convention.[92]

92. "New Pentagon rules ban 'abusive interrogation'" by John Diamond. *USA Today*, 9.7.06:6A.

Predictably, this new manual forbids any kind of *physical* torture (like polishing the family jewels up with a few thousand volts!), mock executions (Oh, did you *think* the guns were loaded?), near-drownings (can you say waterboarding), sensory deprivation, and that ol' standby: sic'n dem dobbies on 'em![93]

These newly approved questioning techniques are mainly *psychological* approaches and include:

- ***Mutt-n-Jeff, a.k.a., "Good Cop/Bad Cop":*** One of the interrogators plays the tough guy, barking at the prisoner-suspect, while the second interrogator—Good Cop—tells Bad Cop to "back off!" and offers the prisoner a smoke, something to eat, etc. When this works—and you'd be amazed how often it *does* work (out of gratitude and the human urge to bond with fellow human beings)—the prisoner gives it up to the "good cop." Evidently whoever drew up these guidelines doesn't think they watch *Starsky & Hutch* re-runs over in the Middle East!
- ***The "Kiss Your Family Good-bye" torture*** threatens the prisoner with never seeing his family again unless he starts cooperating. Contrary to what you might think, just because they wear C4 underwear and crash planes into buildings doesn't mean they don't care about their own families. Keep in mind some such fanatics believe they are killing *your* family in order to make the world safe for *their* family.
- ***The silent treatment, a.k.a. "The Arabic Method":*** Bad Cop just sits and stares at the bad guy until the bad guy breaks under the pressure. It is said the CIA favors this method . . . uh, that is, *if* they were ever actually into this sort of thing . . .
- ***Rapid-fire questions*** are thrown at the prisoner until he becomes so confused he confesses. Complete opposite of the Silent Treatment.
- ***The "You're Never Gonna See Daylight Again!" approach*** threatens a terrorist with being prosecuted for committing atrocities and spending the rest of his life in solitary. Believe it or not, while such

---

93. Many of the physical tortures now forbidden for use by the U.S. military, including turning Doberman pinschers loose on prisoners, are still routinely used—including by many of our Middle Eastern "allies." See *Theatre of Hell: Dr. Lung's Complete Guide to Torture* by Dr. Haha Lung and Christopher B. Prowant (Loompanics Unlimited, 2003).

fanatics don't mind dying a "glorious martyr's death," the idea of "disappearing" and "rotting away" inside a prison cell doesn't have the same appeal. Gotta remember, many such fanatics are in a hurry to get to Heaven and "get busy" with those seventy-two virgins!

Police use the same sort of argument on street punks, reminding the junkie how he's not going to be able to get his drugs or telling a "ladies man" how he's no longer gonna be able to play the ladies. Find out what a person loves and then threaten to take it away from him, and/or promise him a reward for cooperating: the old "Carrot & Stick" approach.

- ***Divide and conquer*** separates prisoners so they can't coordinate their stories. (Or share a good laugh about how the Americans are killing them with kindness.)
- ***False-flagging*** intends to make prisoners think they're being held in another country.
- ***The "All-Seeing Eye" attitude*** implies that the captors are all-knowing and that they know more than they actually know about the prisoner, his terrorist organization, and their pending operations.

You're not alone if you're just a little skeptical as to *how* effective these new politically correct interrogation guidelines are going to be against some hardcore, suicidal fanatic who looks forward to blowing himself up and taking as many "Godless infidels" with him as possible. However, to give credit where credit is due, these psychological ploys *have* proven useful for law enforcement down through the years so, with minor modification (and the occasional waterboarding), they still might prove effective on suicidal terrorists.

For our more immediate purpose at hand, taking into account time and circumstance (as well as pesky local, state, and federal ordinances against holding someone against their will), we can adopt, adapt, and apply these same interrogation ploys to our Mind Slayer agenda:

- A combination of *Mutt-n-Jeff* and *divide and conquer* will give our enemy the choice of negotiating with us or with our more "evil" cousin. Militant groups use this ploy all the time, spinning off "rogue factions" from the parent organization that engage in heinous acts of terrorism, making sitting down at the table with the "more reasonable" parent organization more palatable. Would you rather pay me—a reasonable guy—now, or have to deal with a couple guys in pinstriped suits from the Linguini Brothers Omerta Collection Agency later?

- *Rapid-fire* spiels are used by salesmen of every ilk to sell us everything from wastepaper baskets to wasteful wars. (See "Mini-Masters," p. 134.)
- Threatening to take away our enemy's beloved "nouns" (a person, place, or thing) is powerful incentive for him to either cooperate or capitulate and vacate.
- *False-flagging* is part and parcel of the Mind Slayer's trade: making our enemy think we're one thing, when we're something entirely different; making them think we're slapping them on the back, never realizing there's a knife in our hand!

There's no telling how well these techniques will work on international terrorists, but you can guarantee they'll all work on that dumbass next door!

CREATING YOUR OWN "TRUTH TESTER"

Lying is essential to the survival of nations and to the success of great enterprises, because if your enemies can count on the reliability of everything you say, your vulnerability is enormously increased.

—Michael A. Ledeen

Use the following exercise to help you set your own "Truth Tester," to better help you spot when someone is lying and then craft your approach to them accordingly.

Unless there are massive, overt inconsistencies in a person's story, it's not that easy to tell if they're telling the truth just by watching their body language. For one thing, you have no idea what a person looks like and acts like when they are telling the truth. For another, what you might think are overt signs of lying, might simply be signs of nervous stress.

To create your Truth Tester, you first have to ask the person a series of *questions you know they know the answer to* and are expected to answer truthfully to. Professional interrogators call this "establishing a baseline" (i.e., recording a set of *truthful body reactions* that can later be used in comparison to untruthful body reactions).

This is not as hard as it might at first sound. All you need do is keep

“DIRECTIONS OF LYING”

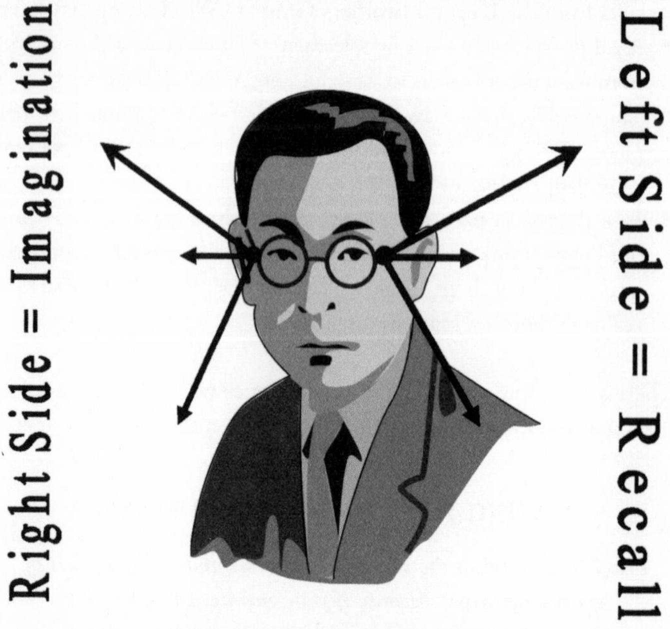

DIRECTION OF LYING

Looking Up and to the Left: Recalling a memory of something actually seen before.

Looking Up and to the Right: Trying to imagine what something looks like.

Looking Left and to the Side (towards his ear): Searching for the memory of a sound.

Looking Right and to the Side (towards his ear): Trying to imagine the sound.

Looking Left and Down: Remembering the feel (touch/smell/taste) of something.

Looking Right and Down: Trying to imagine what something would feel (touch/smell/taste) like.[1]

1. Trying to imagine taste is often accompanied by unconsciously swallowing and/or licking the lips.

Figure 9.

track of where the person’s eyes go when they’re searching for the answer to each of your questions.

Glancing at the sample questions that follow, notice how the questions *deliberately engage the senses* (sight, hearing, and touch—including taste and smell). You don’t have to use the exact questions that follow (i.e., you don’t have to ask him about automobiles). Simply craft your baseline questions (1) around something you know he knows and, hopefully, likes to talk about, and (2) a subject that will force him to access his senses.

Remember that for ninety percent of people, looking to the left means a person is actually remembering something, and looking to the right means they are accessing their imagination—in other words, trying to make something up, like a lie.

Sample questions and responses:

> **Question:** "Do you recall what the first car you owned *looked* like, what model and color it was?"
> Response: He looks up and to his left, recalling the picture of the car in his mind.
>
> **Question:** "Do you remember what the radio *sounded* like?"
> Response: He looks to his left side, toward his ear, searching for a remembered sound.
>
> **Question:** "What kind of seats did it have, leather or fabric?"
> Response: He looks left and down, remembering the feel (touch and possibly smell) of the seat.
>
> **Question:** "Can you imagine what a car would be like if it didn't have wheels and instead flew?"
> Response: He looks up and to the right, creating (imagining) a picture in his mind.
>
> **Question:** "Did you ever wonder what a flying car's engine would sound like?"
> Response: He looks to his right side, trying to imagine the sound.
>
> **Question:** "Do you think a ride in such a car would be bumpy or smooth?"
> Response: He looks right and down, trying to imagine what it would feel like.

Keep in mind that these directions are reversed for about ten percent of people, most often lefties.[94] When encountering a leftie, use the same strat-

---

94. By the way, Miyamoto Musashi, the greatest swordsman to ever live in Japan—some say, *in the world!*—was a leftie. See "Musashi: Taste the Wind, Ride the Wave" in Part II.

egy to establish their baseline, simply noting if they are reversing directions in their responses.

FYI: the quicker the responses a person gives to right-side "imagination" questions, the better the chances they will be excellent candidates for hypnotism.[95]

One final way to trip up a liar is to "overload" their brain. Since lying is just naturally more mentally taxing, more stressful than telling the truth, it takes our full concentration to pull it off.[96] Therefore, the more you can give a suspected liar to do while he's trying to keep his lying mask on, the better your chances of causing him to slip up. Performing an extra task while lying or telling the truth should therefore affect the liars more.

For example, police might give an anxious suspect a release form to fill out while he's being questioned. Anxious to leave the police station, concentrating on filling out the required form, the suspect becomes lax in keeping up his lies.

Or, using the old standby "Good Cop/Bad Cop" routine, Good Cop will question the suspect while Bad Cop walks threateningly around the room snarling and occasionally making lunging motions toward the suspect, unnerving the suspect, making it harder for him to keep track of the lies he's telling Good Cop.

Performing an extra task is not the same as giving the suspect something to do with his hands, or giving him a cigarette to smoke, both of which will help relieve his anxiety, making it easier for him to maintain his lying.

The extra task you give him to do has to be something that *divides* his attention—for example, trying to maintain his lying face while also trying to write what's required on his release form, or constantly flinching from Bad Cop's aggressive threats while trying to "truthfully" answer Good Cop's questions.

---

95. For a complete training course in hypnotism, see *666 Devilish Secrets of Hypnotism* by Dr. Haha Lung. (publication pending).

96. See "*The Load of Lying*," by Marina Krakovsky. *Scientific American Mind*, July/August 2009:10.

THE FIVE RULES FOR LYING SUCCESSFULLY

In her highly informative and user-friendly 1989 *Success with the Gentle Art of Verbal Self-Defense*, Dr. Suzette Elgin aptly, if somewhat metaphorically, declares lies to be "malpractice of the mouth."

Dr. Elgin then goes on to teach us the Three Types of Lies:

- **Polite lies:** Lies that help us "get along" in society
- **Survival lies:** As the name implies, lies that help us survive
- **Incompetent lies:** Lies that don't need to be told . . . but people just can't seem to stop telling them!

Rather than try to bullshit us with some pie-in-the-sky, "Can't we all just be honest with each other" philosophy, Elgin tells it like it is:

> I will be absolutely truthful with you here—in my ideal world, you would never lie. But none of us live in my ideal world or anybody else's. We live in the world of our reality consensus, in which many compromises have to be made. In that world, lying is going to happen, and both you and I are going to tell some lies. Our problem is therefore to function in this world without being perceived as liars.[97]

Having acknowledged the reality that, sooner or later, we're gonna have to belch out some blarney, Elgin's nice enough to give us the five rules to follow if we need to lie successfully:

- **Lie only as a last resort:** Seek an alternative to lying. Delay is less costly in the long run than deception and a whole lot easier to keep track of.
- **Don't lie on the telephone:** It's too easy for the person at the other end of the line to pick up on hesitations and trembles in your tale. If you have to lie on the telephone, place a mirror in front of you to provide you with feedback.

---

97. Ibid. 238.

- **Watch your natural body language** when lying face-to-face. Try to relax, so as not to appear tense.
- **Insert deliberate body language** designed to distract the listener from what you are saying. Poker players are notorious for using this tactic, tossing in a phony "tell" of apparent disappointment in the hand they've been dealt before folding. Then, having conditioned your opponent(s) to pick up on this obvious tell you show every time you draw a bad hand, you are now ready to purposely show your "disappointment tell" the next time you're holding onto a royal flush!

And Elgin's final rule:

- **"Practice, practice, practice!"**

Review "The Ten Commandments of Lying" in Mind Control (Citadel, 2006).

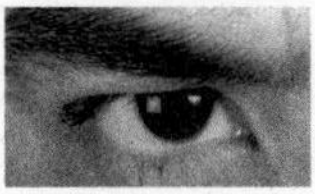

4.

The Power of Persuasion

Remember that this which pulls the strings is the thing which is hidden within: this is the* power of persuasion, *this is life; this, if one may say so, is man.
—Marcus Aurelius, *Meditations*

IN *DOUBLE YOUR BRAIN POWER* (1997), author Jean Marie Stine defines *persuasive communication* as "the process through which people attempt to influence the beliefs or actions of others." Whether aware of it or not, we practice this kind of persuasion every day: every time we haggle with the fruit vender, argue with the car dealer, try talking sense to the crackhead holding hostages at the 7-Eleven, negotiate with a "rogue nation" about giving up their nuclear weapons program, or just try to convince that babe at the bar that we know what's in her best interest.

The Mind Slayer's craft is—lock, stock, and barrel—the study of the power of persuasion.

Mastering the art of persuasion isn't difficult, so long as you remember these two—indisputable—truths:

- **People like people who like them.**
- **People like people who are *like* them.**

So if you sincerely pretend to like someone and sincerely pretend to like the same things they like (which, of course, includes hating the same things they hate), there's a pretty good chance you can get your foot in their front door, your hand into their wallet, and your *never mind* into their pants anytime the mood or that fresh bottle of Viagra in your pocket[98] moves you.

It should come as no surprise that people are more swayed by the opinions and behavior of those who are like them.[99]

Xenophobia—that initial reaction of *fear* of strangers—being natural, why shouldn't an initial reaction of *liking* those who are like us also be a gift from Mother Nature? Ah, but doesn't wise and wily Hannibal's Truth XCII warn us that "No true gift comes with tax, toil, or tail attached." Lest we forget, Mr. Darwin says *we* once had tails!

Across all communication modes, people are usually more successful at winning over members of their own sex, with men overall being slightly more successful in persuading *both* sexes than are women. Perhaps this is because men are perceived, overall, to have higher credibility and expertise.[100] The exception to this being when the topic is stereotypically feminine (e.g., child care and tampons).

How do we personally become more persuasive?

By learning to recognize (1) where others *think* they stand in the great cow-pie-laden field of life and (2) where those people *actually* stand in the great cow-pie-laden field of life. It's what we call "reality" versus how we'd "really-like-it-to-be." Would it really surprise you to find out the two perspectives don't automatically coincide? All right, they seldom even come close!

So once you've learned to recognize the self-serving sentences, syntax, speeches, and scripts playing in your enemy's head, all you need to do is master a couple of simple techniques for first *getting his attention* and then *getting what you want*—we call it Spank'n, Thank'n & Yank'n!

And, when need be, if need be, apply a little old-fashioned bribery—because everybody has something they *need* or *want* (just remember not to confuse the two in your own mind).

Finally, for the overachievers in the family, we'll dedicate ourselves to the ongoing study of any and all tactics and techniques, tried-and-true tricks of the trade, from past and present master persuaders—*Mind Slayers!* We'll relentlessly, ruthlessly, and without regret pick clean the brains of those

98. Or are you just happy to see me?

99. See *Scientific American Mind*, July/August, 2009:71.

100. Ibid.

people who already know what we need to know to move a little farther up the food chain.

How do we *know* they know? Because they *survived* long enough—and have remained *unindicted* long enough!—to pass their tricks of the trade along to us.

THE CRAFT OF "RE-WRITING" PEOPLE

We are all working together to one end, some with knowledge and design, and others without knowing what they do.
—Marcus Aurelius

Every published writer knows that the secret to good writing is re-writing. This applies to "re-writing" people as well.

The gods may have "written" us, but I don't know anyone who couldn't benefit with a little "editing." (But under no circumstance should you ever keep a written list of people you think should be permanently deleted!)

In the same way a novice writer starts by picking up a single pencil, so too the would-be Mind Slayer sets out to acquire those basic skills he or she needs to master the craft of "re-writing" people: mastery of words and symbols that move people both consciously and subliminally, the manipulation of both physical and psychological nuance, all adding up to the power of persuasion.

And like the would-be writer whose trusty red No. 2 pencil seems constantly in need of sharpening, so too the future mastermind must continually be alert for ever better ways to sharpen the skills he acquires—skills necessary for pressing his enemy's mind into a blank receptive page, upon which the now-literate Mind Slayer can then write his own thoughts and, in the process, re-write his enemy's destiny!

In the beginning was the word . . . A single word? Oh, how much chaos and confusion . . . and *creativity* sprang from that single word! Single words beget sentences—unfortunately sometimes *prison* sentences! Well-honed sentences strung together become speeches, spoken dreams, and dramas, begetting ideologies. These ideologies, in turn, become the screamed slogans and battle cries that inspire us to subdue the earth!

In the beginning was the word . . . and, in the end, people are like words, single words joining together to become sentences—yes, sometimes *prison* sentences. Benevolent or malevolent, sentences that can hold their own go on to form paragraphs and speeches—cries for freedom! Or else calls to enslave those whose words don't quite fit the time or the place, those who forget—or flatly refuse—to stay within the approved parameters of the assigned essay called life.

Each of us writes his own story in life—be it script, screenplay, or resignation. And nobody's good enough to be their own editor.

To communicate, people not only use the various accepted parts of speech to convey their needs and desires, the various parts of speech are also convenient keys for classifying how—and whether or not—certain people play well with others. For example:

- **A Noun Person** is a *concrete* (as opposed to *abstract*) thinker. Slow but dependable, just give him the facts about people, places, and things and he'll (eventually) come to the right conclusion because Occam's razor[101] is his Bible. If he's your boss, diligently get the facts for him and trust his decision. If he's your partner or employee, make sure you provide him plenty of time and leeway to weigh all the variables. In fiction: Tony Soprano. In real life, Colin Powell.
- **An Adjective Person** is colorful and dashing, leaning toward the flamboyant in deed and the overly descriptive in wit. He always "talks the talk"—just keep a close eye on him to make sure he follows through and "walks the walk." Charming, beware, for he can be hypnotic at times. His "too good to be true" deals . . . *sometimes* pan out, but are *always* hard to resist. In fact and fiction: Giovanni Giacomo Casanova and Don Juan. In real life: Bugsy Siegel.[102]
- **A Verb Person** is action-oriented. He's your "go-to guy" to get things done—fast and *usually* discreetly and efficiently. He's Machine-gun Jack McGurn[103] to your Al Capone. Has short patience and an even shorter attention span—or perhaps just a notoriously focused

101. Occam's razor in a nutshell: don't make a problem more complicated than necessary. The simplest explanation is usually the best explanation. The straightest path gets you there the fastest. Or as Stalin said: "No man, no problem!"

102. Suave gangster credited with founding Las Vegas, later assassinated, reportedly for not paying his bills on time.

103. Masterminded and carried out the infamous St. Valentine's Day Massacre that left Big Al the undisputed (i.e., last man standing!) crime boss in Chicago.

field of vision. Any mission you send him on had better be challenging. Show him the money (the goal, the mission objective, etc.) worthy of his considerable talents to get him moving and he'll stay moving. Weakness: he's a sucker for still waters. Works well with a Noun boss to "slow" his impetuousness. Real life *and* fiction: George S. Patton.

- **An Adverb Person** makes a loyal "soldier," from chauffeurs and accountants to leg-breakers. Good workers, always diligent to details, they dot the *I* and cross the *T*. Weakness: unimaginative. Spell out in clear, simple terms what you require of them. In fiction: Stacy Keach's Frank James in *The Longriders* (1980). In real life: Frank Nitti.[104]
- **A Pronoun Person** is a mercenary, plain and simple. Self-centered, everything's "I," "Me," "mine" with this guy. No altruism in his game.[105] Show him the carrot that's in it for him and keep whatever that carrot is dangling in front of his face at all times. He's loyal, so long as it's in his best interest—so long as your bribe is bigger than the next guy's! Greed is his downfall.
- **A Preposition Person** is an innovator. He likes to think outside the box—sometimes *too far* outside the box. Works well with Nouns and Conjunctions. In fiction: Viktor Frankenstein. In real life: Robert Oppenheimer.[106]
- **A Conjunction Person** is a born negotiator.[107] Likes everything to fit together smoothly, likes to tie up loose ends. Works well as advisor to Nouns. Makes a great lieutenant to a Noun boss. Helps direct and coordinate Adverbs and Prepositions. In fiction: Robert Duvall's Tom Heyden, Corleone family consigliere in *The Godfather* parts I & II.[108]
- **An Interjection Person** can be frenetic, frantic, often fanatic, and

---

104. Al Capone's soft-spoken second-in-command. Committed suicide rather than face a federal conviction for income tax evasion—same financial faux pas that took down Big Al! FYI: the real-life Nitti was *not* as portrayed in Kevin Costner's 1987 *The Untouchables*.

105. Not that altruism actually exists. Remember: everybody gets paid, one way or another.

106. Coordinated the creation of the first atomic bomb.

107. See "The 6 Rules of NO-gotiation" in *Ultimate Control* by Dr. Haha Lung & Christopher B. Prowant (Citadel, 2010).

108. If only they'd have brought Robert Duvall back for *The Godfather* III . . . Nah! Nothing coulda saved *that* movie!

thus often (initially) mistaken for a Verb Person. Easily excitable and just as easily distracted. Send him to distract your enemy. A sucker for a "get-rich-quick" scheme. A "one-time use" operative.[109] In fiction: Polonius in *Hamlet*. In real life: All the 9/11 hijackers.

SPANK'N, THANK'N & YANK'N!

One of the most succinct ways to sum up—and employ—the power of persuasion is to use the black science "Spank'n, Thank'n & Yank'n" process:

Step One: *Spank* 'Em

You never get a second chance to make a good first impression, so put everything you've got into your "meet-'n'-great" skills. A firm handshake—or, as they say these days, "Spank that hand!"—along with good eye contact and a big smile do make a good—lasting—impression.

When meeting someone—not just for the *first* time but *each time*—you should always (1) acknowledge the other person's existence, (2) make that other person feel important, and (3) show them that you like them. Because . . . Right! We like people who like us.

Everyone wants to feel good about themselves. Make them feel good about themselves and they'll feel good about *you* and they'll come back for more.

Lepers—real "A piece of my liver just fell off" lepers—don't feel very good about themselves, and most of us aren't too keen about having lepers hanging around. Yeah, we are "leper prejudice." Like everyone else, lepers need a hug, too . . . but there's a pretty good chance they ain't getting one!

Conversely, when we go out of our way to make physical contact with another person, we're saying, "I acknowledge that you exist in time and space, my friend. You're real." And we're saying, "I'm not afraid to touch you because I'm pretty sure you don't have any disease I can actually catch—unlike leper boy over there!"

So whether it's spankin' that hand each time you meet, pattin' that back in appreciation for a job well done, a friendly "We're on the same page"

---

109. What Sun Tzu calls an "expendable agent." See "Sun Tzu Storms the Gate!" in the section on Asian arts of espionage, in Part II, pp. 206ff.

high-five, or a sporting "Good game!" ass slap, *physically making contact* with another person triggers actual *physical changes* within their body, stimulating them in ways a more cerebral, lukewarm "Que pasa?" in passing doesn't.

FYI: while a snowball is better than no ball, an old-fashioned handshake is better in the "spank'n'" department than the current "hit-that-rock" fist-bump, an actual—*situation appropriate*—hug, even better.

For most Westerners, anything closer than three feet is considered "intimate distance." A handshake literally reaches across and bridges this distance, a hug even more so.

Step Two: *Thank* 'Em

Everybody likes to be thanked. Think of being thanked as a verbal hug. Because that's what it is. And everyone wants——nay, *needs*—to feel appreciated from time to time.

- Send those Thank-you flowers to that secretary who bumped your name to the top of the interview list.
- Send that Hallmark card (or small plaque) to your personally favorite "employee of the month."
- Become a big tipper. People are more likely to do something for us if they've already done something for us before—and especially after we've remembered to thank them appropriately.
- Thank people for things they do for you. Thank them for doing a good job.
- Thank a person *to others* unexpectedly. Example: Catch good ol' Bob standing round the watercooler shootin' the breeze with his coworkers and make a show of thanking him with a hearty handshake and a "Now, Bob here is a modest guy and he'd never think of blowing his own horn. But if it weren't for him, I wouldn't have gotten that promotion. So, thank you, Bob. Thanks a lot!"

This kind of *public* praise accomplishes two things: first, Bob is now going to try to do *even more* things to help you (especially if he can't for the life of him remember exactly what it was *specifically* he did to help you in the first place). Second, everyone within earshot now realizes how big you are, a humble and gracious human being, willing to give other people credit where credit is due. If they're lucky, maybe *they* will be next! They *envy* Bob's recognition so they'll want to be around you and they will want to work for you—follow you.

Show appreciation for others and you show appreciation for yourself.

Step Three: *Yank* 'Em!

You've "spanked 'em" (i.e., gotten their attention) and you've "thanked 'em" (and they've figured out they like being thanked and appreciated by you), so now you're in a prime position to "yank 'em," as in "yank their chain," to send them off (willing and eager) on missions of your choosing. That's both their conscious and *unconscious* way of thanking you.

The true gift is in graciously accepting.

"COINS AND LOINS": THE MUCH UNDERUSED ART OF BRIBERY

No true gift comes with tax, toil, or tail attached.
—Hannibal, Truth XCII

The value of a well-placed bribe has been known since ancient times:

> Fish take the bait and they are caught on the line. When men take their salary from you, they will submit to you. Catch a fish with bait, and that fish can easily be reeled in. Hook a man with gold and he will spend all his talents for you.
>
> —T'ai Kung

Sun Tzu understood the use of bribes in recruiting fortuitously situated agents.[110] Likewise, the great conqueror Hannibal, who took several walled Italian cities during his campaign against the Romans without firing a shot, using instead the timely bribing of a guard at the fortress gate.

How often have you heard "You can't bribe an honest man"? Sure you can. It happens every day.

You bribe your kids with an extra half-hour of television if they'll brush

---

110. See "Sun Tzu Storms the Gate!" (pp. 206ff.).

their teeth. You bribe your teenagers with a new iPod if they get good grades all year. What's that paycheck your boss hands you for doing all his dirty work and heavy lifting if not bribery?

When threats fail, countries bribe other countries not to grow dope and not to go nuclear.

Bribery has gotten a bad rap down through history. What is bribery but temptation? I have something I think you might like to have. Nobody's forcing you to take it.[111]

Perhaps you recall from our previous discussion on altruism that, ultimately, there is no such thing as altruism. Everybody gets paid—if not in gold, then in feeling good.

Psychologist Carl Rogers (1902–1987) said that we judge all actions and experience in terms of their value (use) in "facilitating or hampering our actualization growth." In other words, we want to know "What's in it for me?" Far from being a cynical view of mankind, this is a vital *survival mechanism* that evolution has programmed into us. Ultimately, we all, first and foremost, look out for number one[112]—or at least we should.

Logic should tell you that you're not much use to others unless you first get your own house in order.

So, yes, we never do anything unless there's ultimately something in it for us. But sometimes helping other people works to our advantage.

The point to all this? *All of us have our "price,"* our potential bribe. The good news is, chances are that you'll never be tempted by an enemy waving that one particular bribe you are especially susceptible to. Your particular bribe might not be something concrete, like money or sex. It might be something more abstract, like . . . ending world hunger. But rest assured, there's a bribe out there with your name on it!

Many times people aren't even aware of—and will adamantly deny—the fact that they're susceptible to bribery—not until it's literally sticking in their face. And when that's the scenario, there inevitably follows "moral" arguments about who's the most at fault: the brib*er* or the brib*ee*. This is the argument always leveled against "sting" operations conducted by law enforce-

111. Because then it would be blackmail or bullying, a discussion for another day.

112. Robert J. Ringer even wrote a book in 1977 called *Looking Out for #1*. See *Ultimate Control* by Dr. Haha Lung and Christopher B. Prowant (Citadel, 2010).

ment agencies, where "honest people just minding their own business"[113] are tempted with bribes. And we all know how easy it is to turn down cash and cootchie when either is being rubbed in your face. (Yeah, the human race is weak that way, and this surprises you *how*?)

Thus, Mind Slayers bribe some with *concretes*: money, sex, drugs, or revenge against your enemies. Others they have to bribe with more *abstracts:* love, power, or the "family they never had." Cults and gangs are good for all three.

When it comes to having to bribe someone, you're simply showing that person what's in it for them. Curiously, this is pretty much the same conversation that takes place when applying blackmail: "You want to keep these pictures out of the media, right?" and bullying: "Here's what's in it for you . . . I let you keep your teeth!"

Bribery being yin to blackmail's yang, they are rightly listed together as one of the six dreaded Killer "B"s:

Blind
Bribery and Blackmail
Bloodties
Brainwashing
Bullying
Bury

When our best efforts to blind an enemy to our intentions fail, the next best thing is to bribe him into looking the other way.

Basically, bribery comes down to what adroit Mind Slayers call "coins or loins," money or sex, or some combination and/or rate of exchange therein. Whereas you can make money with sex and you can use money to buy sex, the two aren't interchangeable. Of course, you can also use sex, just like money, as a bribe[114] . . . so maybe the two *are* interchangeable.

Whether drachma or dollar, from a stack of cold, hard Benjamins to a dowry of musk oxen, *money still rules*. We need money—or something similar—in order to survive. And while we can't do a Blanche du Bois and depend on "the kindness of strangers" . . . we can always count on the greed of

---

113. The other side of the argument is that those people targeted for the sting either have a past record or else have "criminal intent" in their heart . . .

114. Have you so soon forgotten your ex-girlfriend?

others—if not your enemy's personal greed, then the greed of those he's surrounded himself with.

Thus, when you can't directly bribe your enemy, you "cut at his edges" by bribing someone close to him.[115]

While disgruntled family members and ex-friends can sometimes be used for this, unlike using a "cutting-at-the-edges" blackmail or bullying tactic, it's much harder to bribe family members and *true* friends into betraying one of their own. Fredo from *The Godfather* (1972) being the exception.

A person's enemies usually don't need much bribing to conspire with you against someone they're already plotting against—your bribe is merely the icing on their "hate cake."

You can also often bribe the little people in your enemy's life, those human beings he takes no notice of: the janitor and maid, doorman and driver, little people he's either stepped over—or on!—on his way up or else—worse yet—*ignored*. Sun Tzu Chapter XIII again: folks holding a grudge are easy to bribe, since they'd probably do the job for free anyway.

I repeat: bribery is but temptation. Nobody's forcing you to take it.[116]

When it comes down to having to bribe someone, you're simply showing that person what's in it for them. This is the same exchange of pleasantries that takes place when applying blackmail: "You want to keep these pictures away from the media, right?" and bullying: "Here's what's in it for you . . . I let you keep your teeth!"

Here's a ploy you can employ against someone who flatly refuses to take your bribe:

> Unless that person goes public, reporting the attempted bribe immediately (to a supervisor, to law enforcement, etc.), they put you in a fine position to later (1) publicly reveal that the person was earlier offered a bribe and for some reason failed to inform the proper authorities—implying that perhaps because they were still mulling the idea over? Or (2) you can

---

115. "Cutting at the edges," attacking an enemy's peripheral when a straight-on attack is unwise, is a Miyamoto Musashi method. See "Musashi: Taste the Wind, Ride the Wave" in Part II.

116. Because then it would be blackmail or Bullying, a whole 'nother discussion for another day.

bank the fact they didn't report the attempted bribe in order to blackmail the person later by threatening to go public with what you know.

This blackmail ploy works best when the person doesn't know it was you who initiated the bribe in the first place. Even if the person suspects you were behind the attempted bribe, you still have plausible deniability.

THE POWER PERSUADER'S GUIDE TO MASTERY

So what specifically should a budding Mind Slayer devote himself to studying?

Pretty much everything we've learned so far from reading this book![117] So let's recap, while we add a few more "electives" (see Figure 10) to your already well-rounded Black Science Institute curriculum.

Mastering Body Language

People can seriously misunderstand what it is they're not saying to each other.
—Jack Rosenthal

The latest research estimates that at least seventy percent of the information communicated between humans is passed along through body language rather than through the actual words we speak. This is especially true of emotional content information (ECI), nearly ninety percent of which is conveyed *nonverbally*.

More important than learning to decipher your enemy's body language is learning to *master your own*.

Examine your own itchin', twitchin', and bitchin', your scratches and stalls. "These are tells" that literally tell your enemy that what you're thinking—and feeling—isn't necessarily what you're saying. What comes out of your mouth isn't nearly as important—and revealing—as what pours out your pores.

Animals are born with this body language instinct. They can tell by the

117. As well as each and every other Dr. Lung book you can get your hands on!

THE POWER PERSUADER'S STUDY GUIDE

What to Study	Advantages to Studying It	Masters of This Art
Study body language	People "leak," both in thought and deed, betrayed by both speech and mannerism. Learn to control your own "tells" while allowing others to "tell" on themselves.	Poker players. Muggers.
Study "word war"	Communication is key. Communication is king. Words are weapons.	Hitler, Barack Obama, Bill Clinton and Bill O'Reilly, all professional hypnotists.
Study propaganda	People respond emotionally *first.* Propaganda is whoever gets there first with the simplest for the simple.	Goebbels. The Illuminati. Cults.
Study subliminal suggestion	Get your message across sans anyone realizing and/or being able to challenge it.	Madison Avenue. *Fight Club* (1999).
Study memory manipulation	All we are is our memories. If we can't trust our memories (and we *can't*!), what can we trust?	Elizabeth Loftus, Harry Lorraine and Jerry Lucas, Jack Daniels.
Master "shape-shifting"	"Bad boys, bad boys, what'cha gonna do when day come 'fo you?" Be someone else!	Martin Bormann. Houdini. Aleister Crowley
Study "The Big Boys"	They got to be "The Big Boys" for a reason.	Marcus Aurelius, J. Paul Getty, Donald Trump, Hitler, Stalin.

Figure 10.

posturing of others of their species (1) when a predator is in the vicinity, (2) when territory is being challenged, and (3) when an attempt to mate is being accepted or contested. If we humans could only learn those three things from deciphering our fellow humans' body language, our chances of survival—not to mention our chances of getting lucky with that babe at the bar—would increase one hundredfold.

How we stand, lean, sit; whether we subconsciously choose to rub our chin or crotch; whether we cross our arms and legs or cross our heart and hope to die, every move our body makes gives off signals—perhaps the *wrong* signals, perhaps giving the game away.

Mastering "Word War"

All language is manipulative; all language is attempted persuasion.
—Dr. Suzette Haden Elgin[118]

It's a war out there and words can get you killed. Think of all the examples down through history where the wrong word spoken in haste, or whispered in the wrong ear at the right time, led to innocent—and brilliant—people being burned at the stake—may Giordano Bruno rest in peace. Yelling "Black power!" at a KKK rally probably isn't a wise career move—not unless you have a really good HMO. Neither is yelling the N-word at a reunion of the Black Panther Party.

Words have the power to promote and to prejudice and to get you placed on the "permanently disabled" roster. We can all too easily lose our livelihood . . . or even our lives . . . just by exercising our freedom of speech at the wrong place, wrong time.

Think of all the racial slurs and religious faux pas that can get your head cut clean off if uttered in the wrong country—or in the wrong *company* in a Western country where you supposedly still have such rights.

Accusing your political opponent of making such insensitive remarks ensures he'll have to spend the rest of the campaign on the defensive rather than on the offensive.

"Dis"[119] a name that somebody holds sacred—their own, their mama's, their gods singular or plural—and you could quite easily have a war on your hands.

Admittedly, some names lend themselves to abuse more easily than others.

Every kid in kindergarten knows how to do it. Take the other kid's name and rhyme it with something: "Danny Big Fanny," "Mary Hairy," "Big Head Fred" . . . names that follow you all the way through high school, and sometimes even into adult life. Adults do it, too.

During the 2006 election campaign in Ohio, opponents of Senate hopeful Sherrod Brown came up with the snippy little kindergarten-*esque* rhyme: "Sherrod Brown let us down." FYI: Sherrod Brown subsequently *won* the

---

118. *Success with the Gentle Art of Verbal Self-Defense* by Susan Haden Elgin (Prentice Hall, 1989).

119. Modern street slang for "disrespect."

election, by the way. Proving once more that while everything works . . . not everything works every time!

Madison Avenue's term for this is "catchy." And advertisers use rhyming all the time to positively promote their clients: "Nothin' says lovin' like somethin' from the oven!"

We like rhymes. Rhymes make convenient mnemonic devices: "Thirty days has September, April, June, and November . . ."

People love to talk. We judge people by how they talk. Okay, everybody on the face of this planet *except you* judges everybody else by how they talk. The words that come out of our mouth instantly mark us as educated (or trying to pretend we're educated), cool (or trying to look cool), Harvard or hillbilly,[120] even straight or gay. (Just because you don't *say* it doesn't mean you're not *thinking* it.)

In order to gain the upper hand in a conversation and/or browbeat a verbose opponent, adroit Mind Slayers are adept at dissecting existing names and words (i.e., highlighting innocuous prefixes, suffixes, and anagrams made from the word) in order to cause any verbose opponent to stumble and hesitate in his verbal assault. Like Hannibal on the battlefield, any perceived weakness (i.e., hesitation or stumble) in an enemy provides an opportunity for the alert and articulate Mind Slayer to rush in and seize control of the conversation.

For example, finding yourself trapped on the losing side of an argument with a true believer who insists on quoting you chapter and verse from the Bible to back up his claims, interject that the word "Bible" begins with "bib"—something you tie around a child's neck, and ends with "ill"—as in sick. You might also want to point out that "Bible" rhymes with "libel." And don't forget to mention that you can't write "believe" or "belief" without sticking "lie" smack dab in the middle.

And since we don't want you to think we're singling out only Christians for abuse, you can give similar argument (i.e., insult) to Muslims by pointing out that "Islam" looks a lot like "Is lame" and Muhammad's name sounds a lot like "Moo-*HAM*-head." Of course, you might want to recall how, at the beginning of this discussion, we mentioned the fact that words can get you killed . . .

To piss off (i.e., upset their train of thought) monotheists (Christian,

120. They prefer to be called "Appalachian Americans" these days. How do you know whether you're an Appalachian American? You couldn't spell "Appalachian" to save your life!

Muslim, Jew), anytime you get into an argument with them, simply substitute "She" for "He" when speaking of God. Whatever deep theological point the person was trying to make will instantly be forgotten as they dutifully rush to defend God's "proper" gender.

The first human who hurled an insult instead of a stone was the founder of civilization.
—Sigmund Freud

The True Art of Arguing

While on the subject of arguing . . . Novices often go into battle eager to participate in "an adventure." Veteran military strategists will tell you, "If you find yourself involved in *an adventure* then something has gone horribly wrong with your *battle plan*!" In other words, a well-thought-out battle plan should never become an adventure.

Likewise, if you constantly find yourself in arguments . . . then you're really not very good at arguing. Remember Sun Tzu's maxim that the best wars are the ones you can avoid fighting?

An argument takes place *between equals* . . . and a true Mind Slayer knows—or at least declines to acknowledge—any equal.

It has been said:

- One takes correction from superiors.
- One argues only with equals.
- One lectures inferiors.

Thus, the king does not argue with the peasant, nor the professor with the pupil.

A true Mind Slayer never gets in an argument. He may elaborate and expound on a subject, even on the short-comings of a rival sans ever allowing anyone, particularly said rival, a chance to get a word in edgewise. He may rant and rave on injustices committed—keeping his audience spellbound for hours—while his lessers, those spoiling for an argument, wait in vain for their turn to speak, it never dawning on them that the Mind Slayer's school of diction is a dictatorship, not a democracy.

While wise enough to take instruction from proven masters who have come before him, imperiously he does not deign to argue with those beneath him and, increasingly, he finds fewer and fewer his equal.

Two other factors play doorman to this theater of the mind where the accomplished Mind Slayer regularly performs his exclusive magic act:

1. He plans and conducts his affairs (i.e., schemes!) in such a way that none but the boldest or else the most foolhardy dare accuse his authenticity, challenge his credibility (his affected expertise, impeccable disguise, etc.), or indict his elocution. The "well-publicized" record (i.e., ruthless and shameless *self*-promotion) of his past victories (real or manufactured), including and perhaps most important the ignoble fates of any past detractors, is enough to keep all but the most confident of verbal duelists from crossing swords with him.
2. Should he ever suspect he is about to be ambushed, confronted, or otherwise challenged as to his personal and philosophical value and validity, with a bow and a flourish he adroitly exercises his "Exit, stage left"—distracting and delaying unwanted scrutiny by employing well-rehearsed verbal ploys from the *Art of Confusion*[121] and/or taking advantage of an actual emergency egress, scouted beforehand, designed to carry him out of the line of fire and out from under the harsh limelight of interrogation.

Getting Your Word in Edgewise and Otherwise

How does a Mind Slayer get the other guy to shut up long enough to seize control of the conversation?

- Interruption ploy one: To stop someone talking, nod your head knowingly/patronizingly and breathe an audible sigh of impatience while forcefully exhaling: "Ah, William James!" (Make it seem as if the motormouth hogging all your airtime had just quoted William James.) When he stumbles over what he was saying and/or hesitates, and everybody looks at you, seize control of the conversation by actually quoting William James:

> It is as important to cultivate your silence power as it is your word power.

121. For a complete course in "The Craft of Confusion" see Dr. Haha Lung and Christopher B. Prowant's *Mental Dominance* (Citadel, 2009).

- Interruption ploy number two: Interrupt the same way, but this time say, "African *dik-dik*!" (Pronounced *dick-dick*) When all heads turn to you like you've just said something dirty, innocently explain that a dik-dik is a very small African antelope, *genus Madoquo*. Now, while everyone, including motormouth is wondering what the hell dik-dik has to do with anything, launch into your own much more fascinating diatribe.

> His soft, precise fashion of speech leaves a conviction of sincerity which a mere bully could not produce. —Sherlock Holmes complementing his nemesis, Professor Moriarty

Where Communication Is King? (Hint: Everywhere!)

Chanting the mantra "Communication is king!" savvy businesses and advertisers deliberately choose words and images with "resonance" in mind (i.e., sounds and syllables incorporating within their seemingly innocuous meaning evocative meanings that "resonate" on a deeper—often subconscious—level).

Ask most people what "Nike" means and they'll tell you it's synonymous with tennis shoe, which, in today's world, isn't far off. The word *nike* comes to us from the Greek (in case your next guess was that it was a Japanese word). Nike was the Greek goddess of victory.[122] Of course, unless you know this—or even care to know this—*nike* to you will ever mean tennis shoe. To ancient Greeks this word—this name—evoked all sorts of images, images of not only the goddess herself but also of great battles the Greeks had won in her name.

A modern-day Nike would be America's Uncle Sam. Uncle Sam started out as a nickname for the government and was made popular during the Civil War and then cemented into the collective consciousness during World War I by that famous recruiting poster with Uncle Sam pointing his accusing finger at passers-by with a stern "I Want YOU!" So when Americans hear "Uncle Sam" it can have resonances, reverberations, and echoes in our mind of any number of emotions: pride in having served our country, thoughts of loved ones who sacrificed themselves, patriotism, nostalgia, sadness, and loss.

Consider: What reaction does 9/11 stir up? To some in America, sadly,

---

122. Which we still keep alive today as "Winged Victory" and that bare-breasted lady leading the French Revolution.

nothing. To others, at the mere mention of 9/11 thoughts of sadness, still maybe fear and still maybe anger flood across the mind. Most of us can still vividly recall the images of that day—the planes striking the Twin Towers, brave first-responders, the bodies, strangers reaching out to help one another . . . and then, soon, images of our enemies dancing, celebrating in their streets. Strong—*emotional*—images.

Remember from our initial discussion of our untrustworthy amygdala how *emotion overrides rational thinking* if only because incoming information gets processed (and reacted upon) by the amygdala emotional center long before it ever makes it to the higher reasoning part of our brain.

In the same way, wily Mind Slayers pepper their speech and promotional images with double entendre, innuendo, and subtle meaning, sometimes using words and images from shared childhood experience memories and even cultural images we may not be fully aware of but that affect us on—you guessed it—a *subliminal* level.

Of course, Mind Slayers also use words and images we all consciously already know are evocative and controversial. Yet even when we suspect others are deliberately trying to use words and images to rile us, get our goat, and yank our chain, we are often powerless to prevent having an emotional reaction to some words and images. For example, for Americans the following can stir up emotions:

- The N-word, "child molester," "sex-offender," "Satanist"
- Images of 9/11
- Images of the Holocaust
- Pictures of JFK can trigger feelings of sadness (and for older Americans, interestingly enough, guilt)
- Pictures of missing children and abused animals

Some of these words and images evoke the same universal reactions of horror and sadness in all human beings. Yet other images, for example, the Twin Towers on fire or images of the Holocaust, while images of horror, sadness, and loss to most civilized folk, in some countries are cause for celebration.

Thus, Mind Slayers choose their words and images to specific effect, depending on whom those words and images are directed toward.

Sometimes our natural attraction or repulsion from a word and a person associated with that word is not even that deep. Ask any child whom they would rather have for a teacher: Mr. I. B. Pleasant or Mr. I. M. Shitimire (pronounced *shit-ee-mire*). Of course an adult would never judge and discriminate against a person based on a . . . *shitty* sounding name, right?

Sometimes people's names just cry out for abuse, and alert Mind Slayers are on the job. For example: Nation of Islam leader Louis Farrakhan becomes "Lucifer A. Con" and Saddam Hussein becomes "Sodom" Hussein.

And if your name just happens to be "Bush," you have to put up with all the puns about "beating around the . . ." and bumper stickers like "I love Bush . . . just not that big pussy in the White House!"

Our modern word "nightmare" means simply a bad dream but the word originally meant exactly what it said: a night mare, a black (sometimes pale) horse you saw while fully awake that, crossing your path like a black cat, meant you were going to die soon. So, back in the day, when you said "nightmare" a person actually saw in their mind's eye a "death horse."

And just as overt words we're consciously aware of have the power to flood us with emotion—Zap! Straight to the easily excitable amygdala—so too are we susceptible to deliberate albeit subconscious/subliminal stimulation and manipulation by words and symbols having "resonance" beyond the mere letters making up the word.

For example, suppose you were to choose the name "Archipelago" for your company.[123] Look at all the positive "hidden" resonance within that name:

- *Arch:* A strongly supported entrance way
- *Chi*: Pronounced *key,* something required to help you open doors. In Japan *ki* (pronounced *key*) means "vital force." The same word is spelled "*chi*" in Chinese—excellent to include in your name if you're heading into Asian markets
- *Pela*: Pronounced like the name Pele, the greatest soccer player ever. While still growing in America, soccer is the number one sport worldwide—something an American company wanting to expand overseas needs to keep in mind
- *Go!* Not only a call to action in the West, but also the name of a centuries-old, still-popular Asian game of strategy.

123. "Archipelago" is used by a company listed on the New York Stock Exchange and specializing in electronic transfer systems.

Mastering Propaganda

Every day we swim in a sea of brainwash, albeit a diluted one. Every time we rally around a flag or logo, or pop a Prozac, or accept a marketing campaign into our lives, we are dancing with the forces of control, or at least with the "consensus trance" that unconsciously seeks to keep us, for all intents and purposes, dazed and confused.

—Erik Davis, *Technosis*, 1998

Whether we call it "propaganda" or simply "product placement," there's no escaping the fact that 24/7 we're being targeted—bombarded!—with a whole pack of someones trying to sell us a whole bunch of something, from Diet Coke to pork-belly candidates and from sex to SUVs.

In 2006, marketers spent a record $175 billion for advertisements in major media, including TV, radio, newspaper, magazines and other print, on outdoor billboards and signs, in movie theaters (and in the movies themselves), and on the Internet. Today, more and more information assails us, flashing at ever faster speed, as advertisers compete for our brains' (1) short attention span and (2) limited processing time. Unfortunately, while both hardwired and software ways of getting information to—into!—our head keep increasing, it's been pointed out that the "wet wear" we have to work with, the human brain itself, hasn't improved much in the past thirty thousand years. In other words, we still process information pretty much as we did back then, and at the same speed.[124]

It's said that one of the most profound philosophical questions ever uttered was "What is truth?"

We're still trying to figure that one out, and it doesn't help matters any that, while trying to decipher the "truth" of the universe, we have to constantly fend off the less-than-honest advances of our fellow man:

> To be sure, every intellectual is normally and above all a servant of the truth. But one cannot effectively serve truth merely by proclaiming it. It must be presented in an attractive manner; the audience must be convinced. The word "propa-

---

124. Laura Pentrecca, *USA Today*, 10.11.06:B6.

ganda" has of late been devalued by many abuses; yet it pertains to the intellectual vocation to propagate the truth.
—Ignace Lepp, 1968

The Three Types of Propaganda

So right about now you're asking yourself, "Why do I need to study propaganda? It's a multisyllabic word so that probably means it's really complicated to learn, right? Wrong. There are only three basic types of propaganda and, right off, you'll undoubtedly notice that these *three types of propaganda* are pretty much the *three types of lying* you're already familiar with in everyday life:

- ***Real information***: The truth and nothing but the truth, so help you God. But the truth is not always a good thing. Sometimes the truth hurts. And sometimes we mean it to hurt, for example, exposing a politician's extramarital affair, or the fact a politician has previously undergone psychotherapy for depression. This is hardly the "career killer" it was in 1972 when it was revealed that Presidential hopeful George McGovern's running mate Senator Thomas Eagleton had been hospitalized three times for treatment of exhaustion and depression. Eagleton chivalrously withdrew from the race, but not before the revelations of his "mental illness" did irreparable harm to McGovern's campaign.

  We're told Jesus was filled with "truth and grace." Grace means you need to know when to keep your mouth shut. "No, honey, those slacks don't make your ass look fat."

- ***Mis*information:** Sometimes you get the facts wrong. It's shoddy reporting, not double-checking all the facts, and/or allowing yourself to be spoon-fed crap by the powers-that-be. But that doesn't always stop an overeager news editor from running with the story.

Did you know the CIA purposely created and introduced crack cocaine into black neighborhoods, and with every three dime rocks you bought you got a free case of AIDS (something the CIA created)? Once this kind of *misinformation* got out of the bag, did you think it was ever/is ever gonna crawl back into that bag? Key: *emotionally evocative* propaganda takes on a life of its own. The second shooter on the grassy knoll?

- ***Disinformation:*** You're lying. You're deliberately putting out what you know to be false information. Whatever the reason for such inaccuracies, it's important we remain aware of how easily such false information can be leaked and/or slipped into otherwise useful and timely information.

> Let's hear it for rumors, for sources anonymous, for dark innuendo, and all things synonymous!—The Joker[125]

Sometimes, these three types of propaganda overlap. People pass along gossip, innuendo, and propaganda sincerely believing it to be the truth—not even anticipating the harm they may be unleashing and/or perpetuating.

Other times, it's hard to tell whether the person disseminating the information is (1) a willing agent provocateur deliberately sent to stir up a hornet's nest, or else (2) an unwitting participant in a propaganda ploy not of his or her making.

Take, for example, Colin Wilson's otherwise informative 2000 book *Rogue Messiahs*, where Wilson comments on fellow author Paul Brunton's claims concerning ancient Egypt:

> [Brunton's] assertion that the Sphinx was built thousands of years before the Great Pyramid, by survivors from Atlantis, has recently received some scientific support from a study of the weathering of the Sphinx by Dr. Robert Schock, of Boston University. (Schock believes it was weathered by rain, not by wind-driven sand.)[126]

Let's examine this paragraph a little closer.

To get our attention, and establish credibility, this paragraph assures us the information contained therein comes from (1) a recent scientific study, (2) done by a reputable scientist named Schock, (3) from the well-respected Boston University, who has discovered (4) convincing evidence (5) derived through sound scientific research, concluding that (6) when the Sphinx was constructed the weather in Egypt *was* drastically different—much wetter—than it was thousands of years later when the Great Pyramid was built.

From this perspective, Wilson's paragraph appears to be well-researched

125. *Batman Inferno* by Alex Irvine (Graphic Audio/DC Comics, 2009).
126. Wilson, 2000:57.

good reporting based on sound scientific work, performed by an unimpeachable scientist, backed up by a respectable institution of higher learning.

Ah, but did you notice the insertion of the phrase "by survivors from Atlantis" sandwiched in between the logical assertion at the beginning of the paragraph that the Sphinx is thousands of years older than the Great Pyramid and the impeccable sources for information given at the end of the paragraph?

If you weren't paying attention (or didn't have Dr. Lung to point these things out for you!) this uncorroborated piece of "information" about the lost continent of Atlantis would have gone straight into your brain's "facts file"—without notice, without question—because, even if your brain was going to send "by survivors from Atlantis" to its fact-check department to be verified, this unproven assertion (that Atlantis actually existed) was immediately followed by mention of sources for the erroneous information that your brain recognizes as "authority figures"—a scientist, a university—making it most unlikely you'd remember to do that fact-check later. So, without realizing it, you would inadvertently—subconsciously—store "by survivors from Atlantis" in your "T for true" file.

Get your facts first, then you can distort them how you please.
—Mark Twain

The Eight Ways to Distort Information

Propaganda can target us in both spoken and in written form, both easily susceptible to being twisted and distorted in one of eight ways:

- ***Appeals to authority*:** This is what happened in the *Rogue Messiahs* paragraph. We are so dazzled with the authorities quoted at the end of the paragraph, we could all too easily be lead to trust and believe that those authorities were "co-signing" for the existence of the lost continent of Atlantis, rather than merely relating their theory/discovery about weather conditions in ancient Egypt. Hello! *Weapons of mass destruction?*

  As much as we'd like to think we're James Dean in *Rebel Without a Cause*, Marlon Brando in *The Wild One*, and the last hippie, the sorry fact is we're raised from birth to obey authority figures—mommy, daddy, our teachers, coach, drill instructor, boss, president. On a good day, this agreed-upon pecking order is what keeps society from chewing its paw off. On a bad day, we're "Isaacs"[127] and it's Jonestown, Waco, or 9/11.

- ***Ambiguous language:*** Ill-defined words and phrases are always open to interpretation—until the speaker provides *his* "proper" interpretation. For example, I use a word you are either not familiar with, or I use a word you are familiar with in a novel way.[128] Now you're confused (just where I want you) and giving me your undivided attention (really where I want you!) until you can figure out what I meant—because you don't want to look stupid (or like you weren't paying attention) later.
- ***Analogies, metaphors, similes, and symbols*** that make people think one thing is connected to another. But, upon closer examination, the two are in no way connected. "Since my opponent has taken office, teenaged pregnancy has nearly tripled!" Well, either your opponent is a *very* busy man . . . or the two are not really connected. Correlation does not mean causation.

  Or how about, "My grandfather fought his way all across Europe with his buddies to defeat fascism, and there's no way he would have voted for my opponent!" Grandfathers, brave veterans, World War II, defeating the inhuman Hun . . . the use of all these evocative symbols implies the opposite: that your opponent is a fan of fascism. In this same vile vein, gadfly Michael Moore once compared the U.S. Patriot Act to *Mein Kampf*[129] and Rush Limbaugh likes to compare Obama to Hitler.[130] Such analogies have been called just "a lazy shortcut to secure *an emotional response*."[131] (Ibid.)

  Remember that *emotionally charged* examples and arguments go straight to your jump-the-gun amygdala before—if ever—giving your higher reasoning mind time to critically examine the facts.

---

127. Synonymous with the psychological term "patriarchal castration," e.g., authority stifles creativity. Someone who follows authority without question. Derived from the tale of Abraham's unquestionably obedient son Isaac. Term coined in the 1930s by Eric Neuman, a student of Carl Jung.

128. See "Cult Speak" in the Glossary.

129. Hitler's opus, blueprint for destruction.

130. "Trivializing the evils of Nazism" by Michael Gerson. *The Washington Post*, see *The Week*, 9.28.09:16.

131. Emphasis added

- ***Selected proofs:*** We control the flow of information, leaking only selected sound bites. This is also known as "lying by omission." Often what we *don't* say is more important than what we do say.
- ***Red herrings:*** We distract our detractors by changing the subject, preferably switching to another hot, *emotionally charged* topic. For example, your opponent is getting the upper hand in a debate and you switch gears and suddenly challenge him on where he stands on "family values" (a vague, hot potato topic). Or you "play the race card," accusing (or better yet implying) that something he said was racist or otherwise ethnically offensive.

  The ears of everyone in the vicinity (even those only half-listening) will suddenly perk up, immediately forgetting the crux of the debate, their attention immediately captivated by the allegation of racial insult or insensitivity.

  Remember a little earlier how you learned to "exit stage left" when prudent?
- ***Mudslinging (a.k.a. ad hominem attacks):*** When you can't poke holes in your opponent's theories, you poke holes in him (most of the time figuratively). Everybody's got dirty laundry. Threaten to hang his out to dry. Personal insults are a time-honored tool.
- ***Quoting spurious sources*** that can't be checked for accuracy. Cult leaders often get their "divine revelations" from sources that can't possibly be verified—from dreams, visions of angels, UFO encounters, and the ancient continent of Atlantis. For example, Elijah Poole, self-styled "Elijah Muhammad," controversial founder of the Nation of Islam cult claimed that what he called "the original Black man" came from the moon *sixty-six trillion years ago!* Poole's successor, the equally controversial Louis Farrakhan once claimed to have received instruction from the (by then) dead Elijah Poole Muhammad when, on September 17, 1985, while in Tepotzlan, Mexico, he was beamed aboard the "Mother Plane," a UFO[132] of gigantic proportions whose existence is—or rather *was*—known only to black Muslims.

---

132. This craft doesn't actually qualify as a true "unidentified" flying object since Farrakhan (and others of the NOI inner circle) still teach Elijah Poole's story that this Mother Plane was built by the superior technology of what Poole refers to in all his writings as the "original Asiatic Black man" who came from the moon sixty-six trillion years ago! For more on

- ***Faulty conclusions*** are drawn, based on faulty information dramatically presented and strategically positioned, using any and all the aforementioned ploys. Again, this is sometimes done inadvertently, when people act on the "best available information at the time,"[133] only to later be given additional information that reveals just how wrong they were in their initial conclusion. Other times, Mind Slayers deliberately lead us by the nose, spoon-feeding us only bits of information, partial truths, allowing us to come to our own faulty conclusion. This is what happened to Othello.

  Sometimes, falling back on this "best available information at the time" excuse amounts to plausible deniability.

Mastering Subliminal Suggestion

Propaganda is often so effective because it concentrates on influencing us at a *subliminal* level, employing potent words and symbols to evoke vaguely remembered and/or vaguely defined cultural and religious memories that nonetheless stir us *emotionally* often without our being *consciously aware* we are being influenced. If we're not *consciously aware* of something . . . then it must be *subliminal*.

I'm sure you recall from the previous section "The Beast Within (Who Doesn't like to Do Without!)" that what is often touted as the oh-so-mysterious craft of "subliminal suggestion" is really nothing more than our midbrain "animal brain" jumping the gun by sending signals out to shoot first and ask questions later—actually, to let the higher brain ask questions later. Recall our example of mistaking a piece of garden hose for a snake? And the more *emotion filled* the sensory information coming in to the midbrain, the more the likelihood of this happening.

We now know there's more to those sensational and cautionary tales from the 1950s about moviegoers being "brainwashed" and "programmed" into buying more soft drinks by unconsciously viewing secretly flashed messages on the movie screen (e.g., the word "thirsty" in between frames), "sub-

---

Farrakhan's fantastic journey, see the Nation of Islam's official newspaper *The Final Call*, November 30, 1989. For more on the mind manipulation techniques of the NOI cult, see *Wormwood: The Terrible Truth about Islam* by Joshua Only (Only Publications, 2009).

133. Review "Ten Good Excuses . . . but Not One Good Explanation!" section above.

liminal messages" that flashed too fast for the person to consciously register them. It turns out there's more validity to those stories—or at least to the techniques used—than at first thought because we now know that just because a sensation is registered in the amygdala doesn't mean it's automatically passed along to the higher, conscious level of the brain. Our amygdala can get excited by any stimulus perceived as threatening (e.g., the image of an angry face or a loud noise) and/or by primitive urges (hunger, thirst . . . sex), all the while our higher brain remains blissfully—sometimes *dangerously*!—unaware of what's going on in the more primitive—more *subliminal*—parts of our brain.

Far from being science fiction, subliminal messages are being beamed into your head every single day of your life. It's called radio and television, magazine ads and billboards, and the Internet. Any time something *isn't* said, but we still somehow "get the message" . . . that's *subliminal suggestion!*

- The hot babe in the new-car commercial doesn't say she'll climb into the backseat with you if you buy the car, but you get the message.
- Cartoon spokesman Joe Camel's nose was modeled on a penis and scrotum because it was determined that the number one concern of Camel cigarettes' target audience—young, white males—was (big surprise) getting laid. And to do that, it helps if you got "the package" for it. So every time they saw Joe the Camel they subliminally saw a hefty "package," which they, in turn, subliminally associated with a happy feeling from getting laid. So Joe the Camel made them subliminally feel good. They got the message.[134]
- Somebody figured out that women equate baking with giving birth . . . that's why the Pillsbury doughboy is a fetus—only partially formed. Why a fetus? Because "Nothin' says lovin' like something from the oven." Hello! "Bun in the oven" = pregnancy, get it? And the last action on every crescent roll commercial is someone poking doughboy in the belly, *giving him a belly button*. Women got the message.
- *The play behind the play.* Everybody's favorite friendly basketball superstar gets to reminiscing and decides to visit his old 'hood and play some B-ball on the old neighborhood asphalt court. After some spirited play, they all enjoy a cold Coke. Nice commercial. But did you

134. And let's not even consider the Freudian "oral fixation" component to smoking.

happen to notice the brightly colored, heavily graffitied wall backing the court? Just your typical inner city wall, right? One the producers were just driving down the street and happen to see, and think, "Gee, this would make a great backdrop for my new commercial!" right?

Now did you ever wonder why you never see any of the usual inner city street graffiti: plenty of F-U's, plenty of gangbanger tags proudly proclaiming the latest brother to die a foolish death? That's because—first, assuming the commercial was actually shot in the inner city, and that's a big assumption!—before any kind of shooting started (the camera kind, not the gun kind!) the producers brought in professional artists to repaint those walls. Oh, they still resemble cool graffiti walls, but you can bet your bottom dollar (because the producer already invested his!) that those walls are now filled with all sorts of subliminal messages.

What's that you say, you never *consciously* thought about it? Exactly. While you were *consciously* concentrating on your favorite B-baller flashing back and forth across the screen, simultaneously, you were being flashed multiple *subliminal* messages from the walls behind your hero. Think of this as the play behind the play. And you just been "played."

These subliminal flashes are specially edited so that they flash by at a speed ignored by your conscious (higher) mind, while stimulating your more animal midbrain urges: eat, drink, wear the same shoes as your B-ball hero and you too will get the girl. Keeping it simple: suppose he's advertising Coke. By the end of the commercial, when you finally—*consciously*—see him and his bros sharing a Coke, you've already been exposed to dozens of *subliminal* flashes that trigger your midbrain's "thirsty" trigger.

Yeah, just like they did in those movie theaters fifty years ago. The more things change . . . the more people stay the same.

According to Armen Victorian in his 1999 *Mind Controllers*, in 1989 a U.S. Department of Defense consultant and contractor revealed how he'd been given the task of devising more efficient operational methods for transmitting subliminal messages via TV. In 2009, it became mandatory for all television stations in the United States to replace analog signals with more up to date, clearer digital broadcasting.

Mastering Memory Manipulation

There's no such thing as "photographic memory." The closest talent to it is called "eidetic memory," where someone is just really good at remembering *vividly*. But even these "eidetikers" don't have a photographic memory.[135] In other words, some people are just better at remembering. The good news is you can, and should, take the opportunity to improve your memory every chance you get. The bad news is, there's a whole lot of really smart—potentially ruthless—people out there doing all kinds of scientific research on how to manipulate your memory.

So much of who and what we are is simply our memory, so the very idea that someone would—or even could—deliberately tamper with our memory is frightening. Yet the state of science today has brought us to the point where we can alter memories.

Today, an alchemist's lode stone of "cogniceuticals"[136] has been discovered that can literally erase harmful and traumatic memories, which promoters claim will help speed the healing process in some patients.

Another avenue of memory manipulation therapy aims to deliberately create artificial phobias in a person's mind, with the intent of helping them overcome self-defeating behaviors (e.g., overeating) by implanting false memories in their mind of their having had a "distasteful" experience with that food in their past—in effect creating an artificial phobia. The proviso to this process being that it's likely that false-memory phobias such as these can be implanted only when the subjects targeted are *unaware* of the mental manipulation taking place. According to Elizabeth Loftus[137] of the University of California at Irvine who conducted the experiments, there's nothing to stop parents from using this technique of implanting false memories to help their obese children.[138]

Query: if parents can become adept at implanting false memories about food, what else might parents—or others?—be able to implant in a child's mind?

---

135. "The Truth About Photographic Memory," *Psychology Today*, March/April 2006.

136. Cogniceuticals: drugs deliberately designed to enhance or entrance the mind.

137. Best known for her controversial work at debunking "repressed memory." See Dr. Haha Lung and Christopher B. Prowant's *Black Science* (Paladin, 2001) and *Mind Manipulation,* Dr. Haha Lung and Christopher B. Prowant (Citadel, 2002).

138. "Can Memory Manipulation Change the Way You Eat?" by Rebecca Skoot. *Discover*, January, 2006:30.

Is it just me, or does the very idea of deliberately "erasing" parts of a person's memory and/or implanting artificial phobias (and, in the future, implanting who knows what other kinds of *false* memories?) instantly conjure up a shadowy circus tent with the smiling, sharp-eyed barker outside bellowing, "Hurry, hurry, step right up! Welcome to Big Brother's Bizarre Brainwashing Horror Show!"?

And while on the subject of Dr. Lung's paranoia: the Alpha-Learning Institute in Switzerland has developed a pair of glasses with light-emitting diodes (LEDs) that pulsate at varying speeds while, simultaneously, a pair of headphones emit a beat synchronized to the pulsing lights. This combination of light and sounds reportedly "tunes" the mind to "optimal frequencies" for relaxation and concentration, thereby increasing the wearer's capacity for memory and making the brain more susceptible to learning.[139]

Scientists have figured out that the human brain is capable of retaining close to 100 billion bits of information, the equivalent of five hundred encyclopedias.[140] And while a lot of the information floating around in our head is based on true past experiences, our brain is constantly editing and re-writing those true experiences—all too often into unrecognizable events.

As a general rule, our brain tosses out the bad stuff (memories of hurtful or uncomfortable events) while clinging tightly to stuff (events, experiences, people) remembered as good—we call that "nostalgia." We especially like to get rid of any past memory about ourselves that doesn't quite fit with our present view of ourselves. Psychiatrists call this kind of selective memory revisionism "self-delusion" or, at the very least, "avoidance."

The kind of memories that have the best chance of surviving this constant culling process are (1) memories that had novel or unexpected consequence and/or (2) memories associated with strong emotion. This accounts for post traumatic stress disorder (PTSD): arising from the trauma of unexpected consequences (e.g., war experience, unforeseen disasters) and the arousal (flooding/overload) of the strong emotions elicited by same.

But even after we've sifted through those memories we want to keep, when we try to call these memories back up, it's very likely *what went in* (actual experiences) is not necessarily going to be *what comes out*:

---

139. See *Learning to Remember* by Dominic O'Brien (Chronicle Books, 2000).

140. *Double Your Brain Power* by Jean Marie Stine, 1997:95.

> When we want to remember, our brains quickly reweave the tapestry by fabrication—not by retrieving—the bulk of information that we call memory. In other words, we recall the best of times and the worst of times, instead of the most likely of times.—Daniel Gilbert, Ph.D.[141]

The kind of selective memory we call "nostalgia" partially explains how Hitler so easily convinced a whole nation to follow him. Hitler's mesmerizing speeches took the German people back to a time, before the defeat, disgrace, and depression following World War I, when they were a powerful nation.

Ironically, Hitler the failed artist was a master when it came to painting a bright—once more powerful—future for his Fourth Reich. More important, he was a Mind Slayer extraordinaire at dredging up Germanic "memories" that were, in fact, reconstructions, reinterpretations, or else complete fabrications of an idyllic time that never existed.

All cult leaders (and all too many politicians) do this same thing: *talking* their followers back to that "perfect time" (the Garden of Eden, the lost continent of Atlantis, the 1950s—when blacks and women "knew their place" and "gay" hadn't been invented yet!).

So what are the basic rules to follow if you deliberately want to screw with someone's memory of the past:

- ***Don't try changing their memory all at once:*** Begin by "tweaking" it a little here and there. One of the key axioms of the brainwashing craft is "We are what we do." In practice, this translates into getting the brainwashee (POW, cult member, abused wife, etc.) to change their behavior just a little at first, then a little more, then a little more. Physics 101: objects in motion tend to stay in motion. Once you get that object moving, it is easier to guide its advance with a slight adjustment here, a turn of the screw there.

  People look back with 20/20 hindsight at Nazi Germany and wonder, "Why didn't they see what was coming?" People look back at nine hundred dead in the Jonestown cult and ask, "How could they have fallen for that line of malarkey?"

---

141. *Bottomline/Personal*, October 15, 2006:9.

The key is they didn't, at least not all at once. This is why Sun Tzu harps on stamping out *little problems* before they become *big problems.* Likewise with memory manipulation, you change a memory gradually, first by introducing elements not present at the actual making of the memory.

- ***Make them question their details of the event*** by quickly providing your own details of what happened—or how something might have happened—any time you hear them hesitate in their recollection. By inserting your own details, you force the person to either (1) stop and backtrack in their narrative to correct you or (2) choose the easier path and continue on with their narrative by ignoring your comments (perhaps promising themselves to correct you later). Most people will choose the latter path of least resistance—never realizing that, by not stopping to correct the details you've inserted, those details will pass into the brains of listeners as unchallenged truth.
- ***Always show them in a good light*** when challenging (and changing) their version of the truth, making them "remember" what an important part they played in what happened. In other words, exaggerate their contribution to good things that happened.

  Remember the last time your friend was bragging on you, entertainingly embellishing your heroics—lying about how big that fish was, about how good-looking that girl was you went home with last night? And, instead of correcting his exaggeration, you just humbly shrugged it off, since you were as caught up in hearing about *your* exploits as everyone else in the room.
- ***Downplay any bad*** they might have done or allowed to happen (until they soon become dependent on your version of the event to look good and/or to maintain their newfound sense of self-respect).
- ***Inject emotion and animation*** into your details to make your version of the story more exciting than the old boring truth. Using emotion and animation engages the right-side imagination hemisphere of their brain, which will automatically begin creating even more exciting images to replace the vague and dull—albeit true—left-side memories.

Notice how, again and again, we keep coming back to the vital role *emotion* plays in the overall influence of people in general, and in such things as helping people form (and helping the Mind Slayer *re-form*) memories in particular.

- ***Distract and shock them:*** Not only do memories with strong, unexpected, novel, and emotional content literally make more of an impression in our permanent long-term memory, it's also been shown that our being startled or otherwise receiving a shock to our system immediately after experiencing an event, and even after merely studying for an exam, helps lock in information we're trying to commit to memory.

For example, test subjects who had their hands plunged into freezing water immediately after studying were found to remember the information they'd studied at a higher percentage rate. The reason ice water (and other similar shocks, such as loud noises) helps us remember is because it causes our old buddy the easily excitable amygdala to trigger the release of stress hormones, helping solidify memories forming in the brain. Recall that even innocuous, harmless stimuli (our garden hose snake, for example) can cause the amygdala to freak out, literally leaping before taking a second look.

In the same way, a sudden, somewhat painful icy shock or a sudden loud noise can cause the amygdala to react instantly, out of proportion to any actual threat. As a result, information that might have otherwise been mulled over, questioned, and collated by the higher brain gets immediately brushed whole into the "permanent" file in the amygdala's haste to initiate "fight or flight."

This may be the reason listening to loud rock music while studying helps some students learn better—the loud music slightly raises the student's stress level and triggers the release of stress hormones, aiding memory. Another tried-and-true college study technique: when taking a break from exhaustive studying, eat hot peppers, really hot peppers—hot peppers are known to raise stress levels.

Asian martial arts instructors have long intuitively known the benefits of pairing the technical (rational) verbal instruction of combat techniques with as-realistic-as-possible stress-filled application—sparring, board breaking, and other activities designed to (1) raise the students' stress level in order to (2) help them better lock in those techniques. This is also why you'll often find traditional martial arts practitioners meditating under icy waterfalls or while sitting in snow.

One example of this is Tibetan monks' mysterious *tumo* heat-generating practice, whereby they meditate nearly naked, seemingly unconcerned and unharmed, outside in freezing weather while wrapped in sheets soaked in near-freezing water. These monks often have contests among themselves to see how many water-soaked sheets they can dry!

Marine drill instructors also find this "shock them into remembering" technique useful—show recruits how to do something . . . and then scare the *bejesus* out of them by screaming in their face!

So the next time you insert an inventive "fact" into the conversation, immediately follow it with a distraction—a loud clap of your hands, for instance, or a sudden "What the hell is that?" look over the shoulder of your listener(s) (causing them to turn quickly to see what's the matter). In more complicated "long-con" situations, the Mind Slayer speaker often employs a confederate to create a distraction. This is the principle behind that lovely, scantily clad magician's assistant.

(More on this in the "Mastering the Techniques of the Mini-Masters" section that follows, pp. 134–42.)

Try this memory manipulation experiment: have your subject sit across the table from you as you read the following list of words to them:

> *"Sundown, sleep, moon, shadow, black, darkness, twilight."*

Now ask them to repeat the words back to you. Chances are they'll inadvertently add (i.e., remember) the word "night" to the list or, at the very least, modify moon into "moonlight" and shadow into "shadows" plural. Small changes to be sure, but now multiply those small changes in memory a hundredfold, to more complicated situations with several points of sensation coming into your brain at one time. Now add to that the weight of years, with similar experiences being jammed helter-skelter into the same file cabinet in your brain. Still think you can trust the memory of an eye-witness, especially one from years ago? What about trusting your own memory?

When you can make an enemy distrust his memory, you are halfway to victory. When an enemy can make you question your own memory, you are three-quarters of the way to defeat!

> Guard your memories well, that your memories may well guard you.—Vlad Tepes, *Dracula's Art of War*

Mastering "Shape-Shifting"

I walked a million miles just to slip this skin.
—Bruce Springsteen, *Streets of Philadelphia*

In 2009, the Connecticut Nursing Association (CNA) held an elaborate dinner to honor their choice of "2008 Nurse of the Year," one Betty Lichtenstein of Norwich. Only later did authorities discover that (1) Lichtenstein wasn't a real nurse and that (2) she created the CNA and had staged a dinner in her own honor as part of a scheme to bolster her resume and get a job.[142]

During the course of a lifetime, we may change our identity many times. To you, your identity may be who you are. To everyone else, it's just a few pieces of laminated ID you carry in your pocket, that embossed diploma hanging on your office wall, perhaps the stethoscope hanging around your neck.

Sometimes, people change their identity out of boredom. Others do so out of necessity—avoiding alimony or indictment!

Whatever your reason for shape-shifting, benevolent or belligerent, you can change your outward appearance in the blink of an eye. If, on the other hand, you're looking for true "inner change," e-mail the Dalai Lama.

We are free to re-fashion our identity until finally—somewhere between rehabilitation, reincarnation, or a hasty witness protection program relocation in the dead of the night—we get it right.

But don't confuse *personality* with *identity*.

Personality you're pretty much stuck with. If you're an asshole now, there is not much chance of your smelling any sweeter any time soon. Experts still argue nature versus nurture, whether Mother Nature carves our personality into our DNA with a rusty butter knife at conception or whether, instead, how we're raised—or not raised—determines our personality later in life. Most people just split the difference.

Identity, on the other hand, is infinitely malleable and for the most part voluntary. You're pretty much free to use any made-up name you want and give yourself any made-up title, short of police officer or President of these United States, just so long as you are not doing it for illicit and/or immoral purposes such as:

---

142. Reported in *The Week*, 8.21.09:6.

- Running a confidence scheme, long con, short con, any con where someone gives you money because they think you're someone else.
- Avoiding paying alimony, child support, and other sundry bills. Nobody likes a deadbeat, particularly a deadbeat dad.
- Impeding law enforcement in any way.

Yes, you can legally use another name to avoid talking to your five ex-wives. No, you cannot use another name in order to *marry* five wives! Likewise, you can call yourself "doctor,"[143] but you better not be caught performing gynecological exams.

Beyond any laminated verification, even a brass-buttoned uniform, there's how you carry yourself. Dress a gorilla in a three-piece suit and the first thing he'll ask for will still be a banana.

A variation of "You can take the boy out of the country, but you can't take the country out of the boy." This would be a case of *personality* (who you really are) giving away your *identity* (who/what you're trying to portray yourself as being). Or, to put it simply, a lot of people are just crappy actors!

We've all watched really bad movies, cringing at how stilted the novice actor's lines were delivered, at how the costumes were all wrong (did cowboys even wear thongs?), and how the background scenery looks like a five-year-old finger-painted it. As a result, we never really forget that the actors are just that . . . *actors acting*.

But when a movie's really good we get caught up in the story, forgetting for an hour or two that we're watching a movie.

The background scenery is convincing, the wardrobe detailed, the dialogue *perfecto*—so much so that we forget who the famous actor is as we become caught up in his masterful shape-shifting into Gandhi or Hannibal the Cannibal.

Confidence schemers are all actors. Cult leaders are all actors. Politicians are all actors. The Bernie Madoffs, the Charlie Mansons, the would-be Mussolini—*Mind Slayers* all, all shape-shifters.

But lest we judge those identity entrepreneurs too quickly, playing the critic too harshly, we must once again thank the Immortal Bard for reminding us *we're all actors*.

---

143. Dr. Doom, Dr. Fu Manchu, Dr. Dre, Dr. Seuss, Dr. Feelgood . . .

Every time you try to pick up a hot babe in a bar, or go on a job interview, you're acting like an actor. If you're a *good* actor, you get the job—in both instances. That's not to say, in either instance, that you're automatically lying per se or that you don't have the credentials and credibility to handle the job. Ideally, your credentials (i.e., IDs, diplomas, etc.) are unimpeachable and you bring plenty of skills and references (i.e., credibility) with you to the interview. But still, you're smart enough to bring your biggest smile with you and to be on your best behavior. No matter whether your goal is office or orifice, hopefully you stand up straight and have a best foot to put forward in both instances.

After all, sincerity has always been pretty easy to fake. It's the bread and butter of the Mind Slayer's craft.

So admit it, sometimes you wish you were someone else.

Sure, it'd be nice to have Bill Gates's billions (probably trillions, by now), but sometimes it would also be nice just to be someone else, take a breather, to have less pressure and responsibility in your life, at least for a while. When most people get to feeling this way, they settle for a vacation or, barring that, they get stinkin' drunk or high. Drugs are not the answer . . . but they damn sure make you forget the question!

Nowadays, it's a whole lot easier to literally become a self-made man, especially when any teenager with a PC can print passable IDs, diplomas, and even college degrees . . . and then go on to fabricate the online universities necessary to verify the authenticity of that diploma or degree. Of course, the counter to this is that anyone with half a brain knows how to use the Internet to confirm references, do credit checks, and track down the vacant lot of your alleged alma mater.

Thankfully, for con men, cultists, and others so shiftily inclined, *most people are too lazy* to turn their computers on,[144] to take the time to double-check letters of reference, or to read the crayon on the credentials. As a result, sundry con men with false IDs, cult leaders with phony "reverend" degrees from Rapture U, and a whole lot of other shady characters prosper at honest folks' expense.

Worst-case scenario: well, we've already seen it, haven't we—some

144. To anything but porn and video games, that is!

Middle Eastern gentleman with that questionable boarding pass slips by some yawning airport screener when he ought to be more thoroughly screened. (That's assuming that the airport screener didn't get his or her job by doing a little shape-shifting of his own!)[145]

When it comes to shape-shifting successfully, you can always count on the right people in the right place at the right time being distracted and/or lazy.

On those rare occasions you do unexpectedly run up against someone daring to question (1) your right to be in the room, (2) your right to have your say, or (3) your right to have your way—whether trying to pass yourself off as an expert in God-knows-what, or ambitiously trying to jump-start your own cult—there are three fears that always make people think twice about challenging someone (who appears) in charge:

- ***People want (need!) to believe someone's in charge, that someone's running the show.***
- ***People are scared to death to question "authority."***
- ***People are scared to death of taking on "responsibility."***

Knowing someone else is in charge lifts a great burden from their lazy and insecure shoulders. It also gives them a feeling of relief—because they're scared to death some sort of responsibility is going to fall on them. They're more than happy to go back to watching basketball while you run the country.

We all like to think we're badasses, but the truth is, when push comes to shove and there is a liability lawsuit pigeon flying around looking for the bull's-eye on the head of whoever's responsible, few people actually have *cojones grande* enough to question authority.

Mind Slayers count on just this sort of hesitation, this sorrowful observation of the human race, since it allows them to use the fear of authority to stifle comment, query, and investigation. This fear used to be called the Sword of Damocles. Nowadays, it's just called "talk to the hand":

- "If you're going to question *my* authority in this matter, then *you* can be the one who explains to (the boss, all the people involved,

---

145. For a complete course in shape-shifting see the section on "How to Be an Instant Expert" in *The Truth About Lying* by Dr. Haha Lung (publication pending).

God Almighty Himself) why the job didn't get done right and on time?" Or . . .

- "I guess you'll be the one explaining to the judge and jury in a court of law why *you* prevented me from doing my job . . . ?" And, "You want to question what I'm doing? Fine. How about I just step aside[146] and let *you* be *responsible* for getting the job done? Think you're *ready* to handle that *responsibility*?"

When using this type of ploy, always leave your obvious threat dangling in the form of a question.

Consequently, once you've established your authority in a situation, should you suspect someone is thinking about questioning your authority, immediately confront and threaten them with the dreaded R-word: *responsibility*.

Don't confuse power with responsibility. Everybody likes having power[147] but nobody wants the responsibility that comes with having power.

Taking control—taking power—isn't as difficult as you might at first fear. Down through history, being (1) willing, (2) able, and (3) the first to start slinging copious cowpies has turned more than one farmer into a fuehrer.

Recent studies have verified what we've all pretty much suspected: *squeaky wheels* really do get the grease. For example, when leaders emerge in a group (e.g., test subjects involved in solving an assigned task), those leaders are not necessarily more intelligent than the other group members; they are simply those people who speak up more often.[148] Students asked to critique such outspoken leaders during one such study done at the University of California, Berkeley rated the people who spoke up more often as the "smartest" in each group—even when those people offered more incorrect answers than did others in the group who were less talkative and consequentially rated by the students as being of "average" intelligence and "not so creative."

According to psychologist Cameron Anderson:

---

146. This threat works best with a dramatic flourish of physically stepping aside.

147. Nietzsche called it "Will to Power," the innate desire all human beings have to self-actualize, to become the best they can be.

148. "Confidence Wins over Smarts" by Robert Goodier. *Scientific American Mind*, Sept./Oct. 2009:15.

> The main reason dominant people took charge is they jumped in first and nobody questioned what they said. Dominant people seem really good at things because they speak with such confidence.

Did you notice Anderson's three provisos? Dominant people (1) jumped in first, (2) nobody questioned/challenged what they said, either because the potential questioner(s) had personal doubts about their own ability to lead (e.g., fear of being held responsible), or (3) would-be challengers were intimidated[149] by the speaker's air of confidence.

In other words, act like you're in charge and someone—perhaps *many* someones—is likely to put you in charge.

> We have made you a creature neither of heaven nor of earth, neither mortal nor immortal, in order that you may, as the free and proud shaper of your own being, fashion yourself in the form you may prefer. —Pico della Mirandola

Mastering the Tactics of the "Big Boys"

No less than one of the "biggest boys" of all, General George S. Patton Jr. himself, advised us:

> Prepare for the unknown by studying how others in the past have coped with the unforeseeable and the unpredictable.

Why would *I* stick my finger in the light socket after I've seen *you* get the shit shocked out of you for doing the exact same thing? Yeah, that is the very definition of stupid.

By studying those who've come before us, those who've *failed*, we need not fall into the same hole, we need not meet the same Waterloo. But instead of adopting a passive, defensive—after the fact—method of study, we should dedicate ourselves to actively and aggressively seeking to discern and decipher the secrets of those who have *succeeded* before us. Sure, we can learn from faux pas and failure, especially our own—if we survive!—but how much more satisfying to learn from success, especially our own, perhaps a success patterned after the master of the past.

---

149. An optimists would say "inspired."

No matter the particular arena of art or artifice you aspire to matriculate and master—study the masters, the "Big Boys," both the respected and the feared, those acknowledged adepts who've previously mastered that same area of study. No matter if the apple of your ambitious and envious eye be glory on the battlefield or a success in less overt—albeit no less deadly!—venues like high finance or politics, study the masters. And don't only study the "good guys": the Donald Trumps, the Bill Gates, the Yataro Iwasakis,[150] the Hannibals, and the Julius Caesars. Also study the "bad boys": the Genghis Khans, the Attilas, the Rasputins, and the Stalins—con men and conquerors alike. And don't neglect the counsel of the shadowy minds between the two: the Machiavellis, the Max Stirners, and the Nietzscheans.

Ignoring the success of another simply because he wears a different style toga, uniform, or a red primary pin versus a blue one is the height of ignorance. "IGNORE-ance," get it? So often, we learn so much more from our enemies than we do from our allies. From Hannibal's "The 99 Truths":

> Enemy! I watch your every move as if you were the most beautiful of dancing girls: I watch your every step forward and back and to the side, each bend of your knee, every sway of your ample hips. I study every gesture of your hand—closing, opening; the practiced smile of your brightly-colored lips, the wide and the narrow of your painted eye. Soon enough we dance! —Hannibal the Conqueror, Truth X

Mastering the Techniques of the "Mini-Masters"

Before I can craft my greatest victory, I must win the trust of the lowest village smith who crafts my sword.

—Vlad Tepes, *Dracula's Art of War*[151]

---

150. Founder of Mitsubishi Motors, 1917. See "The Three Diamonds Way" in *Mind Control* Dr. Haha Lung and Christopher B. Prowant (Citadel, 2006).

151. Vlad Tepes, Christian warrior-prince who fought back Muslims attempting to invade Eastern Europe and who (ruthlessly) ruled the Walachia region south of Transylvania (in present-day Rumania) circa 1400. The factual inspiration for Bram Stoker's fictional blood-sucking Count Dracula.

The forest and the trees. There's a danger that while you're busy studying the latest "art of the deal" takedown by Donald Trump you'll miss the lowly Artful Dodger slipping a hand into your pocket.

In our admiration (envy?) of the "Big Boys" who slide through life like the soles of their shoes are greased with beluga caviar, we all too often miss the "Little Masters" of manipulation all around us: that impossibly hot babe in the bar, that homeless panhandler on the sidewalk, the used-car salesman, the telemarketer and the televangelist—all of them have something to sell us and all are as adept at the art of distraction as the best professional magicians. That's right. The same sleight of hand used by Hermann the Magnificent and his lovely assistant Marcia to bedazzle an awe-struck audience is the same sort of distraction used by Pete the Pickpocket and his lovely 38D-cup assistant (the one who's just suffered a sudden wardrobe malfunction! Please, let me help you with that . . . with those big, bouncing . . . while Pete plucks my wallet!).

Since ancient times, both the cutpurse and the cutthroat have used the methods of the master magician to play their tricks and thuggery.

Be it some shady charlatan to the accomplished showman, the sundry con man to the prosperous car salesman, whether tomorrow is feast or famine depends on how well they ply their trade today. And this means mastering both "the body and the bull"—those friendly, even seductive, mannerisms and bold-faced blarney guaranteed to draw us in, the magician's art of fooling us and the salesman's craft of making us willing to pay for being fooled!

For years, magicians have been a step ahead of the rest of us—including psychologists.[152]

Now You See It, Now You Don't!

According to master magician and accomplished showman Logan Hawke, to be a good magician you have to also be an even better psychologist. The master magician uses both his words and his body to captivate us, to force us to follow his every move. He leads, we follow, our focus fixated on him (or more precisely on *where he makes us look*).

In every other endeavor in life we value truthfulness. Yet here we sit having paid good money in the hopes that this man (or woman), this magician, will be able to deliberately trick us. And that's precisely what he does

152. "Quicker Than the Eye: How Magicians Toy with Your Powers of Perception" *Psychology Today*, Sept./Oct. 2006:15.

because his livelihood depends on his skill to fool us. If he stumbles or fumbles or we succeed in seeing through his legerdemain or illusion, he's failed. And so we'll not be recommending his show to our friends. And he'll starve (or maybe have to go back to selling used cars).

Thus, the moment he steps foot on the stage, the magician has his job cut out for him: using amusing banter, elaborate flourishes of cane and cape, colorful backgrounds decorated with often mysterious but always distracting symbols, and scantily clad assistants—all designed to deliberately capture, contain, and continue to entertain his audience.

Even fans of the Masked Magician's tell-all TV program *Greatest Secrets of Magic Revealed* still love to watch magic shows, trying to catch the would-be magician literally "in the act"—while simultaneously, secretly—perhaps subconsciously—hoping to be fooled just one more time.

But as masterful, as endlessly dazzling, as the magician's craft at first appears, open any *Beginner's Guide to Magic* and you'll quickly realize that all the magic tricks ever performed, that ever *will* be performed, all come down to a few simple psychological principles, principles you can use to put a little *magic* into your personal power of persuasion:

- ***People like to be entertained:*** Even when they know how the trick is done, they'll still applaud if the trick is done well. The magician keeps up a nonstop barrage of cute—distracting—talk called "patter" by professional showmen. Ironically, the modern "patter" (meaning "senseless, repetitious talk" and "to speak glibly and rapidly") comes from that most sacred of Western scriptures "The Lord's Prayer"—in Latin "Paternoster," shortened to simply "Pater." The word took on its current negative connotations in medieval times when the Lord's Prayer was required to be recited in Latin, a language few people understood, especially when it was all too often recited badly, to the point where it was unintelligible—hence, "patter" took on the meaning of senseless chatter.
- ***People want to believe in magic:*** So much of our religious and cultural identity is based in magic—real magic, the stuff of witches and flying carpets and dragons and giants—archetypes burned into our brains at an early age. Add to this the fact that, as children, we believe wholeheartedly in magic. So perhaps being fooled by a magician tickles some long dormant memory of pleasant, trusting child-

hood in an otherwise cynical adult? Not surprising, this principle carries over into the rest of reality: so long as you're entertaining—even if you're an entertaining rogue—people will forgive you of anything.

- ***People like people they can like:*** Remember that (1) we like to be liked, (2) we like people who like us, and (3) we like people who are like us. Be a user-friendly magician. That mysterious Manson-scare-the-children look was played out a long time ago. This explains the current popularity of so-called street magicians who dress and (for the most part) act like normal people. Bottom line: people will forgive you of anything if they like you. Case in point: Bill Clinton.
- ***People look where other people are looking:*** Figuratively and literally, physically and philosophically. A show of hands: Who remembers the classic Three Stooges skit where the man exits a doctor's office after being ordered to keep his head tipped back? As he walks down the street looking up, before long everyone in the street has stopped to look up, trying to spot what he's watching so intently. Chaos ensues! (It's the Three Stooges. Chaos *always* ensues!). Try this skit yourself.

Countless psychological studies have been done to prove people pretty much "go along to get along." Nietzsche cursed this tendency to follow along behind "the herd."

- ***The magician looks where he wants you to look:*** If he's looking left—look right; that's where the real action is taking place. Politicians and propagandists use this same ploy ad nauseum. Convince everybody you're heading for Afghanistan, then take a sudden left at Iraq. Can't teach what you don't know, can't lead where you don't go.

Likewise, veteran news personality Ted Koppel once drew the distinction that "the news media doesn't tell people what to *think* . . . It tells people what to *think about*."

- ***The magician points where he wants you to look:*** Your eyes obey his finger. This same rule applies to advertising. What's that you say? You didn't know you wanted one of *those* (actually, you didn't even know *those* existed) until you saw it advertised on TV. You *followed the finger* and, yet again, Madison Avenue *gave you the finger!*

- ***The magician's hand (and/or his whole body) moves away from where he doesn't want you looking:*** Eyes naturally follow movement. The magician's hand goes in one direction and you follow, while he's busy doing something with his other hand he doesn't want you to notice. Bernard Madoff. Can you say, "A $65 billion Ponzi scheme that went undetected for more than 20 years"?
- ***Beware of the magician's distracting assistants*** (on the stage or on the street!): The pretty girl moves, your eyes follow. An anonymous caller phones in a "Building on fire!" or "Officer down!" on the west side of town while the First National gets hit on the east side of town.
- ***People see what they expect to see:*** On a good day, we call this "hope" and "expectation." On a bad day, it's "prejudice" and "discrimination." You go to a magic show because the little kid in you *wants* to see the beautiful girl turn into a tiger. Don't disappoint him. And in the big, bad grown-up world: prospective investors like to see flow charts (replete with all the bells and whistles) that prove to them how they're going to make a ton of money investing in your latest project.

The magician pretends to throw a ball up into the air (while actually dropping it), and the audience "sees" the ball flying into the air.

According to a recent poll, ninety-five percent of Americans believe car salesmen have "low ethical standards." As a result, twice as many people trust lawyers more than they trust car salesmen.[153]

Go Ahead, Kick the Tires: How to Be "Salesman Savvy"

However, it would be using broad strokes indeed if we were to paint all used-car salesmen as sleazy. On the one hand, you might find your particular used-car salesman to be friendly, helpful, and upfront in helping you buy a good, reliable used car. On the other hand, if you stroll onto every used-car lot believing that ninety to ninety-five percent of used-car salesmen are

---

153. "Battle on the Car Lot" by Willow Lawson. *Psychology Today*, Sept./Oct. 2005:28.

shifty and that they will say anything to sell you a car, then you're walking onto that car lot alert, with eyes wide open, and so there's less chance you're gonna get taken for a ride.

In many ways, the microcosmic experience of buying a used car can be seen as a metaphor for life in general. And you should always go into life alert with eyes wide open. Let's review our previous discussion on why it's okay to be xenophobic . . . Right, because it kept our paranoid[154] ancient ancestors alive long enough to get us here. If only those ancestors had been just a little more trusting . . . Well, we probably wouldn't be around to have this conversation.

Likewise, if you walk onto a used-car lot (or into any exchange/encounter, for that matter) paranoid to the gills, there's less of a chance of you being blindsided by some smarmy salesman. And if your particular salesman does turn out to be the nicest, most honest man on Earth, what harm has been done by your paranoia? But heaven help you should you walk onto that lot with your wallet wide open, with an opposite—*Here I am, come and get me! I trust the world until the world gives me a reason not to trust it*—attitude.

First, the used-car dealer is not your friend. You did not come to this car lot to make friends. If later you drive off the lot with both a reliable used car and a new BFF—all the better, but that's not what you came for. Focus.

Second, as with the magician's craft, for the sleazy used-car salesman, getting you to focus where he wants you to focus is key. The salesman's job is to distract you. Your job is to stay focused.

Mr. Sleazy Salesman knows superfluous fast-talking patter makes it less likely (1) you'll notice dents and details—both in the car and in his spiel—and/or (2) you'll remember to ask all those questions you rehearsed on the way to the lot. Keep in mind people hate/fear to question authority and, on that car lot at least, Mr. Sleazy is the authority when it comes to previously owned vehicles.

FYI: The average person talks about one hundred and fifty words per minute. An accomplished fast-talker can easily spit out two hundred words per minute. In addition, it's been noted that only ten percent of what most speakers say is crucial, the rest being (1) illustrative anecdotes, (2) attempts

154. "Only the paranoid survive": Intel founder Andrew Grove, quoted in *The Wall Street Journal*.

at humor, (3) additional explanation, and (4) transitions from one topic to another.[155]

Keep this in mind when fending off these other tried-and-true tricks of the used-car salesman's trade:

- ***The Bait and Switch, a.k.a. Low-Ballin':*** The salesman quotes you an impossibly low price just to grab your attention. But then, once he's got you all revved up, he "sadly discovers" that this particular car has already been sold and offers you a similar (albeit more expensive) car as a replacement. Another variation of the Bait and Switch is to low-ball the price of the car and make the difference back with hidden charges.
- ***Bonding, a.k.a. Matching:*** The salesman goes out of his way to find something in common with you—real or not.

  We all like to talk about ourselves. He distracts you by getting you to talk about yourself, family, your last vacation, pleasurable things you will associate with the car he wants to sell you. He takes you back to your "happy place," easing your anxiety (and/or suspicion). This kind of bonding also helps him "peg" you.
- ***Pegging:*** The salesman figures out ("pegs") your sensory orientation: Watcher, Listener, or a Toucher—so he'll know how best to frame his approach to you.

  Having correctly pegged you as a Watcher, he'll "show" you a car, emphasizing the shiny paint job and how cool you'll "look" driving around in it.

  If you're a Listener, he'll take time to let you "listen" to the engine revving and the stereo blasting, emphasizing how "solid" the auto sounds when you slam shut the doors.

  If he pegs you a Toucher he'll encourage you to ease back in those fine leather seats, and "feel" how your hands fit around that steering wheel.
- ***The Turn and Walk:*** After showing you a car, the salesman suddenly, almost absentmindedly, walks away from you and toward the sales office. If you follow him without question, he's got you hooked. You can likewise use this ploy if you can successfully make Mr. Sleazy

155. *Double Your Brain Power* by Jean Marie Stine, 1997:147–149.

think you're actually going to walk away from his offer-you-can't-refuse. He'll change his tune "toot-sweet."

- ***The Test Drive:*** He hands you the keys and tells you it's time to take her for a test drive. This ploy works especially well if he's pegged you as a tactile-influenced Toucher.
- ***The Either/Or:*** Novice salesmen are taught to always ask "either/or" questions. Never ask a customer a question that can be answered with a no.[156]
- ***Time Investment, a.k.a. Guilting:*** You'd think a salesman would want to make a quick sale, but that's not always the case. Stall tactics work well for him. The longer a sale takes, the better the chances you're gonna buy. The more time you invest, the less resistance you have. This is sometimes called "guilting" because the more guilty you feel about wasting the seller's time, and/or wasting your own time, the more likely you'll drive off the lot in the car he's already chosen for you.

  Thus, it's to his advantage to deliberately drag out the process. Mr. Sleazy might actually tell you, "I know that after an obviously busy person like you spends all this time looking for just the right car, you're not going to want to leave without what you came for."

In the end, it's all the same, no matter what you're trying to sell—whether a used car or the invasion of a Middle Eastern country. It all comes down to your being able to sell yourself.

The Salesman's Four Rules of Thumb

- **The Reason Rule***:* On average, people are more cooperative when given a reason for any action or request. Adding "because" makes people *think* there's a reason: "I can see you're gonna buy this car and not just *because* your wife is going to love you for it, but also *because* you're obviously the kind of person who knows a good deal when he sees it."

  Always use the word "because" in any request. The word "because," in and of itself, even without any logic or substantive evidence, helps elicit a positive response. "*Because* I can see you've gotta lot of chutz-

---

156. Lawson, 2005:28.

pah, and *because* I like that in a man, I'm gonna let you in on the best kept secret on this lot . . ."

- **The Scarcity Rule (variation of Limited Time Offer):** This rule approach assumes (with good reason) that people are more motivated by the thought of losing something than they are of gaining something. Thus, a limited time offer works better than a rebate. "I can't promise this car's gonna be here tomorrow. And I'd really hate to see you lose out on a beauty like this." "If we don't do this now, the situation over there is only going to deteriorate further."
- **The Reciprocity Rule** makes us feel we have to do someone a favor in return for a favor done for us. It's called feeling obligated.
- **The Matching and Mirroring Rule:** Recall how people like people who are like them. Intentionally put yourself in synch with the other person by matching their body language and actions (e.g., tapping a pencil in rhythm with the other person's breathing, etc.) and mirroring their movements (e.g., imitating their body language and patterns of speech). Having successfully picked up on and then mirrored their patterns, you can now begin to subtly lead them in the direction you want. If you've ever taken Psych 101, you know this is called "operant conditioning."

Your Only Rule of Thumb for Not Being a Sucker

Thumb your nose at his pressure tactics. There's no urgency to quickly "seal the deal" no matter what the salesman tells you. (This applies pretty much to *everything* in life by the way.) Before you ever get to the car lot, tell yourself: "No matter what, I'm *not* going to buy a car *today*." No matter what Mr. Sleazy says, odds are the car is still going to be there tomorrow.

Mastering the Tricks of the "Little People"

A little man with a big knife is still a little man . . . but it's still a big knife.

—Vlad Tepes, *Dracula's Art of War*

No, we're not talking about mastering the cute little dance steps of the Lollipop Guild from *The Wizard of Oz*. We're talking about learning from the people you find so easy to ignore: the guy who watches—or doesn't watch—over your car in the underground garage; the doorman and security guard at your apartment building; the clerks behind the counter at all the stores you frequent; the garbageman who empties the Dumpster with *your receipts* in it out behind all the stores you frequent; waiters at restaurants; the gardener; pool boy; and postmen; that blind homeless guy who sells pencils outside your office building who nonetheless seems to see everything that goes on; the maid who cleans your hotel room; the janitor who empties your wastebasket at the office—all the "little people" you come into contact with every day whom you barely take notice of but who, for the right price—money paid by your enemies or simply their own personal revenge for a slight you've unknowingly done them—have the power to make your life miserable.

These little people see every move you make. These little people have the ability to make you late for that vital meeting. They know personal information about you that your enemies, the police, or a private investigator might pay handsomely for: what time you arrive at and leave from work—via the crowded street exit or that dark, underground parking garage where no one can hear you scream. They know what stores you favor, what foods you prefer, and your favorite drink down at your favorite bar.

And they know what time—and where—you pick your children up from school . . .

All such inside information can be used to track you and trap you, information a wily Mind Slayer can use to ingratiate himself with his intended target.

The ancient East Indian *Kama Sutra* extols the usefulness of not only frequenting all the places the subject of your interest frequents, but also instructs on how to ingratiate yourself with your target's siblings and servants, in order to eventually get closer to them.[157]

Sinan, Grandmaster of the medieval Syrian Order of Hashishins (Assassins), was notorious for manipulating the little people surrounding his enemies.[158] How easy it was for his agents to bribe (or threaten) an otherwise

---

157. For a complete course on sex and seduction techniques of the *Kama Sutra*, see *Mental Domination* by Dr. Haha Lung and Christopher Prowant (Citadel, 2009).

158. For their complete sordid history, as well as the espionage and martial arts techniques of the assassin killer cult, see *Assassin! Secrets of the Cult of the Assassins* (Paladin Press, 1997) and *Assassin!* (Citadel, 2004) by Dr. Haha Lung.

loyal servant into leaving a door or window unlocked. Striking up a casual conversation with a servant at the local market, within short order a wily assassin could have all the information he needed on the travel itinerary of the servant's master, even what types of "harmless" fruits and vegetables their master favored.

Likewise, François Eugéne Vidocq, master criminal-turned-detective, knew the importance of giving the little people their due, mentioning milk-men, bakers, fruit venders, mercers, grocers, and especially porters. Says Vidocq, "All porters are students of faces; it's part of their job."[159]

So what can/should we today learn from the little people in our lives?

First, they're human beings with feelings; ergo they might just harbor a grudge for being ignored and/or insulted by us, a grudge that could all too easily be exploited by one of our enemies.

Second, because they are so often "in the background," they are for the most part ignored by those in the foreground and, as a result, these little people see things and hear things and retrieve things from the wastebasket those in the foreground might miss. By the very nature of being little people they must "keep their place" quietly, unobtrusively in the background, and be more alert to offending the big boys in the foreground.

Those of us in the *foreground* should be so alert.

Mastering *Everything!* (or at Least *Studying* Everything)

Miyamoto Musashi admonished us to "Study the *Ways* of all professions." By this he meant not only the physical skills of the various crafts, but also the attitude with which craftsmen within various jobs carry themselves.

When can we ever know enough? A bored man is merely walking through empty rooms in his head. Fill those rooms! We *specialize* to make a living; we *generalize* to go on living.

You never know what specific piece of trivial information will come in handy, what obscure factoid might save your life. Yeah, kinda like that MacGyver guy on TV.

Musashi also cautioned his students from having a favorite weapon and from favoring habitual strategies, in order to make it harder for an enemy to develop a counterstrategy.

---

159. Vidocq, 1857/2003:168, 186.

You never know what tool you're going to need for certain. But you can know for certain that the fuller your toolbox, the better your chances of having the right tool—or tactic or technique—on hand when the time comes.

The more you know, the harder it is for an enemy to pigeonhole you.

It's a no-brainer: the more you know, the better you throw; the more options at your disposal, the better your chances of thinking your way through the unexpected by thinking *outside the box* . . . in order to more easily put your enemy *in a box!*

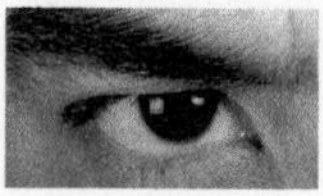

5.

Yu-kami: The Seven "Spirits" of Success

You know the day destroys the night, night divides the day. Try to run, try to hide, slip on through to the other side!
—The Doors

WAS IT NOT wise Plato who first postulated that this world we see and hear and touch and taste is but a *pale* reflection of a higher, more perfect existence?

But perhaps this world is not so much pale as it is a chiaroscuro intercourse—or, better yet, *combat*—sometimes subtle, all too often violent!—twixt the light and the darkness.

Tis true shadows flee when exposed to the light. Yet just as often it's the case that too much light blinds as surely as too little. Thus, through the initial machinations of the gods, and through not a little of our own constant maintenance, for each iota of light in us, there is a corresponding—*competing!*—speck of darkness. Most likely the universe has need for both.

So there's the world you see . . . and then there's the world you don't see. And where the two tentatively touch, *duality* appears precariously balanced—if only for an instant. And it is just that delicate balancing—and the sometimes *deliberate* upsetting of that balance—that provides the backdrop against which the hesitant actors of this world play their parts, the all-accepting canvas in front of which the artist prances, and the applause for which the magician struts his manipulations of both body and mind.

And, in the final analysis, before we're all said and done, will we not all test the fit of the mask and mantle of "actor," and of "artist", and perhaps even of miracle-performing "magician"?

Duality is the stark white stage with jet-black curtain upon which we play these parts.

Or, if you prefer, duality is the ocean in which some swim freely and in which others barely tread water. It is likewise the blood that seeps through our veins, the sweat dripping from our troubled, tested, and all-too-tempted brow.

Indeed, it seems the design of nature—nay, *destiny!*—that we humans dive and delve into, deal with, and dance in duality:

- Behind our own troubled brow: *the conscious and the subconscious*—some thoughts apparent to all, other thoughts hidden even from ourselves.
- In our expression: *the spoken and the unspoken*—what people say and what they don't say.
- And in our dealings one with another: *respect paid aboveboard . . . or money paid under the table*.
- The living and the dead: Or, if you're not paying close enough attention to the quiet cautions and whispered warnings of the universe, *the quick and the dead*.

In Asia, yin-yang is the rule. For everything in existence, there is an equal opposite: *the seen* and that which by nature must remain *the unseen*.

In Japan, there is *Gen*, the manifest world of human beings. But there is also *Yu*: the unseen world of the *kami*-spirits.

The material world and the spirit world, juxtaposed to one another, influencing one another: a sensual celestial dance by two lovers that can never dare be joined—though that hardly dissuades the one from all too often offering unwanted advances toward the other. But, oh, the dangers should these two worlds overlap . . .

In the West we warn, "Beware of offending strangers, lest you entertain angels unawares."[160] The Japanese have a similar caution, *marebito*, "super-

160. Hebrews 13:2: "Be not forgetful to entertain strangers: for thereby some have entertained angels unawares."

natural guests" sometimes turn up at the oddest times, often with the most obscure of agendas.

Yu-kami both move people and move through people, a kind of "possession," influencing us to act in certain ways, perhaps peculiar ways—thoughts and expression free and familiar to that other world but often at odds with the mask we wear daily in this world. In fact, the worlds of *Gen* and *Yu*, men and spirits, overlap to such an extent that it is easy to find parallels and correspondences between the attitudes of the dwellers in both.

Individuals "possessed" of one (or more) of these spirits exhibit easy-to-spot traits and characteristics. Thus, these ancient "spirits" often manifest as modern traits and states familiar to any student having weathered Psych 101.

Learning to recognize these psychological traits and states within both friend and foe provides the Mind Slayer (and us) yet another way to successfully read and re-write others:

- ***Bakemono* (a.k.a. *Mono-no-ke*),** "evil and low spirits," at best bring chaos and confusion; worst-case scenario: they herald total disaster, destruction, and death. These types of spirits come in two basic types:

  Mono are the kami of animals and lesser spirits (called "elementals" in the West). Worst case, these spirits are mischievous and bothersome, but seldom threatening. They are mostly the stuff of children's stories and of myth. When a person comes under the influence of one of these, they are often occupied by "lower" bodily desires (eating, sex, sloth), not especially dangerous but hardly productive or conducive.

  Magatsuhi, on the other hand, are full-fledged demons up to no good. This class of spirit includes the fearsome ogre-like *oni* and the wily half-man, half-crow *tengu,* the latter rightly linked with the Ninja clans of central Japan.[161] These demons play on our unfulfilled wants and desires, tempting us.

  Once the Mind Slayer recognizes that your personal psychology reflects the thinking of someone "possessed" by a Bakemono, the Mind Slayer does all he (or she) can to encourage your self-destructive bad habits.

---

161. For the complete history and training methods of the mysterious ninja of Japan, see *Nine Halls of Death* by Dr. Haha Lung and Eric Tucker (Citadel, 2008).

Japanese Name	Meaning	Example of Spirit	Influence on Humans
BAKEMONO	"Evil and low spirits"	a) *Magatsuhi* (*Oni and Tengu*) b) *Mono* (kami of animals and other "lower" entities.	Base desires, unfulfilled wants and desires. Lust.
ONRYO	"Angry spirits"	*Konjin*, a kami that, once offended, demands seven deaths to appease it.	Resentments. Desire for revenge for real and imagined slights.
GORYO	"Unquiet spirits"	Similar to what Buddhists call *pretas* (Hungry spirits).	Promises left undone. Positive: encourages commitment. Negative: creates despair.
KETSUEN-SHIN	"Blood-relation spirit"	A kami that is worshipped by a group linked by blood.	Familial obligation, also trauma resulting from childhood abuse.
UJIGAMI	"Clan spirits"	Collective spirit of an *uji* (clan).	Positive: filial loyalty to culture, tradition and community. Negative: toxic identification with gang, religious cult, racial identity.
NAOBI	"Repairing spirits"	Spirit intent on restoring balance and status quo.	Positive: negotiator, peace-maker. In extremis: totalitarian. Stagnates in defense of status quo. End justifies means. Not necessarily kind, does whatever it takes to restore balance. Careful what you ask for. God always answers prayers, sometimes he answers no.
SHINIGAMI	"Death spirit"	Debt collector (souls, etc.).	Positive: allows no debt to go unpaid, no trespass unchallenged. Negative: old unpaid debts (dark secrets) come back to haunt you.

Figure 11.

- ***Onryo*** are rightly called "angry spirits" who fan our resentments into thoughts for restitution, reparation, and revenge—three masks all hiding the same angry face. For example, *Konjin* are vengeful kami that, once offended, demand seven deaths as recompense.

  Psychologically, the Mind Slayer easily fans the flames of resentment dominating an Onryo-possessed person until those resentments flare into a desire for full-blown rage to revenge real and imagined slights.
- ***Goryo*** are the "unquiet spirits" that hound us, reminding us of all

the things in life we've left undone, all the promises we've made to others (and to ourselves) that we've failed to keep. Goryo are always whispering in your ear what a failure you are. It is easy for a perceptive Mind Slayer to keep those whispers coming, to magnify any doubts and insecurities we harbor, no matter how well we try to hide them, often even from ourselves.

Curiously, there can be a positive side to Goryo "possession": when we allow our guilt at not having fulfilled a promise to finally goad us off the couch and into positive action. On the positive side, a Goryo attitude encourages commitment. Negative: it creates despair.

- ***Ketsuen-shin,*** "blood-relation spirits," are similar to Goryo in that they remind us (*guilt us!*) into remembering past promises made but not acted upon. In this particular instance, these are promises made—our duty, what Hindus call dharma—to the groups that influence our lives as "patriotism" to clan and country. Negatively, adopting the mind-set of a Ketsuen-shin spirit makes us feel obligated[162] to a dead relative and to outdated traditions and archaic cultural mores and tribal prejudices. Psychologically, a Ketsuen-minded person can still be "possessed" by family trauma from childhood. Think Anthony Perkins in *Psycho* (1960).
- ***Ujigami,*** "clan spirits," link the person to their clan, community, and to a lesser extent their country. This term originally referred to the collective spirit of an *uji* (clan), those associated by the physical blood pumping through their veins. Today, psychologically speaking, this "blood" relationship is more metaphoric than actual, and so incorporates any "blood" affiliation—family, friends, cadre.

  On the positive side, this "spirit" engenders filial loyalty to culture, tradition, and community. Negative: toxic identification with gang, religious cult, and racial identity.

  Once the alert Mind Slayers spots this "spirit" in a person, they have no difficulty encouraging and enhancing faux feelings of *uji* loyalty and obligation, in effect, leading the ujigami-possessed person around by the nose.
- ***Naobi-no-kami*** are "repairing spirits" whose job it is to restore bal-

162. "Duty" is the debt you owe yourself. "Obligation" is a debt (usually erroneous) thrust upon you by others.

ance. Not necessarily kind, this kind does whatever it takes to restore balance and reinforce or reinstate the status quo. On the positive side, this kind of mind-set can manifest as a negotiator and peacemaker. In extremis on the negative side, this mind-set promotes totalitarianism and often stagnates in defense of the established order and status quo. For this kind, the end always justifies the means.

- ***Shinigami*** are the spiritual IRS, come to collect outstanding debts. Mythologically, Shinigami is the Old Grey Mower himself, albeit with a Japanese accent, come to cart away your soul. Psychologically—*metaphorically*—shinigami are those spirits that refuse to stay buried, those rattling skeletons in our closet that refuse to stay quiet, the mistakes of the past trying to stake a claim to the present. In other words, old debts and dark secrets come back to haunt us.

In many ways similar to Goryo kami, Shinigami are also unpaid—and in many cases *unindicted*!—trespasses we've yet to answer to. Thus, Mind Slayers love Shinigami, those past actions and inactions that he can ruthlessly use to literally guilt you to death. But, long before that happens, the Mind Slayer will have exhausted you with *extortion* and *blackmailed* you into bankruptcy!

While we'd all like to think we're pristine and untouchable, the truth is none of us is immune to attack from this direction. What was it Francis Bacon (1561–1626) pointed out: "Some things are secret because they are hard to know, and some because they are not fit to utter."

We all have certain indiscretions in our past we'd rather not see in the running for *America's Funniest Videos*. And even when we manage to successfully exorcise our own restless Shinigami spirits, a determined Mind Slayer can still get at you through the past indiscretions of friends and relatives.[163]

Perhaps you recall from *Mind Manipulation* (Citadel, 2002) the chapter titled "Digging Up Dark Secrets," where we first revealed the seven kinds of dark secrets people keep:

- ***Something you did:*** The past comes back to haunt us. The truth is you *did* inhale and you really *did* have sex with that woman. Remember how your little sister threatened to tell

163. Right, Miyamoto Musashi's "Cutting at the Edges" ploy.

mom and dad about your sneaking back into the house late unless you gave her a quarter and promised to do her chores . . . for the rest of your life? Same principle. You offer to sell your enemy a full photo spread of him and his new girlfriend (or boyfriend) . . . before you sell them to his *wife*.

- ***Something you're made to think you did:*** Using this approach, your enemy makes you feel responsible for an actual screw-up, or for an "accident" he helped arrange for you to participate in. This arranged accident could be anything from you crashing the boss's computer to your enemy making you think you inadvertently killed someone.

  Professional con men known as "bump-n-hump artists" specialize in staging fake auto accidents: first literally bumping into you, before then figuratively humping you by making you think you've given them whiplash or some other hard to dispute injury. In the same vein of con-artistry, other hustlers stage stuntmenlike accidents (e.g., slipping on a spilled bottle that has "accidentally" fallen from a store shelf, store displays collapsing onto them, etc.), making it look like you or your business is liable. All too often, in order to avoid trouble (or scandal) for ourselves (or for our business), we quickly settle out of court.
- ***Something someone close to you did:*** Nothing's more important than family and friends. We drop everything to come to the aid of loved ones. This reflex holds true when someone threatens to expose a friend or loved one's misdeeds (e.g., that guy your alcoholic brother doesn't remember beating into a coma, that visit to the abortion clinic your little sister doesn't want your parents or priest to find out about).
- ***Something they make you think someone close to you did:*** Same strategy as making you think you did something.
- ***The hint of scandal:*** For some people (e.g., politicians) the mere hint of scandal is enough to scuttle a promising career. Remember the 2007 disappearance of Washington intern Chandra Levy? Her real killer was eventually caught and, while no real blame ever attached itself to her boss and lover Congressman Gary Condit, Condit's confession that he had had an affair with Levy added to the initial suspicion he was placed

> under following her disappearance, and was enough to effectively ruin his chances for reelection. Likewise, Michael Jackson was never actually convicted of any impropriety against children. Yet once the allegation(s) was lodged against him . . . Years later, though now dead, he's still the butt of jokes.[164]

In many instances, merely the *threat* of having his name (or the name of a loved one) associated with such scandal is enough to bring an enemy around to your way of thinking:

> Dateline: June 2002, the FBI charge three men from Ohio and Kentucky with conspiracy to extort money via e-mail from patrons of a child-pornography Web site. The extortionists, calling themselves "Hacker Group 109," made contact with their targets in Internet chat rooms by expressing an interest in discussing child pornography. The men then "followed their targets home" via e-mail, sending them a blackmail letter threatening to expose their dirty little secret to the police unless they paid through the nose. Twenty-one people, from as far away as California, reported the attempted extortion.[165]

Consider: if twenty-one people reported this attempted blackmail, how many more people were not only targeted but had paid up? The best ally blackmailers have is silence—the fear and shame of their targets.

In his 1974 book *Aftermath*, author Ladislas Fargo maintains that Nazi Party secretary Martin Bormann's obvious influence (i.e., hold) over Adolf Hitler stemmed from the fact that Bormann's eldest son, Krönzi, was actually the bastard of Hitler by a young woman named Uschi who may have once been a nun named Pia! Such a scandal could have stopped Hitler's rise to power before it ever began.[166]

"Fuku wa uchi, oni wa soto!"[167]

---

164. Q: How were Michael Jackson and K-Mart alike? A: Both had little boy's pants half off!

165. Associated Press, 6.14.02.

166. Fargo also claims to have actually met Martin Bormann in Argentina in 1973, some twenty-eight years after he'd reportedly faked his death during the fall of Berlin. (Ibid.)

167. Ancient Japanese blessing: "Good luck in! Demons out!"

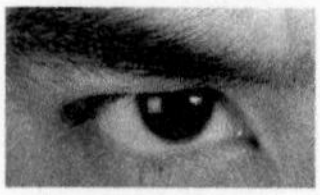

6.

Hannibal's Six "Movers of Men"

What a man loves, what he hates, what he needs, what he desires: These are the four pillars that support his house.
—Hannibal the Conqueror, Truth IV

IT HAS BEEN SAID that no other single man was more responsible for building the Roman Empire than Hannibal—its most intractable *enemy*!

Hannibal Barca (247–183 B.C.), better known as Hannibal the Conqueror, has been called "The Sun Tzu of the West," and rightly so. In the second and third century B.C., three Punic[168] wars were fought between the emerging empire of Rome and its only real rival, the North African city-state of Carthage, with Rome emerging victorious all three times.

By far the greatest military strategist to emerge from this more than a century of slaughter was the Carthaginian general Hannibal. Considered Rome's "public enemy number one,"[169] during the Second Punic War (218–201) Hannibal unexpectedly succeeded in crossing the "impassable" Alps from Spain at the head of an international mercenary army of more than

---

168. The Roman name for Carthage.

169. "100 Greatest Generals" by Brian Sobel with Jerry D. Morelock, *Armchair General*, March 2008.

twenty-six thousand men, replete with elephants, to attack Rome's lightly defended northern border. For the next sixteen years, Hannibal's army wreaked havoc up and down the Italian peninsula, subverting many of Rome's allies, and handing Rome its most devastating defeat ever at the battle of Cannae in 216 B.C.

Unfortunately, like so many accomplished military commanders before and after, ultimately Hannibal was betrayed by bureaucracy at home rather than beaten by blades on the battlefield.

Hannibal lived roughly one hundred years after Alexander the Great (355–323)[170] and, growing up, young Hannibal was greatly inspired by tales of Alexander's conquests, as he was by stories of his own father's exploits.

Hannibal's father, Hamilcar, who had been Carthage's much-heralded military commander during the first Punic War, not only taught his sons, Hannibal, Mago, and Hasdrubal, the art of war but also instilled in them an abiding hatred for all things Roman. Reportedly, with the bitter taste of defeat from the First Punic War still fresh in his mouth, Hamilcar took young Hannibal to Carthage's main temple where he made the boy swear on his father's sword undying enmity with Rome. Hannibal kept that vow till his last day.

By all accounts, Hannibal was a well-educated man. A lifelong scholar, as a young man Hannibal studied the Greek classics and, like his fellow Carthaginians, knew the Earth was not flat.[171] He was also undoubtedly familiar with Middle Eastern Phoenician[172] writings, as well as writings from farther east. How *far* to the east no one can be certain but it's quite within the realm of possibility that, because of Carthage's far-reaching sea trade, the man who was to become the "Scourge of Rome" may have chanced across—or, given his nature, deliberately sought out—the strategies of such Far Eastern masters as Kautilya[173] of India and the T'ai Kung, Sun Tzu, and Cao Cao of China—writings available in Hannibal's time.

---

170. And one hundred years before Julius Caesar (100–44 B.C.).

171. Two hundred years before Hannibal's birth, the Greek philosopher Philolaus (circa 450 B.C.) had declared that the Earth was round. Coincidentally, during their sixteen-year "Roman holiday," Hannibal and his army spent considerable time in Philolaus' home town of Tarentum, on the heel of Italy.

172. Carthage was originally an outpost of the Levantine Phoenicians.

173. Called "The Machiavelli of India," Kautilya was author of the *Arthasastra* (Treatise on Material Gain) and chief advisor to Chandragupta, India's first emperor who founded the Maurya Dynasty (322–185 B.C.).

Later in life, Hannibal would also prove himself an able administrator, diplomat, and—when need be, though much to his disliking—politician.

But Hannibal is of course best known to history for his brilliant battlefield exploits and insights. Today, he continues to impart his hard-won wisdom to us through his "The 99 Truths." Like Sun Tzu masterwork *Ping-fa*, Hannibal's "The 99 Truths" are universally applicable, capable of fitting into any time and place, capable of *dominating* any time and place, as applicable in the boardroom as they are on the battlefield. For example, in his Truth LX, Hannibal gives us "The Six Movers of Men," the six basic motivations he saw as (1) naturally influencing man's actions and (2) basic motivations that could—in the right or wrong hand—all too easily and effectively be used by one man to influence—*control!*—his fellows. Truth LX reads:

> He who fights for blood soon finds it dripping from his own heart.
>
> He who fights for glory never lives long enough to hear the victory songs.[174]
>
> He who fights for gold is already blinded by the glitter and glare of his own greed, all too soon led astray by all things shiny.
>
> He who fights for sport seldom finds The Gods in a sporting mood.
>
> He who fights for love must leave the one he loves the most behind so he can dance with the one he hates the most.
>
> But he who fights for honor cannot be led astray.

The first thing we notice is that all six of Hannibal's "Movers of Men" possess the positive attribute of "focus." That's because these are six prime motivators, those things—one or the other or several together—we all obsess over to some extent.

No surprise then that positive "focus" in extremis all too easily becomes negative "obsession." For example, while we might, especially in our modern, politically correct, oh-so-sensitive times, eschew fighting for morbidly attractive topics like blood, glory, gold, and cruel sport,[175] few would or

174. It's obvious just from looking that, at least in the English translation, only a single, thin line separates "glory" from "gory"!

175. UFC, bull-fighting, and National Conventions every four years being the exception.

could successfully argue against fighting for such high-minded virtues as love and honor.

Yet even when these two highly esteemed motivations (excuses often used to justify whacking our fellow man on the head with a rock!) are taken to extremes,[176] when we lose focus of our original chivalrous quest or, worse yet, when we allow love and honor—or any of the previous four movers for that matter—to become obsessions, even they can become liabilities and invite indictment (see Figure 12, p. 164).

BLOOD

Blood attracts two types: (1) the revenge-minded (admit it, like we all were immediately following 9/11) and (2) serial killer types who get off on seeing the red stuff. It's obvious Hannibal is speaking here of the former, though he undoubtedly ran into more than his share of the bloodthirsty latter during his admittedly sanguinary campaigning.

Hannibal was well aware that, like any good knife, revenge cuts both ways.

Down through the years, revenge has gotten a bad rap. People try to soften it up by using euphemisms like "justice" and "karma" but the truth is there's an innate desire/compulsion within us to seek balance—*lex talionis*, an eye for an eye. When we've been wronged the universe feels out of whack, off-balance. The only way to right that balance is for the perpetrator of our suffering to suffer an equal (or perhaps greater) proportion of the suffering and loss than he has inflicted on us. Admit it, we'd all like to see Osama bin Laden's head on prominent display on a pole at Ground Zero . . . after we've had a really long—leisurely—"talk" with him.[177]

This desire—need—for "rebalancing" is basic to the human animal and is thus found in all cultures. As previously mentioned, it's usually under such euphemisms as "justice," "karma," and, occasionally, "God's will."

More personal, one-on-one, hands-on "rebalancing" we call payback and vigilantism.

The man out for revenge, out for blood, is, if nothing else, *focused*. Since

176. This simply means we get to liking the "whacking" part!

177. For a complete course on how to negotiate with terrorists, see *Theatre of Hell: Dr. Lung's Complete Guide to Torture* by Dr. Haha Lung and Christopher B. Prowant (Loompanics Unlimited, 2003)

before Hannibal's time we've written ballads and told tales of wronged men (and women) who focus and take to the blood trail seeking righteous revenge—justice. Scotland's William Wallace (at least Mel Gibson's version) and Gotham City's Batman.

All societies condone revenge (under the heading of justice) to one extent or the other. Though societies generally frown on vigilantism, preferring instead a general consensus, usually requiring a blessing by the Elders[178] before embarking on revenge:

- Dinah is raped and, days later, a group of Israelites first trick and then slaughter all the men of the rapists' tribe.[179]
- The assassination of the entire Romanov dynasty
- The atomic bombing of Hiroshima and Nagasaki
- The invasion of Afghanistan

So, as a society, we do condone bloody vengeance, uh, "justice," so long as at least fifty-one percent of us are in agreement.

The other type of blood motivation—spilling blood simply because we like seeing "Ohh, the pretty color!"—is generally not sanctioned by civilization. When not fed by some "Mama made me wear her old dresses to school" psychological glitch, this kind of rogue "vampirism" usually bubbles up in someone already predisposed to anger.[180]

Once the Mind Slayer recognizes that their targeted person is prone (i.e., vulnerable) to anger, they will either (1) fan the flames of the target's already existing anger or else (2) engineer a scenario designed to "bring out the beast" (i.e., deliberately enrage that person)—timing/coordinating their target's outburst for the most inconvenient and most embarrassing and career-damaging time possible for that person.

Whenever possible, the Mind Slayer further influences his target by also providing the enraged person with a convenient scapegoat to blame, thus encouraging (i.e., justifying) the target's newfound thirst for revenge . . . uh, justice.

One might imagine that soldiers out for vengeance would make the best

---

178. Today we call them Congress.

179. Genesis, chapter 34.

180. One of our five Warning F.L.A.G.S.

soldiers, but this is not necessarily the case. A wily commander like Hannibal understood that there are times when inflaming someone's anger and need for vengeance is useful for galvanizing them against the common foe, but that too much of a lust for vengeance can turn an otherwise disciplined force into a lynch mob. Thus, at other points in "The 99 Truths," Hannibal again touched on both the need for revenge and the need to reign in—or at least more finely hone—one's need for revenge.

For example, fleeing from Carthage with a Roman bounty on his head at the conclusion of the Second Punic War, Hannibal was given asylum by King Prusias of Bithynia, who during a banquet assured his honored guest that he was welcome to live out his days in peace in Bithynia if he chose—even though both men knew the Carthaginian would never rest in his quest to bring down Rome. Reportedly, Hannibal toasted his gracious host with what became Truth LIII:

> The wine of a true friend is fine indeed. But some thirsts can only be satisfied by the blood of a foe!

In hindsight, Hannibal's words ring ironic, given that Roman bloodlust (fueled by fear) for their aging Carthaginian foe could likewise only be satisfied by blood. Hannibal's final words before taking his own life,[181] even as a crack Roman hit team was breaking down his door, ring ironic:

> It is time now to end the great anxiety of the Romans who have grown weary of waiting for the death of a hated old man.

Hannibal goes on in "The 99 Truths" to lay out at least four other "rules for revenge":

- *Revenge should wait until both your sword and your wits have been sharpened.* (LV)
- *Revenge demands a steady hand and a steadier eye.* (LVI)

181. Roman sources record that Hannibal drank poison (as befits a Roman statesman), and others maintain that he fell on his sword (as befits a Roman general). Mostly, we have only Roman versions to go by. Given his reputation for efficiency, leaving nothing to chance and little to the benevolence—whim—of the gods, perhaps he did both.

- *Revenge demands a long blade . . . and a longer memory.* (LVII)
- *Revenge, like fine wine and Royal Blood, takes time to ferment properly.* (LVIII)

GLORY

Stephen Crane's *The Red Badge of Courage* (1893) tells the universal tale of a young man who naïvely soldiers off to war in search of glory only to discover that the truth of war is men left broken and bloody and buried, the medals pinned to their chest scant recompense for the metal lodged in their heart.

The Mind Slayer knows that many of the people motivated by dreams of glory, or of fame and recognition, probably never have, and probably never will have, ventured near an actual battlefield. As a result, we class glory seekers into two types:

- The young and naïve who crave to carve their place in society, to find themselves. These kinds of naïve glory seekers are really "identity seekers" who lack focus and self-esteem and so are easy fodder for gangs, cults, and ruthless military recruiters.
- And those who crave glory out of all proportion to any potential talent they actually possess. More often than not, such people are frustrated, angry, and resentful at a world that fails to recognize their destiny and genius. How difficult are people like this to manipulate? Not very.

Offering a way for someone to achieve the glory (recognition, fame, etc.) they so crave puts the Mind Slayer firmly in their favor, securely in the driver's seat.

The first type, the identity seeker, the Mind Slayer dazzles with tales of past heroes, showing them how they too can be a hero, a winner, or one of "the chosen"—all along the way being sure to constantly reassure the seeker how special they are.

This kind of glory seeker falls into the category Sun Tzu calls "Expendable Agents."[182] Send him on a one-way (i.e., suicide) mission "only he" can

182. *Ping-fa*, chapter XIII. See the chapter "Sun Tzu Storms the Gate!" in Section II.

accomplish. This kind was (figuratively or literally) born to "die for a cause" . . . Why not *your* cause?

The second type of glory seeker, those who feel frustrated that the world doesn't recognize their talents, is easily drawn to the Mind Slayer (and his cause) simply because the Mind Slayer does appear to recognize their talent. In this way, the Mind Slayer adroitly strings the glory seeker along with the promise of making him famous, until the glory seeker becomes dependent on the Mind Slayer for his self-esteem.

GOLD

Focused. Obsessed. Greedy. Reckless. Mercenary. His loyalty is contingent on profit. Convince him you know where the mother lode of his particular brand of "treasure" is and he'll follow you anywhere . . . until he finds out different. See Bogart's *Treasure of the Sierra Madre* (1948).

However, "Dr. Lung's Altruism Rule" states: there's no such thing as altruism. Everybody gets paid. If you want someone to do something, simply tell them what's in it for them.[183]

Where one gets paid in gold—cold, hard cash—another gets paid in that warm feeling that they're a good person for stopping to help a stranded stranger. So gold in some instances doesn't mean the heavy, shiny stuff (though it's nice to have plenty of that, too!).

Your particular gold (the apple, or rather *obsession* of your eye) might be all kinds of things—from physical symbols of wealth (a fancy car, fancy girlfriend) to knowing in your heart you've done a good deed for your family and friends.

For the Mind Slayer, it's simple push-pull: find out what kind of gold a person wants and then either pull them in with promises of showing them where there's plenty of it to be found, or else threaten to withhold their gold from them.

183. However, if the truth of the matter is that there isn't anything in it for them . . . you might want to invest in a couple more "Dr. Lung" books first!

SPORT

Except for the expedient extraction of information in the face of a looming "dire threat situation" where life is in immediate peril,[184] cruelty has no place on the battlefield. Battle, by its very nature, is cruel enough without our making sport of a defeated enemy. Okinawan Grandmaster Gichin Funakoshi, founder of *Shotokan* karate, taught his students to "Slay . . . but never humiliate a man."

Deliberately indulging in cruelty—sans justifiable excuse—making sport of those no longer able to defend themselves, marks us as petty and cruel. When a Mind Slayer discovers this sadistic cruelty trait in others, they immediately fan the flames, encouraging that person's obnoxious acts—in the case of a cult leader, or ruthless dictator, actually giving their blessing to such cruelty. This in turn sets up a "feedback loop" that only benefits the Mind Slayer: the more obnoxious and offending the person's acts are (1) the more he will find himself shunned by other—normal—people, and, therefore, (2) the more he will be drawn into the Mind Slayer's camp (or cult) and the more he will take the Mind Slayer into his confidence and, most important, (3) he will soon become dependent upon the Mind Slayer for validation and vindication.

Many of this type are natural bullies (though they may lack the physicality to play out their bully fantasies). Such people are easily bored and easily led, especially when their Mind Slayer enabler provides them an excuse, or better yet, a whole venue (gang, cult, rebel army, etc.) in which to freely practice their perversions.[185]

LOVE

No one is more focused than those motivated by the love of kin, kind, and country. Of Hannibal's six "movers," love is trump—as if that comes as a big surprise to anyone.

On the positive side, such people are loyal, attentive, caring, and self-sacrificing. However, in negative manifestation, love all too easily becomes

184. Right, *Theatre of Hell: Dr. Lung's Complete Guide to Torture* by Dr. Haha Lung and Christopher B. Prowant (Loompanics Unlimited, 2003) again!

185. Read the Marquis de Sade's *120 of Sodom* . . . if you dare.

myopic, obsessed, possessed, overly possessive, and Othelloean jealous. The self-sacrificing aspect on the positive side of the equation, corrupted by *perceived* neglect, all too easily becomes martyrdom . . . and that martyrdom thing seldom ends well.

Machiavelli hit the nail on the head, telling his prince that (if forced to choose) between being feared or being loved, the prince should prefer the former, since fear is at least more constant than love. In other words, if someone truly fears you, there's little chance that fear is suddenly going to blossom into love. Love, on the other hand, can turn to hate in an instant, at just the drop of a former lover's name.

For the Mind Slayer, manipulating a target is often as simple as finding the thing he covets and offering to help him obtain it:

> What a man loves, what he hates, what he needs, what he desires: These are the four pillars that support his house.
>
> —Truth IV

Or else finding the thing he treasures the most and threatening to take it away from him. Hannibal's Truth I:

> Enemy! When you look at me don't see something you hate . . . see the very thing you love the most. For that is what I will surely rip from you if you ever rise against me!

HONOR

It is telling that Hannibal, by all accounts an honorable man himself, should reserve honor as the final and, by default, most worthy of things worth fighting for.

The man who fights for honor fights not only for himself but for those things he loves outside himself, for his honor is intricately linked to the honor of his loved ones, those who call him friend, and the cause and country he fights for.

The honorable warrior is focused, truthful, and loyal to the clan, cause, and country to which he has pledged that honor.

On the negative side, too sensitive an honor can make a man hesitant when, instead, he should be hurling himself headlong into the fray.

His honor called into question, or otherwise trespassed, at the very least,

HANNIBAL'S SIX "MOVERS OF MEN"

Mover	Positive Traits	Negative Traits	Mind Slayer Approach
BLOOD	Focused.	Bloodthirsty, prone to rage. Revenge-minded.	Feed his blood-lust. Fan the flames of his anger. Encourage (justify) his thirst for revenge.
GLORY	Focused.	Naïve. Easily led. Lacks self-esteem.	Dazzle him with tales of past heroes, "show him" how he too can be a hero ("winner," "one of the Chosen," etc.). Assure him he's "special." Send him on a (one-way) mission "only he" can accomplish. *Red Badge of Courage* (1893).
GOLD	Focused.	Obsessed. Greedy. Reckless. Mercenary, his loyalty is contingent upon profit.	Convince him you know where the mother lode of his particular brand of "treasure" is and he'll follow you anywhere . . . until he finds out different. *Treasure of the Sierra Madre* (1948).
SPORT	Focused.	Cruel. A natural bully. Easily bored. Easily led.	Give him a venue in which he can freely practice his perversions.
LOVE	Focused. Self-sacrificing.	Obsessed. Myopic. Martyr.	Find the thing he loves and offer to help him obtain it or else threaten to take it away from him.
HONOR	Focused. Truthful	Hesitant. Revenge-minded. Loyal. Just. End justifies means so long as it restores honor.	Make it appear to him that he's lost his honor (lost face) and then trap him by offering a way to regain that lost honor.

Figure 12.

steps are taken to reclaim that honor. In extremis, vengeance becomes the order of the day—as it was for the forty-seven ronin.

The Mind Slayer can play on the honor of only a shallow mind, one with an equally shallow sense of honor, by making it appear that person has lost his honor (or lost face, if you will), further entrapping him by offering a way to regain that lost honor.

Shallow men often fail to see their own shortcomings, inflated and imagined entitlement, and their own lowness in attitude and inattention to detail as the true cause of their being dishonored, preferring instead to point their finger at other, more honorable men as the cause of their affront.

But so long as we are honorable, no other man can ever make us lose that honor. Figuratively and literally, that honor is left to ourselves.

Only by our taking action when decorum and common sense call for counsel and quiet, or else through our inaction when it is time for honest and battle-honed men to step to the fore, can we ever cause our honor to be called into question.

Duty flows out from my breast. Obligation pours into my ear! Skin cut a thousand times eventually heals. Honor wounded but once never heals. War always begins with deceit. This is why war is always the final recourse of an honorable man. War always ends in desperation and death . . . and the death of honor is the most tragic of these.

—Hannibal

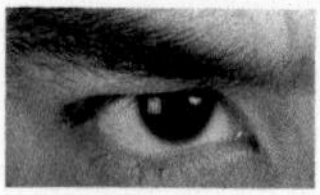

7.

Cao Cao's "Nine Strategies"

Let the enemy create your victory.
—Cao Cao

DURING HIS LIFETIME, Cao Cao was called China's "Martial King" for his undisputed mastery of the art of war. The most successful general of China's Three Kingdoms Period (220–280 A.D.), a self-made man, between his birth in 155 A.D. and his death in 220 Cao Cao rose from obscurity to eventually be crowned King of Wei, a kingdom controlling a sizable portion of China. Cao Cao's son would go on to become Emperor of all China and would humbly proclaim his father to be *T'ai Tzu*, literally "respected founder" of the Wei Dynasty.

Variously known as Ts'ao Kung, Wei Wi Ti, and "Duke T'sao," during his formative years Cao Cao made a diligent study of those strategists who had come before him, most notably Sun Tzu.

Like Sun Tzu, Cao Cao believed in going to war only as a last resort. To Cao Cao, going to war was a sign of failure, all other methods of securing peace, for example, maintaining peaceable relations with neighboring states and/or maintaining impenetrable defenses—having faltered and failed. War is a grim affair, one that must not be entered into halfheartedly:

> Fight only as a last resort. War is not a personal vendetta. Balance gain and loss before beginning . . . Plan well beforehand.

> Know your enemy and choose your lieutenants well. Count your troops, measure the distances you must travel, and commit the lay of the land to memory. Do all this before stepping one foot on the road to war. A wise general seizes victory when first he drafts his troops. He does not gather water at the well a second time.

Sun Tzu and Cao Cao were not the first to espouse the ideal of "winning sans fighting," nor were they the last:

> The right use of the sword is that it should subdue the barbarians while lying gleaming in its scabbard. If it leaves its sheath it cannot be said to be used rightly. Similarly the right use of military power is that it should conquer the enemy while concealed in the breast. To take the field with an army is to be found wanting in the real knowledge of it.
>
> —Tokugawa Ieyasu (1543–1616)

According to Cao Cao, you must "Let your enemy create your victory." To accomplish this, Cao Cao's main maxim was clear:

> Nothing is constant in war save deception and cunning. Herein lies The True Way[186] . . . Just as water has no constant form, so too war has no constant dynamic. As water adapts to each vase, so too those adept at war adopt an attitude of flexibility, thus adapting to flux and circumstance. So much of this cannot be known in advance but must be judged on the spot with practiced eye.

Thus, your battle plan must adapt to circumstance and flux, evolving as it encounters obstacles and opportunities.

Cao Cao literally made "The Rules" when it came to combat. Yet when circumstance and happenstance demanded, he would just as quickly discard "The Rules" in favor of some unorthodox and unexpected *ch'i* maneuver designed to achieve a telling victory. So although Cao Cao admonishes us by saying "Do not call up your army in bitter winter nor in blistering summer,

---

186. The Tao.

since it is too much of a hardship on the common people" don't be surprised to discover he himself successfully attacked the state of Wu in the dead of winter.

In other words, the dynamics of war are ever-shifting, necessitating that we are always adjusting—evolving.

But war is not the time for training. Each man must know his place and trust in his commander, just as any able commander must know the limitations of each of his men:

> Let each sphere be responsible for its officers. Let each officer be responsible to his sphere. Organize your regiments through the use of flags and gongs and symbols, and use loud drums to clearly signal attack and withdrawal.

Cao Cao continues that it is just as important, perhaps more so, that the king (or emperor) settled on the throne must let the commander in the field do his job:

> Court and combat are likewise two separate spheres. Combat is not won by ritual nor by court etiquette. Sometimes it is necessary to deny the emperor a battle in order to win him a war.

Once the battle is joined, once you've set to sea,[187] it matters not whether the prevailing wind is in your favor or against you, you deal with it:

> When all things operate in his favor, the wise general thinks about what can go wrong. When Fortune has turned her back on him, he schemes how best to get her attention again. Advantage alerts him to disadvantage and drives him towards advantage.

Cao Cao's credits reach far beyond the battlefield. He compiled an updated edition of Sun Tzu's *Ping-fa*, breaking Sun Tzu's *Art of War* down into its present (lucky?) thirteen chapters.

---

187. See "Musashi Crosses at the Ford," in *Mind Penetration* by Dr. Haha Lung and Christopher B. Prowant (Citadel, 2007.)

Cao Cao also created an unbeatable style of unarmed *wu shu* (what Westerners call kung-fu) for his army by incorporating the practical lessons he'd learned on the battlefield. Nowadays, this martial art is referred to as "The Nine Hands of Iron Wall Kung-fu."

Legend has it Cao Cao was given the nine principles (i.e., hands) of his Iron Wall fighting style, strategy, tactics, and techniques by the Goddess Nuwa, patron saint of the mysterious Black Lotus secret society.[188] According to legend, Nuwa once saved the earth by using her powers to fix a great gaping hole in the sky that was threatening to swallow up the earth.[189]

According to legend, Cao Cao had a dream (or a vision) in which the goddess gave him nine dazzling stars[190] from her hair. From these, he created his war art, composed of both *cheng* (orthodox) physical formations and tactics as well as *ch'i* (unorthodox) strategies.

Unlike many armchair generals, Cao Cao's art of war and his winning battlefield principles are based on his actual combat experiences, lessons learned the hard way that subsequently form the basis for the "Iron Wall Kung-fu" style he developed.[191]

Cao Cao's Iron Wall Kung-fu, both in strategy and in actual physical application, specializes in building an impenetrable wall of what to *the untrained eye* (and often even to *the trained eye* of an opposing general!) appears to be passive blocking techniques but what are in fact aggressive counterattacks.

For example, in the physical one-on-one self-defense training of Iron Wall Kung-fu, rather than merely blocking or deflecting an attacker's punch with your elbow (known as your "short-wing"), you instead block into your attacker's arm with an unexpected and forceful elbow strike designed to *cripple* that attacking arm! In the twentieth century, a variation of Cao Cao's kung-fu fighting form (Jp. "kata") was subsequently successfully incorpo-

---

188. For the history, tactics, and techniques of this pan-Asian secret society of femme fatales, see "Secrets of the Black Lotus" in *Mental Domination* by Dr. Haha Lung and Christopher B. Prowant (Citadel, 2009).

189. An eclipse, perhaps? Or would you prefer a black hole?

190. Some versions of the legend say nine jewels.

191. See *Iron Wall Kung-fu: Secrets of Winning Martial Arts Strategy* by Dr. Haha Lung (publication pending).

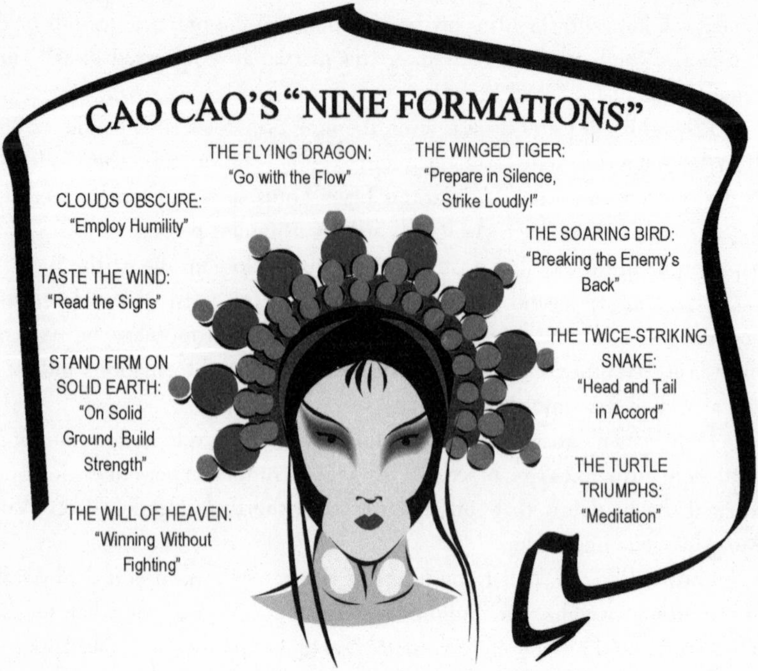

Figure 13.

rated into the formidable fighting arts of the *Cao Dai* cult guerrillas in Vietnam.[192]

This same "Iron Wall" principle applies to Cao Cao's psychological warfare: make the enemy think you are defending when you are really attacking; make him think you are fleeing when you are really leading him into an ambush. Classic Sun Tzu. And common sense.

THE WILL OF HEAVEN

Key attitude: "Winning without fighting." Sun Tzu's ideal, further refined by Cao Cao:

192. For a complete training course in the "Winged Tiger" style of kung-fu combat inspired by Cao Cao, see *Lost Fighting Arts of Vietnam* by Dr. Haha Lung (Citadel, 2006).

> Without engaging the enemy in battle, the wise general accomplishes his goal with his force unscathed. Thus it is said he is victorious under Heaven because he has not sacrificed a single man to the sword.

Win battles with a minimum of bloodshed or, better yet, avoid fighting altogether. What a novel concept—one that still hasn't caught on!

Likewise, in order to be in harmony with the Will of Heaven one does not make war for personal gain. Says Cao Cao:

> Do not embark on war out of personal emotion. Look to the objective gain or loss.

To be in harmony with the Will of Heaven meant not only accepting that there are some things out of our control—events within the dominion of the gods, luck and the weather, for instance—it also warned against committing needlessly foolish or heinous acts repellent to Heaven. Thus, the wise general is not just victorious, he is "victorious under Heaven." His reluctance to go to needless war in the first place and his aversion to needlessly spill blood while engaging in wanton slaughter pleases the gods, who it seems value universal balance[193] above all else.

To achieve this balance means a leader must (1) know himself, (2) know his enemy, and (3) know his AO—area of operation: "the three knows."[194]

To preserve his rapport with the Will of Heaven, a commander of men (by default, a commander of *himself*) must possess five virtues: wisdom, integrity, compassion, courage, and discipline[195] (sometimes rendered "severity").

It stands to reason that if these are the five *positive virtues*,[196] then the wily Mind Slayer must look to uncover—or else create and cultivate—the opposite *negative vices* in his enemy:

- Turn *wisdom* into *ignorance* using *distraction*.
- Turn *integrity* into *treachery and betrayal* using *compromise*.

---

193. Chinese: *Tao* and *T'ai Chi*.

194. Know yourself, know your enemy, know your environment (surroundings).

195. "It is certain, only with either fortune or discipline can catastrophe be avoided. Of the two, the only one you can never run out of is discipline." (General William Westmoreland)

196. For an in depth discussion of Cao Cao's Five Virtues, see *Mind Control* by Dr. Haha Lung and Christopher B. Prowant (Citadel, 2006).

- Turn *compassion* into *ruthlessness* inciting *hatred*.
- Turn *courage* into *cowardice* through inducing *fear.*[197]
- Turn *discipline* into *weakness* through *sympathy.*

A man moves Heaven with his prayers, Earth with his will.

—Vlad Tepes, *Dracula's Art of War*

STAND FIRM ON SOLID EARTH

Key attitude: "On solid ground, build strength." Projecting an air of confidence and commitment, we appear unassailable and so we dissuade insult and do not invite invasion.

From carrying yourself in an alert manner on the street so as to dissuade a would-be mugger[198] to making sure our affairs and accounts are literally in order so as to dissuade a hostile business takeover, how we carry and cavort ourselves determines whether Mind Slayers see us as a fellow predator, hence a potential threat, or else as potential prey, hence *supper*! Thus, Miyamoto Musashi instructs us, "Let your combat stance be your everyday stance and your everyday stance your combat stance."

Both on the battlefield and off, the instant you relax is the instant an alert enemy rushes to fill that opening. Thus, "I make myself invulnerable and await my enemy's moment of vulnerability"—classic The Turtle Triumphant strategy.

Whether in life in general or in the martial arts in particular, maintaining our balance, our firm footing preferably on solid ground, is key. For example, in karate the most important component to proper kicking technique is the landing—landing in a solid, ready-to-rumble-further stance.

In any confrontation, never allow your opponent—whether on Wall Street or out there on those mean streets—to see you off-balance. Whether in high-stakes negotiations or back alley head-knockin', you need (1) firm footing and (2) a firm foundation.

Firm footing is *where* you move. Firm foundation is *how* you move.

Cultivating a firm foundation (i.e., strong legs, balance) will compensate you when you find yourself with an *un*firm footing (i.e., literally or physically on shifting sand, figuratively caught up in a situation of violent circumstance

---

197. *Fear* is one of the Five Warning F.L.A.G.S., as is *sympathy* that follows.

198. For a complete course on street-applicable martial arts, see *Street Ninja: Ancient Secrets for Surviving Today's Mean Streets* by Dirk Skinner (Barricade Books, 1995).

and flux). However, having a firm footing will not necessarily compensate you if your overall foundation (i.e., physical fighting stance, negotiating position) is weak. Ideally, the two work in concert, not unlike The Twice-Striking Snake striking simultaneously.

In a more metaphorical, yet no less important sense, "Standing firm on solid ground" means literally knowing not only "where you stand" but what you stand for on the important issues in life. Thus the first of "The Three Knows" is Socrates's admonishment to "Know yourself" (i.e., "stand firm"), with the third of the Three Knows being "Know your environment" (i.e., "solid ground").

TASTE THE WIND

Key attitude: "Read the signs." Like Sun Tzu before him, Cao Cao preferred to avoid bloodshed. But when conflict was unavoidable and physical confrontation called for, action had to be swift and telling. A good warrior does not pull his sword a second time. But before setting out on any campaign, intelligence was always job one. Thus, in the same way a predator sniffs the air for prey, so too we learn to "taste the wind."

Cao Cao realized early on that with the right kind of intelligence—both the *innate* and the *gathered* variety—bloody conflict could often be avoided altogether.

Think of it this way: *innate* intelligence is the kind you're born with; *gathered* intelligence is the kind you'll die without!

And while, like any able commander, Cao Cao would never let his enemy lead him around by a ring through his nose, he was quick to point out that "Dividing and uniting troops—these changes result from observing the enemy."

By "observing the enemy," Cao Cao is telling us we need to understand human nature on the most basic level—yin-yang:

> Human nature advances towards gain, and retreats from pain.
> Victory lies in understanding the subtleties, in attacking the vulnerable, not the invulnerable.

As for putting (and keeping) one's own house in order, above all else, Cao Cao warns us, a wise general keeps his own counsel since *secrecy must be the first and foremost weapon in our arsenal*:

> Winning begins and ends with keeping dispositions hidden.
> Nothing is constant in war save deception and cunning.

When war was unavoidable, Cao Cao did his best to be first to acquire the most extensive intelligence on his enemies as possible. His catchphrase was: "Cultivate strength, spy out weakness." Thus, he made liberal use of *Lin Kuei*[199] spies to keep him well-supplied with timely gathered intelligence, assassins to make sure his enemies never enjoyed a restful night's sleep, and agents provocateur to "split the enemy's forces" by sowing dissent and confusion.

A grand example of Cao Cao literally using "the whole ball of wax" when it came to defeating his foes is related by Sung Dynasty (960–1126) writer Chang Yu:

> *His army camped for the night not far-distant from an enemy force of equal strength commanded by a formidable opposing general of complementary experience and that general's king. Cao Cao uncharacteristically took a break from planning the morning's pending battle to unexpectedly call for a soldier whom he had just that day condemned to death for cowardice.*
>
> *Once more Cao Cao allowed the soldier to protest his innocence before finally opening his hand to show the soldier a small ball of wax. "It is widely known that when a man lies his mouth becomes dry and, should he eat rice, he will be unable to swallow it," Cao Cao told the man. "Now, since I have little rice to spare from the mouths of my men, if you can swallow this ball of wax without choking, it will prove your innocence and I will grant you your freedom."*
>
> *Quickly swallowing the ball of wax with ease, the soldier smiled triumphantly. Cao Cao congratulated the man: "You have won your freedom but you still must leave the army since some of your fellow soldiers may not be as convinced of your innocence as I am. However, if you are caught in uniform, the enemy will still certainly kill you. Therefore, put on this priest's robe. Not even our vile enemy would dare kill a priest!"*
>
> *Quickly the newly pardoned man donned the priest's robe and was just as quickly turned away from Cao Cao's camp . . . never realizing he had been pointed in the direction of the enemy camp.*
>
> *In short order this false monk was captured and taken before the enemy king. In fear for his life, he told the enemy king the tale of his*

199. (Ch.) Literally "forest demons," think "Chinese ninja."

miraculous pardon by Cao Cao, all because he was able to swallow the ball of wax . . .

Without a second thought the king ordered the faux monk man killed and the mysterious ball of wax cut from his stomach . . . Inside the ball of wax the king discovered a tiny message from Cao Cao, addressed to the king's general, outlining a conspiracy hatched between the two of them. Enraged, the "betrayed" king ordered the immediate execution of the general—his best general—just as Cao Cao had planned!

The following day, lacking a competent general, the enemy king's army was easily defeated.

By the way, Chang Yu's story is an excellent example of what Sun Tzu calls "expendable" or "doomed" agents.[200]

Translated into everyday use, you have a piece of gossip you want to wind up in a third party's ear so you deliberately leak it to a known blabbermouth you're certain will run straight to the person whom you eventually want to hear the information. In this way, you not only accomplish your goal but you do so by placing a layer of "insulation"[201] between you and the gossip.

CLOUDS OBSCURE

Key attitude: "Employ humility." Whenever possible, you want to keep a low profile by (1) not calling attention to yourself as you go about preparing to make your move, while (2) taking steps to distract your foe's attention away from where you are making those preparations. (Yes, this is exactly what we learned when studying the magician's craft in the previous chapter's section "Mastering the Techniques of "The Mini-Masters.")

Whether on the battlefield, in the boxing ring, or else struggling tooth and nail to keep your wallet and quite possibly your life in some back alley,[202] the more that you can hide your intent from your antagonist, the better your chances of winning. Japanese ninja are renowned for blinding others with

200. Sun Tzu's *Ping-fa*, Chapter XIII.

201. "Plausible deniability."

202. Dirk Skinner says, "Give them the wallet. Money isn't worth dying for. You can always make more money. You can't make more life!" (Skinner, 1995)

stealth and misdirection, as were their predecessors, China's *Moshuh Nanren* and the aforementioned *Lin Kuei*,[203] and their many offshots and imitators.[204]

Clouds Obscure goes hand-in-hand with the former Taste the Wind intelligence gathering. Only, in this instance, it's we who are feeding our foe *false* information—called *dis*information in spook-speak.

In the same way a bank of clouds slowly passes in front of the sun, obscuring the light, so too we keep our mission secret, keeping our true goals and actual objectives hidden. The more that we can keep our enemy guessing, the better the chance our enemy will guess wrong.

"Guessing" simply means we don't have enough actual information to go on to make a detailed decision. Sadly, even when given accurate information, and contrary to the inflated opinion average people hold of themselves, most people *aren't* all that good at guessing. Hopefully, your enemy is one of these, but it never hurts (you) to provide him with as much free manure as possible to fertilize his little garden of delusions.

Two of the best examples of Clouds Obscure are the semi-mythical tale of the Trojan Horse and the all-too-real example of World War II's Normandy invasion—where false invasion preparations, including the creation of entire staging bases (replete with straw dummy personnel, wooden planes, and even inflatable tanks!), were set up to distract Axis spies from actual Allied preparations.

THE FLYING DRAGON

Key attitude: "Go with the flow." It is said that by riding the wind, the dragon reaps the whirlwind. This means that instead of foolishly and fruitlessly resisting the wind, the wise dragon (as well as anyone with a modicum of common sense!) first correctly discerns the way the wind is moving and then "goes with the flow," using the wind to his advantage.

---

203. For a complete training course in this ninja art, see Dr. Haha Lung and Christopher B. Prowant's *Shadowhand: Secrets of Ninja Taisavaki* (Paladin Press, 2002) and *Shadowhand: The Art of Invisibility* by Dr. Haha Lung and Christopher B. Prowant (Citadel, 2004).

204. For the complete history and fighting techniques of these groups, see Dr. Lung's *Knights of Darkness: Secrets of the World's Deadliest Night-fighters* (Paladin Press, 1998) and *Knights of Darkness* (Citadel, 2004).

On the battlefield, a general must always be alert for what's called "the ebb and flow" of battle, when the "winds of battle" shift in your favor, or against you, the same way a sailor stays ever alert for shifting winds lest he find himself suddenly crashing upon the rocks.

In one-on-one combat, this reminds us of the Judo Principle: our opponent tries to push us and, rather than resisting him, we pull him. Conversely, he tries to pull us and, instead of resisting his strength, we unexpectedly "go with the flow," thereby doubling the strength of our countertechnique throw or takedown.

This attitude and tactic harkens back to not challenging the Will of Heaven. Or, if you prefer a more Western adage, Jesus' "Resist not evil . . . if a man forces you to go one mile with him, go with him two instead."[205]

A secondary catchphrase sometimes assigned to this tactic is "occupy the mind," entreating us to occupy both our own mind (with timely and true intelligence) while dazzling our enemy's mind by feeding him doubt and disinformation. Dragons are, first and foremost by their very nature, distractingly dazzling. We learn much from the dragon . . .

THE WINGED TIGER

Key attitude: "Prepare in silence. Strike loudly!"

Cao Cao was legendary—and much feared!—for his ability to quickly and efficiently mobilize his forces, so much so that a superstition grew among his foes against even daring to speak his name, similar to the taboo of wishing an actor "Good luck!" rather than "Break a leg!" just before going on stage. Thus, they said of Cao Cao: "No sooner do you speak the Old Dragon's name than he appears!"

The only constant in Cao Cao's world was getting to the party before your foe. A couple thousand years later, on the other side of the world, in another civil war, another great strategist by the name of General Nathan Bedford Forrest bothered by an insistent newspaperman to explain how he won battles, snapped, "It's whoever arrives *first* with the *most*!"

Thus, Cao Cao was rightly famed—and rightly feared!—for how he

205. Matthew 5:39.

always seemed to arrive "first with the most," arriving at the scene of battle before his enemies ever suspected his army was on the move. This component of his Winged Tiger strategy was simple:

> Make a show of being far away . . . then march with all haste to arrive before the enemy even suspects you are on the move! Choose a circuitous route that gives the illusion it requires a great distance to travel. Even when you start out after the enemy does, so long as you calculate correctly, you can still arrive before your enemy.

Arriving at the battlefield of *your* choosing well ahead of your enemy has many obvious advantages over arriving late and being forced to fight on a battleground of your foe's choosing.

Cao Cao well knew that, in order to literally upstage an opponent, he had to bring something new to the table, or as he put it: "Beyond the regular rules . . . One must use subtler origins."

- "Prepare in silence" harkens back to Clouds Obscure, playing your cards close to your chest. It's a no-brainer that the less our enemy knows (or suspects) about what we're up to, the better our chances of pulling it off. Thus, the wise commander keeps his own counsel. This is perhaps what Cao Cao meant when he commented that, while his men could share in his victory, they could never know the pain and sacrifice it took him to get them there: "The troops can share in the joy of victory, but not in the travails of conception."
- "Strike loudly," which on the surface can be seen as practical advice to let loose with your best karate *kiai*, battle cries, and bagpipes in order to unnerve your foe, might just as easily be rendered "Strike swiftly!" "Strike forcefully!" and "Strike boldly!" for Cao Cao's intent is clear—evoking the same effect as of a great stalking tiger who, having already approached us unseen ("Prepare in silence . . ."), now paralyzes us in place with his mighty roar ("Strike loudly!") as he pounces! Compare this approach with the following "Soaring Bird" strategy of circling (overhead) silently, unsuspected, before launching a sudden strike, to win the battle in one bold, telling stroke.

Imagine the effect of striking your enemy without prior warning, sadly similar to the stereotypical "quiet, kept pretty much to himself" coworker who, having nursed his secret grudges for years, suddenly whips out a Kalashnikov and, screaming at the top of his lungs about injustices real and imagined, decides today's the day to show everyone in the office his Rambo imitation! In the same way, you've prepared in secret (or, as Cao Cao says, "in silence") before suddenly, unexpectedly launching your attack. An enemy prepared, one alerted to your preparations, at least has a chance. An enemy who never sees it coming . . . doesn't see much of anything after that! Right. Pearl Harbor. 9/11.

THE SOARING BIRD (a.k.a. "RAPTOR")

Attitude: "Break the enemy's back." Western scholars sometimes translate this tactic as "The Raptor" since, like a predator hawk, the wise commander deftly, often unseen, first succeeds in rising above his enemy, literally taking the "high ground," before suddenly, sans warning, striking down with dazzling speed, the force of the unexpected and perfectly timed impact snapping his target's back! Here, we hear echoes of the ideal of Karate Grandmaster Gichin Funakoshi: *Ikken hisatsu!*—literally "to kill with one blow." Students master the art of executing each *and every* strike—a kick, a punch, elbow, or knee—as if it will be the single contest-ending blow—Force of Will honed to a laser point, slicing through those of lesser focus, determination first distracting, then dominating, until finally decimating the indolent and the indecisive.

Having strategically taken "the high ground" far above the killing field, the predator raptor leisurely circles, the perfect vantage point from which to observe without being observed, until the time comes to strike, when he comes upon his target from an unexpected angle, striking with full and fatal force the first time:

> Mastery comes from the opportunity itself and opportunity is mastered through events. —Cao Cao

THE TWICE-STRIKING SNAKE

Attitude: "Head and tail of one accord." This strategy can be traced to an ancient Chinese myth of a special sort of snake (Ch. *shuai-jan*).

that could attack with both its head and its tail simultaneously.[206] Sun Tzu mentions this unique creature in his *The Art of War*:

> The skilful tactician may be likened to the shuai-jan. Now the shuai-jan is a snake that is found in the Ch'ang Mountains. Strike at its head, and you will be attacked by its tail; strike at its tail, and you will be attacked by its head; strike at its middle, and you will be attacked by head and tail both.[207]

This strategy can be applied to battlefield tactics—for example, meeting an enemy's main force with your own main force (the head) while keeping troops in reserve to shore up any flagging areas of your own line and/or deploying special units (the tail) to harass his flanks.

But beyond this obvious classic strategy, the Twice-Striking Snake also refers overall to the way ancient Chinese military strategy was divided into two components: the kind of direct toe-to-toe *cheng* strategy formations we generally associate with two heavily armed forces facing off against one another, and unconventional *ch'i* tactics, what we today think of as "special forces," "guerrilla warfare," and "terrorism."

"Head and tail of one accord" also calls for collecting your disparate elements into a coordinated whole, with the left hand always knowing what the right hand is doing. For example, the German's final push of World War II, since dubbed the Battle of the Bulge, might have succeeded except for the fact that the Germans literally ran out of gas, literally stopping their Panzers in their tracks.

Employing the Twice-Striking Snake strategy allowed Cao Cao to attack with a direct attack on the one hand, surprise attack on the other. This twofold approach also allowed Cao Cao to employ spies, *Lin Kuei* assassins, and liberal amounts of psychological warfare in advance of any physical attack. In several instances, Cao Cao's use of *ch'i* elements circumvented or outright prevented the need for actual bloodshed.

When attacking, Cao Cao employed both regular troops in conventional

---

206. In the service of clarity and brevity, some translators render the "Twice-Striking Snake" as "Scorpion," since the concept is the same—simultaneous strikes from two directions as the scorpion's claws seize hold, immobilizing the victim, while the scorpion's tail simultaneously strikes the death blow.

207. 1910 Giles translation, XI:29.

direct combat formations (*cheng*), as well as unorthodox and indirect (*ch'i*) spies, assassins, agents provocateur, as well as special forces troops.

For example, Cao Cao's "dragon-wings" were specially trained, specially equipped sappers and shock troops with much in common with modern special forces:

- Traveling great distances in short periods by unexpected routes through hostile terrain in order to slow an enemy's advance
- Surprising the enemy by arriving early at a battle site in order to lay booby traps and ambush
- Relieve and reinforce besieged allies
- Provide rear-cover fire for retreating troops
- These specialized *ch'i* troops could also be called upon to create distracting false attacks designed to draw enemy forces away from Cao Cao's real objective:

> My enemy rushes to the fore, but I am attacking his rear. When he responds by reinforcing his rear, his front again becomes vulnerable. —Cao Cao

Likewise, Mind Slayers often employ unexpected and unappreciated persons to do their bidding. This harkens back both to Musashi's "Cutting at the Edges" ploy and to our previous discussion of all those little people we all too often overlook. According to Sun Tzu, these are exactly the kinds of people who are ripe for recruitment in the enemy camp, a *fifth column* just waiting to turn traitor and help the invading force. More on this in a later section called "Sun Tzu Storms the Gate!"

While the king's soldiers are ever on guard against ninjas slipping over the wall and slipping a dirk in their master's back, it is the overworked, underappreciated servant who slips the poison in the king's cup.

The hammer quickly forgets the nail, but the nail never forgets the hammer.

THE TURTLE TRIUMPHANT

Attitude: "Meditation."

The turtle is hardly as dazzling and awe-inspiring as the dragon, not nearly as fearsome as the tiger, hardly as swift as the raptor, or even as scheming as the snake. As a result, the "lowly" turtle is often overlooked; sometimes, he's even mistaken for a rock.

But the turtle is a born survivalist, one who literally carries both his bunker and bomb shelter around with him on his back. When threatened by overwhelming force, he prudently withdraws into the safety of his prepared shell. Like a wise monk—first drawing in his limbs, then drawing in his senses—he meditates until the danger eventually tires of trying to pry him loose and moves on. And in the event an attack is called for . . . Just how true is that old wives' tale that once a snapping turtle latches on to you, even if you cut off his head, his jaws still won't let go until the sun goes down?

Sometimes, simply surviving is the best outcome. Guerrilla warfare 101: when faced with a superior force, he who runs away *does* live to fight another day.

We can learn a lot from the turtle—and not just "Slow and steady wins the race." Cao Cao learned a lot from the turtle:

> I make myself invulnerable and await my enemy's moment of vulnerability. In an advantageous situation, one ponders disadvantages. In a disadvantage situation, one ponders advantage. Defend, when you lack strength. Attack, when your strength is in abundance. When the enemy attacks me, he becomes vulnerable. When he shows an indication he is advancing, I set an ambush in place for him and pretend to retreat. If he seems eager to retreat, I slow my march so he can do so. Attack where he is empty, avoid where he is full. The easy victory lies in subtleties, in attacking the vulnerable, not the invulnerable. Attack what he holds dear and he will rush to the rescue and to his doom.

Compare Cao Cao's "I make myself invulnerable and await my enemy's moment of invulnerability" statement with a similar sentiment from Sun Tzu:

> The good fighters of old first put themselves beyond the possibility of defeat, and then waited for an opportunity of defeating the enemy.[208]

208. *The Art of War* by Sun Tzu (Lionel Giles translation, 1910).

The final of the Three Knows is "Know your environment." The turtle knows—and controls—his environment because he carries it with him at all times.

Likewise, Cao Cao always controlled his battlefield. And when his strategy called for defensible fixed battlements, he was sure never to allow an enemy to anger him or otherwise draw him out into open ground. On the march, he never allowed himself to be maneuvered into and mired in restricting ground (e.g., a boxed canyon, his back to a mountain, or to the sea).

One battlefield example of Cao Cao's use of the Turtle Triumphant tactic was the day he uncharacteristically found himself at a disadvantage where literally "drawing his head in" turtlelike was called for:

> *His smaller force trapped in a long, narrow canyon by the enemy forces amassed at both ends of the canyon, unseen Cao Cao had his men quickly dig holes into the side of the canyon walls. Leaving half his men hidden inside these holes, Cao Cao then boldly advanced as if to attack the enemy at the front end of the canyon.*
>
> *Realizing he was advancing toward the front end of the canyon, thinking he had in mind to break free, the enemy force at the rear of the canyon quickly rushed forward further into the canyon, intent on attacking Cao Cao's exposed rear. But no sooner had they passed the men Cao Cao had hidden inside the canyon walls than those hidden men leaped from their hiding places, to attack the enemy rear! Simultaneously, Cao Cao suddenly turned his own troops back, crushing the enemy in the canyon between the two halves of his force. Meanwhile the enemy at the front end of the canyon was so stunned by this reversal of fortune that instead of rallying to the aid of their trapped comrades they fled in panic!*

Some three hundred years earlier, half a world away, another great general, Hannibal the Conqueror, faced a similar threat from barbarian hill tribes attacking his army's rear as they passed through narrow canyons while traversing the already treacherous Alps on their way to Rome. To remedy this, like Cao Cao, Hannibal had his men hide in the side of canyon walls where they waited until the harassers passed before emerging to trap the hill tribesmen between themselves and Hannibal's rear guard.[209]

---

209. See *The 99 Truths: Hannibal's Black Art of War* by Dr. Haha Lung (publication pending).

So what can *we* learn from the Turtle Triumphant?

- Learn to meditate. Patience + breath! = meditation.
- Nobody notices a rock until it starts moving.
- Sometimes all you need to do is outlast your enemy.
- Sometimes merely to survive is victory.
- Don't bite the enemy unless you're prepared to hold on till the sun goes down!

Even though Cao Cao himself was heralded as a great general, he never let it go to his head, never lost sight of the most important fact all able leaders know:

> In the end, all victory depends on the skill of the single warrior.

8.

Kuji-kiri: The Nine Doors to Power

BEFORE WE CAN HOPE to influence the minds of others, we must first seize our own mind by the scruff of its unruly neck. Before we can attack our enemy's mind-set, we must first get our own mind set for the task. The Turtle Triumphant isn't the only one who meditates.

Concentration, meditation, visualization, even self-hypnosis are all connected, and all come together to whet our focus, hone our will, and revitalize our spirit. All of these are ways of *self-creation*, of taking the basic stuff we've been given by mother nature and sharpening it to crystal clarity.

Whether you call it prayer or meditation,[210] down through the ages various means for "centering" the human mind (and spirit) have been used with varying degrees of success depending on (1) the dedication of the person doing the meditating and (2) the viability of the technique itself—again, often dependent on the particular technique's compatibility with the particular person doing the meditating.

Ironically, what has proven down through the centuries to be one of the easiest schools of meditation to master, as well as being one that has

210. It has been said "prayer" is when you do the *talking*; "meditation" is when you do the *listening*.

consistently proven *immediately* useful to its practitioners, comes to us from an infamous cadre we more generally associate with *murder* than with *meditation*—Japanese ninja!

It is more properly known as *Shinobi*, the ninja folk of medieval Japan *kuji-kiri*, a form of meditation distilled from ancient taboo "left-hand" rituals from East Indian *Tantra* yoga, mysterious mind-bending methods from Tibetan *Bon-Lamanists*, and shamanistic practices from aboriginal Japanese *Ainu*[211] animism.

Kuji-kiri (literally "nine hands cutting") combines ancient mudra hand gestures with concentration and visualization designed to create specific effects depending on the specific mudra being used. According to tradition, these mudra were originally distillations of full-body yoga positions (called *asanas*).

Tantra yoga teaches that there is a mysterious energy known as *kundalini* (Skt. "serpent force") similar to the Chinese-Taoist concept of *chi* (Jp. *ki*) that fills, flows through, and animates all things. This kundalini "pools" at seven power centers along the spine known as *chakra* (Skt. "wheels"). When stimulated by kundalini, itself "awakened" by regular yoga practice, these power centers blossom open like flowers, granting the yoga practitioner enlightenment and *siddhas* ("psychic super powers").

There are also chakras in the palms of our hands, so when the hands are properly arranged into mudra and used in conjunction with the proper mediation mind-set, we receive the same benefits from doing this "hand yoga" as from performing full-body yoga positions.

Whether you buy into the siddhas "super powers" theory or not, the undisputed fact is that regular meditation cannot but help improve our powers of concentration—a most valuable skill whether you have ambitions of becoming a Mind Slayer yourself with the power to influence those around you or you're only concerned in not becoming some Mind Slayer's next victim!

---

211. *Ainu* (Jp. "Hairy ones") were the original Caucasian inhabitants of the Japanese archipelago.

		Mudra	English Name	Attribute	Key
INTERIOR	YIN	RIN	Power Fist	Strength	Strength
		PYO	Great Diamond	Focus	Direction of energy
		SHA	Pure-Wind	Healing	Healing
		KAI	Dragon Hand	Adaptability	Premonition
BALANCE		TOH	Watercourse Hand	Balance	Harmony
EXTERIOR	YANG	JIN	Hidden Hand	Perception	Knowing the throughts of others
		ZAI	1000 Lotus	Control/Creativity	Control of the elements
		RETSU	Wisdom Fist	Will	Control of time and space
		ZEN	Great Sun	Enlightenment	Enlightenment

Figure 14.

Meditation Exercise #1

Preferably sitting comfortably in a quiet spot,[212] close your eyes and imagine you're smelling a large, beautiful rose. This rose can be any color you wish, only concentrate on actually "seeing" it in your mind's eye as you breathe in as deeply but comfortably as possible.

When we smell something we truly like—flowers, food, etc.—we take in a long, deep breath, pulling our breath to the bottom of our lungs. This is the type of slow, deep breathing you should do now.

Actually filling your mediation space with fresh flowers or burning incense can augment this exercise, although honing your powers of concentration (by imagining the shape and smell of the flower) can never do harm.

212. With practice, it will no longer matter whether you are in a peaceful setting or surrounded by chaos; you will still be able to instantly "center" yourself through this meditation.

Mediation Exercise #2

Having "centered" yourself with this "flower breathing," choose the mudra that represents the mind-set you wish to invoke:

- When feeling exhausted, position your hands in *Rin*, "The Power Fist," as his meditation will infuse your body and mind with renewed *strength*. Each time you breathe in a deep "flower breath" you will literally feel strength and energy entering your body.
- When suffering from aches and pains, *Sha*, the "Pure-Wind" healing mudra, will help you recover. Again, as you breathe in, imagine healing vapors entering your body. Taking your concentration to the next level, in your mind's eye gently direct these healing vapors entering your body to the specific site of your aches and pains. Likewise, as you exhale, imagine your pains being exhaled from your body.
- To help yourself come to a difficult decision and strengthen your determination, you'll want to practice *Retsu*, "The Wisdom Fist."
- For creativity, *Zai* helps get the juices flowing.

9.

Poor Richard's Rich Wisdom

THERE'S A DARN GOOD REASON he's the guy on the $100 bill—the only *non*-president to be so honored. Benjamin Franklin (1706–1790), one of the Founding Fathers of the United States, was a statesman, diplomat, printer, and author. He is credited with the discovery of electricity and was the inventor of bifocals. He also established the first fire department and public library on American soil. And, in typical American fashion, we tend to forget he was also a notorious womanizer, rabble-rouser and scheming Freemason[213] who suggested taking the turkey (rather than the eagle) as the official symbol for the United States, as well as making Hebrew the official language (to further emphasize our split with those English-speaking English). Well, Ol' Ben (in his wise and wizened persona of "Poor Richard") would have been the first to admit you can't always get everything right . . . but you can darn sure try.

And while most streetwise youngsters today couldn't pick Ol' Ben out of a lineup, ask any of them what life's all about and they'll tell you (without

213. In 1730 Franklin wrote the first documented exposé of American Freemasonry. The following year he inexplicably became a Freemason himself, swiftly rising to the position of Provincial Grand Master of Pennsylvania in 1734. He later travelled to France to join other lodges. This abrupt turnaround has raised more than one eyebrow in conspiracy circles. To make matters worse, in 1773, while in England, Franklin coproduced a new revised version of *The Book of Common Prayer* with Baron le Despenser, a.k.a. Sir Francis Dashwood, founder of the infamous *Hellfire Club* and a member of Adam Weishaupt's even more infamous Bavarian Illuminati. (*Conspiracy Encyclopedia*, Thom Burnett, et.al. compilers [Conspiracy Books, 2005.])

skipping a beat while they're rifling through your pockets), "Life's all about gettin' dem Benjamins!"

While it is, admittedly, a worthwhile goal to keep as many portraits of Benjamin Franklin in your pocket as possible, another way of "gettin' dem Benjamins" might be learning to appreciate the man for the insightful witty wizard of worldly ways he was.

"WIT AND WISDOM" . . . AND WHAT ELSE?

Every time someone writes an article, a book, or does a PBS bio on Benjamin Franklin, it's mandatory that the words "Wit and Wisdom" form part of the title—and with good cause.

But all too often, Ol' Ben's biographers conveniently forget to add "wily" to his résumé. All those jobs he held—skills displayed—from inventor to diplomat, required him to be able to come up with unconventional solutions.[214] As difficult—and as dangerous—as one former vocation was (e.g., standing at the end of a line attached to a kite you hope is about to get struck by a gazillion volts of electricity!), success in the latter craft of diplomacy (with emphasis on "craft") was just as demanding—and often just as dangerous.

Diplomacy in Franklin's day required first tipping your hat at convention while, surreptitiously, undermining tradition and challenging that fattest, most indolent of beasts: status quo. Yes, playing this game did require considerable "wit and wisdom" on Ol' Ben's part, requiring such acumen as:

- A gift for gab and gossip, from solicitation and seduction. Advises Ol' Ben: "If you have no honey in your pot, have some in your mouth."
- An uncanny ability to read (and when necessary *rewrite!*) others.
- And a natural inclination toward intrigue paired with a penchant for espionage . . . "Guerrilla warfare" of the mind, if you will.

Franklin was as shrewd a character as they come and a man who had a lot to say on a variety of subjects. A lot of these sayings are well-known American aphorisms: "Forewarned is forearmed"; others are not so well known nor as oft quoted. Yet beneath Franklin's pithy, user-friendly, folksy

214. Right, what Chinese strategists call *ch'i*.

and down home sayings, we sometimes glimpse deeper—near Machiavellian—insights into human nature:

On Self and Self-Discipline

"Deny self for self's sake."
"A full belly makes a dull brain."
"Little strokes fell great oaks."
"Diligence is the mother of good luck."
"He that can have patience can have what he will."
"He that waits upon fortune is never sure of a dinner."

On Human Psychology

"You may be too cunning for one but not for all."
"A cunning man is overmatched by a cunning and a half."
"He is not well-bred that cannot bear ill-breeding in others."
"If you want to convince, speak of interest, not of reason."[215]
"What signifies philosophy that does not apply to some use?"
"If you would have it done, go; if not, send."
"Vessels large may venture more, but little boats keep near the shore."
"He is a fool that cannot conceal his wisdom."
"If your head is wax, don't walk in the sun."
"The proud hate pride—in others."
"Pride dines on vanity and sups on contempt."
"Many princes sin with David; but few repent with him."

On Love

"Beauty and folly are old companions."
"If Jack's in love, he's no judge of Jill's beauty."
"He who speaks ill of the mare, will buy her."
"The proof of gold is fire, the proof of woman gold: the proof of a man, a woman."
"Samson with his strong body had a weak head, or he would have not laid in a harlot's lap."

215. Remember, there's no such thing as altruism.

On Politics and Power

"One sword keeps another in the scabbard."

"An Empire, like a cake, is most easily diminished at the edges."

"Laws, like cobwebs, catch small flies. Great ones break through before your eyes."

"When one has so many different people with different opinions to deal with . . . one is obliged to give in on smaller points in order to gain the greater."

"Sudden power is apt to be insolent, sudden liberty saucy—that behaves best which has grown gradually."

"There never was a good war or a bad peace."

"It is remarkable that soldiers by profession, men truly and unquestionably brave, seldom advise war but in cases of extreme necessity."

"Necessity never made a good bargain."

"Neither a fortress or maidenhead will hold out long once they begin to parley."

"A nation, to keep respect of other states, must keep its own self-respect at home."

On Dealing with Enemies

"There is no little enemy."

"Love your enemies; for they shall tell you all your faults."

"The weakest foe boasts some revenging Power/The weakest friend some serviceable hour."

"Don't think to hunt two hares with one dog."

"Experience keeps a dear school, but fools will learn in no other."

"Let us beware of being lulled into a dangerous security of being weakened by internal contentions and division; of neglect in military exercises and disciplines in providing stores of arms and munitions of war; for the expenses required to prevent a war are much lighter than those that will, if not prevented, be necessary to maintain it."

"The way to be safe is never to be secure."

"Make yourselves sheep and the wolves will eat you."[216]

216. Evidently, Ol' Ben was not a big fan of that whole "Turn the other cheek" approach.

UNCLE BEN'S "LUCKY 13"

Franklin insightfully observed that man's problems were, for the most part, not a result of foul fate nor the whim of the gods, but rather self-inflicted:

> I believe in my conscience that Mankind is wicked enough to continue slaughtering one another as long as they can find enough money to pay the butchers.

However, the scientist in him could easily be more objective, pointing out the components of man's wickedness:

> All our different desires and passions proceed from and are reducible to this one point *uneasiness* though the means we propose to ourselves for expelling it are infinite. One *fame*, another *wealth*, a third *Power* as the means to gain this end.

Being that so many of our ills were/are self-inflicted, it stands to reason we could/can find a cure. To help us self-medicate, Franklin wrote a tract called "Rules for Making Oneself a Disagreeable Companion" in which he outlined what he considered the thirteen principles in what he dubbed "The Art of Virtue":

1. **Temperance**
2. **Silence**
3. **Order**
4. **Resolution**
5. **Frugality**
6. **Industry**
7. **Sincerity**
8. **Justice**
9. **Moderation**
10. **Cleanliness**
11. **Tranquility**
12. **Chastity**
13. **Humility**[217]

---

217. Franklin reportedly added "humility" only after an argument with a Quaker friend.

Conversely, any would-be Mind Slayer will be quick to realize how the polar opposites of each of these thirteen "virtues" can all too easily become powerful "vices" for mercilessly crushing your enemy's . . . dreams:

- **Tempt his *temperance*:** Irish wit Oscar Wilde (1854–1900) knew his limitations, admitting, "I can resist anything but temptation." Hardly surprising, Ol' Ben said it first: "The most effectual way to get rid of a certain temptation is to comply and satisfy it."

Back farther still, on the other side of the world in India, practitioners of the left-hand path of Tantra yoga were/are notorious for their epicurean excesses—believing that only by indulging our desires will we finally "burn up" the "fuel" of worldly distraction that prevents us from experiencing *samadhi* enlightenment.

Anytime an alert Mind Slayer discovers that his targeted victim harbors a shameful fetish or secret desire, he weasels his way closer into his target's confidence by "accepting" the target's desire, assuring his target that, whatever the fetish or desire, it's "normal" . . . but that no one else in the world—except the Mind Slayer, of course—really understands.

This kind of "nonjudgmental," "unconditional acceptance" is a powerful lure often used by cults who, after "forgiving" the new cult member, later uses his "confession" to slander and blackmail him should he ever betray the cult.

- **Disrupt his inner *silence*** with disturbing news of the world. Invade his sanctuary; give him no rest—sleepless men make bad decisions. Both devastating true revelations and confusing *mis*information can be used to *un*balance a foe.
- ***Order* can all too easily succumb to *dis*order:** The more organized your foe, the easier it is to *dis*organize him. A single missing tile and a billion-dollar space shuttle, one of the most sophisticated pieces of equipment ever on the face of this planet, is literally *toast*.

Martial arts wunderkind Bruce Lee valued simple techniques over more complicated ones, reminding his students that "the more complicated something is, the more easily it can be broken." The Battle of the Bulge again: the most up-to-date tank is useless unless you remember to "Fill 'er up!" at the pump. Or, a single "open mic" and you can kiss your political career good-bye.

- **Question his *resolution*** until you make him question his resolution himself. One thing is for certain, human beings are seldom truly certain of anything. The most successful of us simply learn to "fake it till we can make it," pretending we know what the hell we're talking about—hoping no one calls our bluff. Worse still, we all too often say "Sure," when what we meant to say was "I need more time to think it over."

Give your rival plenty of reasons (excuses) to doubt his choices, to go back on his word, to not keep that important appointment—making him undependable, alienating him from others, making him draw closer to you and making your schemes more palatable to him.

For a wise man, doubt is the beginning of wisdom. For a fool, doubt is just another day.

- **Help him spend his *frugality* unwisely:** The more energy you can make your enemy expend today, the less he'll have to throw at you tomorrow. Encourage him to spend his time, his money, and ultimately his life *un*wisely.

This is the principle behind a wise general's "probing" attacks, meant not only to test an enemy's battle line for weakness but also to force the enemy general to hurriedly reposition his defenders again and again in order to give added support to where you've made him *think* you plan on attacking—hopefully as far away as possible from the actual site of your impending attack. Such distractions and faux attacks are mandatory before any major military engagement in order to test an enemy's resolve and, as much as possible, distract him from your true objective.

Likewise, in business and politics, where this same principle is called "putting out feelers"—that is, testing the waters to ascertain how receptive your intended market is for a new product or how receptive the voting public is to a new idea.

- **Encourage laxity over *industry*:** In his 1645 *A Book of Five Rings,* Miyamoto Musashi outlines a combat ploy called "passing it on." Observing that human beings tend to unconsciously mirror one another (e.g., the way a simple yawn can be passed on from one person to another) so too a martial artist's attitude (alertness and stance) can be passed on to his opponent. In application: I deliberately relax my shoulders and consciously lower the tip of my sword, causing my opponent to *unconsciously* do the same. The instant I perceive him doing so—I attack!

This is also part of what Cao Cao (and Sun Tzu before him) meant when advising us to "first make ourselves invulnerable and then await the enemy's moment of vulnerability."

Whether on the battlefield or in the boardroom, one bad apple really does spoil the whole bunch. One lazy employee or soldier—allowed to get away with not pulling his share of the weight—will soon "infect" his fellows with the same indolence. It seldom works the other way around. Fresh meat doesn't cure spoiled meat.

Conversely, whether in an office or on the battlefield, we want to assure our foe that "There's plenty of time to do that later." The lazier he appears to the boss, the better you look. The more we can encourage our enemy to relax on the battlefield today, the better our chances of burying him on that field tomorrow.

- **Test his *sincerity*:** Make him question his own sincerity (dedication and resolve) until others see him doing so and start to question his sincerity (and trustworthiness) as well.

Finagle him into unexpected and demanding social situations where you can foist obligations[218] upon him. Maneuver him into positions where he has to volunteer, where the success or failure of a project is suddenly squarely on his shoulders. You can then graciously offer him your assistance—which puts you in a perfect position to further undermine him.

- ***Justice* becomes injustice becomes revenge:** Convince someone they've been passed over and pissed on and their first *natural reaction* will be to seek justice—recompense, restitution, reparations . . . *revenge* by any other name!

---

218. An "obligation" is a debt someone tells you that you owe them, usually for some real or imagined favor they did you in the past. "Duty" is the debt you owe yourself.

Convince such a wronged individual that you "feel their pain," that you understand and—again—that their need to get some "pay back!" is completely natural, understandable, and that they'll probably even be "doing God's work" and putting the universe back on track by seeking revenge.

It's always better when you can get permission—let alone a "blessing"—to do bad. Moderation in all things . . . except excess! There comes a tipping point where self-discipline becomes self-indulgence becomes self-righteousness. Take him to that precarious point . . . and push him over!

- ***Cleanliness* is next to Godliness . . . and next to impossible!** There's the *physically* clean and then there's the *psychologically* clean.

Outward physical cleanliness is easy to achieve—Ajax plus scrub, scrub, scrub. Inward psychological cleanliness is a whole 'nother pile o' dirt, primarily because there's no objective yardstick anywhere with which to measure psychological cleanliness. Even if you prefer calling it psychological health, you'll still be hard-pressed to find a consensus as to exactly what that means. That's because what worked for the caveman doesn't necessarily work for the congressman—yet both were probably perfectly adjusted to their times—psychologically healthy—if not socially moral.

Machiavelli reminded us "*Quod licet jovi licet bovi*,"[219] what works (and is socially accepted) in one place and time as psychologically healthy ends up getting you labeled thirteen ways from crazy somewhere else in more "enlightened" times.

This harkens back to the fact that we all have skeletons in our closet, dirty little secrets about ourselves (and our loved ones) we'd prefer to keep to ourselves, including the fact that we may still harbor "outdated" ideas that keep us forever on the fringe of the "politically correct" scene—hidden desires and secret prejudices we've learned not to express—at least not openly—in "polite" society.

How nice then when we can find a kindred spirit, someone who thinks and believes (and hates and, yes, lusts) like we do. The Mind Slayer will, smilingly, convince us he is just such a kindred spirit, friend, and confidant we've been looking for.

---

219. Latin: "What is permitted for the king is not permitted for the cattle."

- ***Tranquility:*** Which he should have already lost when you (1) disturbed his *silence* and (2) *dis*ordered his *order*!
- ***Chastity*** was Sony and Cher's adorable little daughter . . . Seen her lately? Nothing stays the same. But change isn't necessarily a bad thing, particularly when you're the one holding the bridle.

"Just say no" works only *before* someone knows what they're missing. This is true whether we're talking sex, drugs, or political power.

Change his world by giving him a taste of what he doesn't know he's been missing and he'll keep coming back to you for his fix.

- ***Humility* is also next to Godliness . . . and also next to impossible,** especially when you have someone constantly feeding your ego until you become fat and bloated on your own importance.

People who have no one to tell them when they've had a little too much to drink (and this includes being drunk on power!), when they're getting a little too "high on their own supply" of self-importance, those people inevitably crash and burn. O.J. Simpson, Michael Jackson, Adolf Hitler.

Everybody needs a posse, family and friends not afraid to tell you when you're screwing up big time—when you're overextending your resources by invading Russia too late in the year or, closer to home, sleeping with underaged boys. And what's with the ski mask, gloves, and razor-sharp hunting knife if you're only going to "talk" to your ex-wife?

Think how much better the world would be if we insisted on applying "Friends don't let friends drive drunk" to everybody in every situation—politicians, for instance? When someone starts "acting drunk"—talking crazy, doing stupid things—we'd take away their "keys" before they ended up hurting someone.

Become your foe's "Yes-man." By assuring someone they can do no wrong, you almost certainly assure they *will* do wrong.

Energy and persistence conquer all things.
—Benjamin Franklin

Part II

UPSTAGING YOUR ENEMY

INTRODUCTION:

"How to Create C.H.A.O.S. (and Get Away with It!)"

To achieve victory we must as far as possible make the enemy blind and deaf by sealing his eyes and ears, and drive his commanders to distraction by creating confusion in their minds.

—Mao Tse-Tung, *On Protracted War*, 1938

IF YOU haven't figured it out by now, *chaos is our friend*.

Sure, there's the usual panic, the running around and flailing of arms and screaming—sometimes *a lot* of screaming!—associated with chaos. But that's the chaotic kind of chaos, the kind we never see coming, the kind of chaos where nobody seems to know what to do and nobody's in charge.

Conversely, the chaos we're talking about creating is the C.H.A.O.S. kind of chaos *we start and we control*, the kind where we deliberately "create hurtles[220] and offer solutions."

It's debatable whether that oft-repeated "Human beings only use ten

220. Or hazards, hardships, Hell on earth, etc.

percent of their brains" claim is true or not, but what isn't in dispute is that human beings create ninety percent of their own problems.

This beggars the question that if we're so darn good at doing bad, at creating problems, why not create a little chaos for our enemies? After all, how hard can it be to first make our enemy's life miserable and then offer to make his life a little less miserable once he starts seeing things our way? Simple addition and subtraction—they do still teach that in first grade.

And you thought chaos—or C.H.A.O.S. at least—was always such a bad thing.

Having decided that chaos might not necessarily be a bad thing all the time, that we might actually be able to use it to our advantage and our enemy's disadvantage, beyond blindly trying to cultivate (unleash?) what seems to be our innate knack for creating problems, we'll also benefit by taking a look at how past masters used C.H.A.O.S. to their advantage. For example:

- How ancient Chinese strategists Sun Tzu and Ssu-ma adapted C.H.A.O.S. tactics to help them conquer armies on the battlefield.
- How "Ace of Spies" Sidney Reilly poured C.H.A.O.S. into his enemies' ears like hemlock.
- How Miyamoto Musashi's masterful use of C.H.A.O.S. technique made him unbeatable in one-on-one combat.
- And how conqueror and cult leader Omar took ultimate power and ruthlessly held onto that power from behind a C.H.A.O.S.-colored cloak of religion—scripture in one hand, sword in the other!

And, of course, the uses of chaos and crisis (whether naturally occurring or craftily engineered) are not lost on modern-day would-be Machiavellis:

> Rule 1: Never allow a crisis to go to waste; they are opportunities to do big things.
>
> —Rahm Emanuel, Obama's White House Chief of Staff

So first we learn how to literally spy out our enemy's weaknesses through our proper use of intelligence—both innate and gathered. Then we'll learn how to put the information and insights we've gathered to work, crafting no-win scenarios for our foes—employing both attractions and distractions—that are guaranteed to add a little more chaos to his life.

Chaos, whether naturally arising from our inattention to life, or else C.H.A.O.S. intentionally crafted by us—*creates opportunity*. But only if we're paying attention.

You might recall one of Dr. Lung's favorite sayings: "Pay attention now or pay the undertaker later!"[221]

221. Yes, Dr. Lung does have a habit of repeating himself . . . but only for *your* benefit!

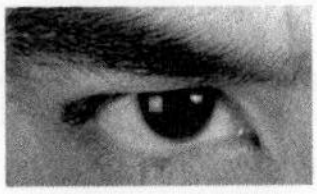

10.

Asian Arts of Espionage

Have good spies; get to know everything that happens among your enemies; sow dissension in their midst. To crush tyranny every method is fair.

—Lazare Carnot, 1793

I KNOW WHAT you're thinking. "Espionage" sounds like one of those big, fancy, "Damn, I'm probably gonna have to study!" words that you'll probably never have any practical use for in your life . . . Wrong. You use espionage everyday of your life:

- Trying to get a heads-up on who in the office is next in line for downsizing . . . and doing whatever you have to make sure it's *the other guy* who gets fed through the shredder.
- Trying to figure out why your wife wore that new, low-cut—"Isn't that just a wee-bit short, honey?"—dress to her regular Friday night "sewing circle" but for some reason didn't pick up when you called *not* to check up on her . . . Can you hear me now?
- Spying on your teenager without them finding out you're spying on them, snooping around for any inappropriate sex, drugs, and rock-'n'-roll, running a background check on their latest boyfriend . . . Ah! A *diary* . . .
- Counterespionage: Keeping your parents from finding out you know

already they're spying on you, that they're snooping around for all your inappropriate sex and drugs paraphernalia and Marilyn Manson memorabilia, while making sure they "discover" that *doctored* bio of your new boyfriend you left purposely peeking out from your diary.

- Finding out why your new Middle Eastern neighbor is stockpiling so much (1) fertilizer, when his lawn is smaller than your lawn, and (2) fuel oil, when there's not an Aladdin's lamp anywhere to be seen in his garage . . . in his basement . . .

In other words, in employing espionage you simply "hide what you have and reveal what you haven't."[222]

The art of espionage is, first and foremost, the twofold art of intelligence: using the innate intelligence you were born with, while gathering all the additional intelligence you can scrounge along the way:

> By "intelligence" we mean every sort of information about the enemy and his country—the basis, in short, of our own plans and operations. If we consider the actual basis of this information, how unreliable and transient it is, we soon realize that war is a flimsy structure that can easily collapse and bury us in its ruins. The textbooks agree, of course, that we should only believe reliable intelligence, and should never cease to be suspicious, but what is the use of such feeble maxims? They belong to that wisdom which for want of anything better scribblers or systems and compendia resort to when they run out of ideas. —Clausewitz, *On War*, 1832

Having acquired real-time information that is (1) sufficient to begin the task at hand while (2) constantly and consistently subject to updating, we can then confidently begin applying that intelligence where it will do the most good—or, from our opponent's perspective, the most harm!

How much better it is to be able to *outsmart*, rather than to have to *outfight* or—God forbid!—have to *outrun* your enemies:

> To those who congratulated him on his victory in the battle against the Arcadians, he said: "It would be better

222. J.F.C. Fuller, *A History of the Western World*, 1956.

> if our intelligence were beating them rather than our strength." —Archidamus III (d. 338 B.C.), King of Sparta

First comes the gathering of *intelligence the noun* (facts and figures, photos and firsthand reports from reliable sources). Then begins the practice of *intelligence the verb* (acting with intelligence by putting our intelligence into action). Intelligence the verb has been succinctly defined as:

> the ability to assess situations never previously encountered and to rapidly come to an appropriate response [that] requires integrated information.[223]

There are many notable Western warrior strategists who were not only born with intelligence but who made a concerted effort prior to battle, in the heat of battle, and in the aftermath of battle to continue gathering intelligence—names like Alexander the Great, Hannibal, Napoleon, and Patton immediately come to mind. Yet when we think of intelligence—innate, gathered . . . and then *ruthlessly* applied—the first name that comes to most already knowledgeable minds is the ancient Eastern master Sun Tzu.[224]

While Sun Tzu himself studied the tactics and techniques of all the strategists who came before him—incorporating proven tactics and techniques, discarding the superfluous—there were few—if any—who came after him who did not bow deeply before "The Master." Down through the centuries, even the Japanese honor the master they call "Sonshi"—ironically using many of his tactics when infiltrating and invading his homeland! (More on the Japanese art of spying in the following chapter.)

And perhaps it was inevitable that a handful of Westerners, those already blessed with intelligence of the innate kind, should successfully master the Asian arts of gathering intelligence. (More on Sidney Reilly in the following chapter.)

> Great advantage is drawn from knowledge of your adversary, and when you know the measure of his intelligence and character you can use it to play on his weaknesses.
>
> —King Frederick the Great, 1747

---

223. Christof Koch, "*A Theory of Consciousness,*" *Scientific American,* July/August 2009: 16–19.

224. The Chinese "tzu" actually means "master;" hence, Sun Tzu means "master sun." While usually pronounced *Sun-Sue* in the West, a more accurate pronunciation is *Swan-Zoo*.

SUN TZU STORMS THE GATE!

How can any man say what he should do himself if he is ignorant what his adversary is about?

—Lieutenant-General Antoine-Henri Baron de Jomini,
***Summary of the Art of War*, 1838**

Your enemy is figuratively—sometimes literally—a fortress. Safe behind his thick, seemingly impenetrable walls, he laughs at the mere thought that a pismire like you could ever pose a serious threat to his position. From high atop what he believes to be unassailable parapets, he tosses the odd insult your way, the way an indulgent master dismissively tosses an already gnawed bone to his mangy dog far beneath him.

Sitting across the negotiation table from you, your enemy snickers at your efforts at securing peace. In his mind, your agreeing to "negotiate" with him only works to his advantage by (1) making him appear your equal, (2) making his past terrorist acts appear legitimate, and (3) delaying any real progress while he figures out how to finally refine weapons-grade uranium.

One of Sun Tzu's staunchest rules was that "Success has never been associated with long delay." Negotiation is never your enemy screaming "I surrender!" Negotiation is simply delay, and delay only works to your enemy's advantage.

While Sun Tzu's ideal was to "win without fighting," for Sun Tzu this meant (1) keeping your own ability to wage war up to par while (2) taking advantage of up-to-date intelligence to keep an eye on your enemy—discouraging and stifling any military adventuring on his part.

Negotiating with an enemy growing stronger—more dangerous—by the day doesn't make sense and so doesn't enter into Sun Tzu's master strategy.

War is not about negotiation. It's not even about confrontation when attempts at negotiation fail. War is first, foremost, and *only* about penetration. The only reason my enemy would even consider negotiation is because he knows that I am more than willing and able to penetrate his borders, penetrate his states, his cities, penetrate the walls of his mighty fortress, and, finally, thrust him through with my rapier! Let Dr. Freud puff away at his "only a cigar" while he ponders the deeper ramifications of all this aggression. I'm too busy celebrating my *victory!*

Before all this, however, I must penetrate my enemy's *mind*, deciding how much of his braggadocio and bluster is just bluff. Through intelligence—both innate and gathered—I may discover that, while his sabers rattle, they do so inside rusty scabbards, or that the rattling of his saber is caused by the *trembling* of his hand—the tremor in his voice matched only by the tremor in his hands. And that the pallor of his face doesn't match the valor of his words.

Ideally, I discover these facts *before* the girding of loins, before I have to beat my plowshare into a sword.

Thus, I use intelligence to burst the bully's bubble to reveal the scared little boy trapped inside, ripping aside the curtain to reveal the "great and powerful Oz" in all his glory.

Our enemy's sneering face is suddenly replaced by a visage carved by fear, his swagger and strut replaced by a stumble and then a final and fatal fall. His patronizing dismissal of our goal is soon replaced by creeping doubt, paralyzing fear, and, finally, realization that we *will* reach our goal.

> "Over my *dead* body!" he squawks.
> We wouldn't have it any other way.
> Master his mind and you've mastered the man.

Jin: The Three Types of Force

Prussian King Frederick the Great (1712–1786) knew the formula:

> The art of war is divided between art and stratagem. What cannot be done by force, must be done by stratagem.

And vice versa: what cannot be accomplished by stratagem (strategy) must be resolved by force. What Frederick called stratagem is just another word for intelligence—both kinds.

But when force must be used—and sometimes it must—from Sun Tzu down to Desert Stormer Norman Schwarzkopf all agree that, first, *only the amount of force necessary to accomplish the mission* should be applied—what's often referred to as a "surgical strike." Don't use a chainsaw when a scalpel will do the job.

Second, any use of force should be *quick, with as little loss of life as possible*.

Even when a use of force was called for—justified and judicial—Sun Tzu differentiated three kinds of *jin* (force):

Zhi jin is straight *yang-cheng* force. Symbolized by the straight line, epitomized by orthodox (*cheng*) thought and tactics (e.g., battle formations arrayed across from one another, in personal combat standing toe-to-toe with an opponent). Metaphorically, *Zhi jin* refers to the "expected," what is rational, logical, and likely to occur given specific parameters.

Bian jin is "ever-changing" *yin-ch'i* force. Symbolized by the circle, epitomized by unorthodox "outside-the-box" (*ch'i*) thought and actions (e.g., the use of special forces units, guerrilla tactics, and spies). In other words, we do the unexpected in order to force our opponent into doing the expected.

Tin jin means "listening force" and refers to developing a "sensitivity" to circumstance and flux, to instantly adjusting oneself accordingly; changing mission parameters to fit changing realities in light of updated intelligence. This is very similar to "The Flying Dragon" in Cao Cao's philosophy "going with the flow."

Proper use of "listening force" then allows us to choose whatever degree of *Zhi jin* and/or *Bian jin* is appropriate to accomplish the mission, win the battle, or end the war.

Kai-men: How to Penetrate

Force has no place where there is need of skill.
—Herodotus (484–420 B.C.)

So we never use brawn when brains will do? Not necessarily.

There are times when you do want to so totally defeat an enemy that he'll be so traumatized he'll never, ever even consider making war against you and yours again.

Ruthless attitude? Yes. Realistic? Hell yes!

Asian strategists often refer to the human body as "The City of Nine

Gates" in reference to the nine "openings"[225] through which you could both physically and mentally attack an opponent (see Figure 15, p. 210).

For example, during physical combat, our eyes and ears can be blinded both literally and strategically through the use of stealth, skullduggery, and subterfuge.[226] Pleasant aromas and pleasing tastes (both of which may disguise deadly poisons!) can be used to trick our nose and tantalize our taste buds. And how many of us are truly immune to the allure of sex?

In order to penetrate these nine gates, ancient Chinese strategists used six principles, known as *kai men*, literally "to penetrate," often simply known as "Opening the Gate."

Kai-men was (is?) the art of the mysterious—and greatly feared—*Lin Kuei* (pronounced *lin-kway*), China's version of the ninja. The Moshuh Nanren, the Chinese emperors's secret police also practiced a variation of *kai-men* craft known as *liu da-kai* (a.k.a. *liu da kai-men*), a catch-all for any and all skills necessary to penetrate defenses—be those defenses physical or psychological.[227]

Down through the centuries, *kai-men* has been used successfully for designing battlefield strategy, winning in individual one-on-one combat, and for crafting psychological ploys guaranteed to penetrate an enemy's nine gates. In the past, various *wu shu kung-fu* styles have also used variations of these six *kai-men* principles for organizing their combat techniques.

Today, savvy Asian businessmen likewise employ *kai-men* to get the upperhand on their competitors.

Before we can begin to effectively apply *kai-men* to our advantage, we have to learn the difference between a reaction and a response.

We all have natural reactions to a perceived attack—be that attack physical or verbal. Take, for example, a physical attack where an assailant tries to bring a baseball bat crashing down onto our head. Instinctively, we react by

---

225. Eyes, ears, nose, mouth, anus, and urethra (generic/symbolic for all the sex organs, and, yes, counting the vagina that would make ten actual "gates" for a woman. Keep in mind that—sorry, ladies—most ancient strategies were designed by, for, and against men).

226. For a complete training course on the uses of stealth, skullduggery, and subterfuge, see Dr. Haha Lung and Christopher B. Prowant's *Shadowhand: Secrets of Ninja Taisavaki* (Paladin, 2002), *Knights of Darkness* (Citadel, 2004), *Ninja Shadowhand: The Art of Invisibility* (Citadel, 2004).

227. The Japanese equivalent is ninjutsu, the "art of the ninja." For a complete training course on ninjutsu, see *Nine Halls of Death: Secrets of Ninja Mind Mastery* by Dr. Haha Lung and Eric Tucker (Citadel, 2007).

THE NINE GATES

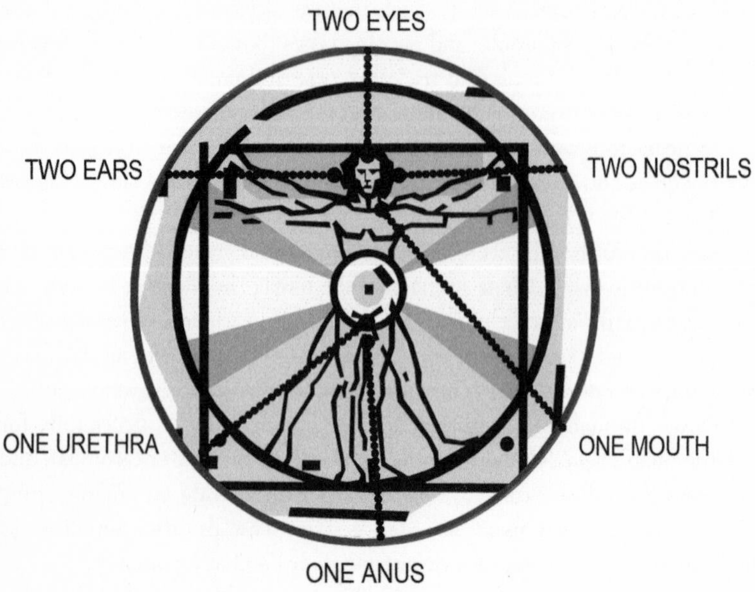

Figure 15.

throwing both our arms up (to block the blow) while crouching-cringing lower (trying to make ourselves a smaller target). This is how we instinctively react.

A trained martial artist, however, doesn't *react*; he is trained to *respond*. Continuing with the above example, having practiced self-defense techniques that take into consideration a human being's already innate, ingrained natural reactions, the trained person being attacked turns the instinctive reaction of our arms flying upward into (1) an angled forearm block (designed to deflect the bludgeon) while (2) simultaneously crouching and striking a blow into the attacker's body.[228]

---

228. For further instruction designed to turn your natural reactions into martial responses, see Dr. Haha Lung and Christopher B. Prowant's *Mind Fist* (Citadel, 2008) and *Lost Fighting Arts of Vietnam* (Citadel, 2006).

Kai-men grew out of, and still retains the priorities of, the ideal fighting strategy of the kung-fu monks of the Shaolin monastery:

> **Avoid rather than check. Check rather than block. Block rather than strike. Strike rather than maim, and maim rather than kill.**

Thus, in any confrontation, be it physical or psychological, use of *kai-men* strategy offers us six escalating levels of involvement:

- ***Chan* ("to reel"):** We avoid confrontation and contact with a superior force (at least until we're strong enough to correctly counter that force). Classic guerrilla warfare: avoid direct contact with the enemy. Fly under the radar.

  In Drunken Style Kung-fu[229] this tactic takes on the form of bobbing the head (making it harder to strike) and weaving (as if drunk and staggering) the body from side-to-side to (1) avoid contact with your attacker and (2) place you in a more strategic position from which to counterattack. Think: Muhammad Ali's "rope-a-dope."

  In a psychological situation, or in a financial situation for that matter, when possible, judiciously avoid those situations and individuals who have the upper hand until such time as you are emotionally (and/or financially) capable of giving them a run for their money.
- ***Dan* ("to brush"):** Unable to avoid confrontation altogether, in a physical situation, instead of backpeddling from an attacker (he'll only keep charging forward) you instead step *forward diagonally*, avoiding his initial attack, placing yourself to the side and *outside* his attack. From this advantageous position, you can either counterattack or else brush past him and flee.

  In a psychological situation, when a superior's suspicion has been alerted to your possibly being/becoming competition to him, you brush past him by convincing him you're no threat . . . until you're strong enough to show him what a threat you can actually be! Classic Sun Tzu: when strong, appear weak.

229. Variously called Drunken Monkey Kung-fu and Drunk Monk Kung-fu.

- ***Ti* ("to take up"):** This is where psychological confrontation and physical confrontation begin to blur into one another. Unable to avoid an opponent altogether, unable to brush past him by convincing him you're no threat, you find yourself forced to confront him.

  In a physical situation, you'll want to ready your body for possible violence, yet do so without taking an overtly aggressive posture[230] that might (1) alert him to your defensive capabilities and/or (2) further enrage him to attack who is as of yet still undecided on whether or not to take it to that next (violent) level.

  There is still a chance at this level to use a *Dan* ploy and convince your would-be attacker you're no threat. However, in the same way you deal with a bully by standing up to him even when you know you don't have a snowball's chance in hell of winning a knock-down-drag-out fight with him, so too you may be able to bluff your way through by deliberately taking a more aggressive stance. Sun Tzu again: *when weak, appear strong.* But beware: street bullies and Wall Street financiers can smell a phony a mile away!
- ***Bao* ("to hold"):** At this point, the confrontation turns ugly. None of your avoidance tactics have worked. Your enemy is on to you. He knows you've been B.S.ing him all along. He's out for blood—whether emotional blood, financial blood, or your actual blood. He's done talking and he starts swinging!

  Viet Cong fighters were taught to seize the belt of an opponent.[231] This tactic was applied both physically and psychologically. Physically, it meant that, in a hand-to-hand confrontation with a larger opponent (e.g., a larger Frenchman or American) Viet Cong fighters stayed in close, "on the inside," to prevent their larger opponent from being able to strike with his more powerful arms and feet.

  Psychologically, *Bao* tactics had Viet Cong infiltrating deep into

---

230. Surreptitiously sliding one foot back, putting a little spring into your legs, finding an excuse to bring your hands nearer your face (e.g., rubbing your chin). For more tips and techniques on fighting back life's bullies, see Dr. Haha Lung and Christopher B. Prowant's *Mind Fist* (Citadel, 2008).

231. To better understand this principle and for a complete training course in Cao Dai kung-fu, see *Lost Fighting Arts of Vietnam* by Dr. Haha Lung (Citadel, 2006).

enemy-held territory, blending in to villages and towns. Again by seizing the belt, by literally staying in close to their opponent, they made it more difficult for more traditional American *cheng* forces to do large-scale bombardment for fear of collateral damage (i.e. wounding noncombatants and/or hitting their own troop with "friendly fire").

In business, as in all matters black science, the *Bao* rule is always "Keep your friends close and your enemies closer."

- ***Kua* ("to carry on"):** Having physically "closed" with an enemy, when he pushes, we pull. He pulls, we push. Instead of trying to stifle his forward momentum (objects in motion tending to stay in motion), we instead add our force to his force, depriving him of his force while doubling our own. This is the principle underlying such martial disciplines as *juijutsu*, *aikido*, and *tai chi.*

  In business, the *kua* rule is "In for a penny, in for a pound." And even though you're warned in business to "never throw good money after bad," it's hard to cut your losses and pull out of a deal after you've already invested time and money. That's why it's so easy for a Mind Slayer to manipulate someone to "stay the course" and even "double-down," to continue to invest in schemes the investor may already have a bad feeling about by implying the investor would be "foolish," "a coward," even a "traitor" if he quit now. Emotionally, this is why good people stay in bad marriages, gangs, cults, and that CD of the month club.
- ***Ding* ("to clash"):** Here is where we meet a threat head-on, forcibly blocking an attack with equal force, using force to defeat force. Mistaking your desire to avoid bloodshed for weakness, your enemy attacks and you forcibly meet his attack with corresponding force. Physical example: he throws a punch and you instantly respond with an aggressive upward turn of your forearm that serves as both your block and your counterstrike, crippling his attacking arm.

  Psychological example: you're attacked verbally and respond in kind with devastating observations and revelations against your detractor you've been banking for just such an emergency—intelligence gained through your astute and timely use of espionage.

  Just remember, even when forced to "ding" with an opponent, to clash toe-to-toe, remember: We fight *smart*. And we fight *dirty*!

Sun Tzu Used Spies (So Why Can't We?)

Be subtle! Be subtle! and use your spies for every kind of business.
—Sun Tzu's Art of War XIII:17

It's somewhat telling that while Sun Tzu is known primarily for his brilliant battlefield victories, the final chapter of his *Ping-fa* (*Art of War*) deals solely with the use of spies. When we consider that Master Sun's ideal was to win without fighting, to avoid going to war if at all possible while still retaining the integrity and validity of the state, it's not unusual that he would see the free use of espionage as not only a precursor to any campaign against an enemy but, best-case scenario, see intelligence—the gathered variety—as the best way to avoid war altogether. Thus, within the twenty-five verses of Chapter XIII, Sun Tzu not only gives us sound reasons for not going to war but also instructs us how, through the proper use of pre-war intelligence, we can avoid war altogether. Again, worst-case scenario and battle is joined, the diligent use of spies, both our own homegrown and those we reap from the enemy, can help bring about a speedy dénouement to the wanton destruction.

Use of Master Sun's Chapter XIII is the surest way to ensure our enemy will in short order be filing for Chapter 11 . . . *battlefield bankruptcy!*

Notice that Master Sun devotes the first two verses of Chapter XIII not to espionage directly but rather to reminding us how quickly a campaign can go if we *don't* use spies, including "heavy loss on the people . . . a drain on the resources of the State . . . commotion at home and abroad"[232] with "as many as seven hundred thousand families" prevented from laboring for the state.

In XIII:3, Sun Tzu continues to point out the obvious (wars can drag on for years), concluding that it's a shame to allow this to happen when, for only the cost of a few pieces of silver, reliable spies can be employed to tip the balance.

> Thus, what enables the wise sovereign and the good general to strike and conquer, and achieve things beyond the reach of ordinary men, is foreknowledge. —XIII:4

---

232. Unless otherwise noted, all Sun Tzu quotes are from Giles's 1910 translation of Sun Tzu's *ping-fa*.

Foreknowledge—*intelligence* by any other name. And how are we to come by such foreknowledge?

> Now this foreknowledge cannot be elicited from spirits; it cannot be obtained inductively from experience, nor by any deductive calculation. Knowledge of the enemy's dispositions can only be obtained from other men. —XIII:5

And those "other men" Sun Tzu refers to are, you guessed it, *spies*, which he immediately arranges into five categories:

- **Local spies**, a.k.a. "Locals," are people already living or working in an off-limits area (country, military base, office) housing information you need. Often, Local spies give up information inadvertently—everybody likes to brag about their hometown and complain about their job. Others do so because they have a grudge. Still other potential Local spies can be bribed or threatened into giving up information and performing a couple "harmless" deeds.

Reading reports and studying aerial maps may give you a general understanding of an area but nothing beats "boots on the ground." And nobody knows an area better than the people who live and work there:

> Whether the object be to crush an army, to storm a city, or to assassinate an individual, it is always necessary to begin by finding out the names of the attendants, the aides-de-camp, the door-keepers and sentries of the general in command. Our spies must be commissioned to ascertain these. —XIII:19

This category of spy includes the little people we discussed earlier, those often-overlooked, unseen individuals who nonetheless see everything.

When trying to gain information on a targeted person, frequent the places he frequents—stores, bars, perhaps his place of work. Striking up casual conversations, gleaning all the information you can about him: work habits, play habits, what and where he likes to eat. Stay on the alert for any juicy tidbits and/or hints of scandal you can follow-up on. Investigative journalism 101.

Remember that little people love it when someone shows them attention, when someone treats them like big people. Trust me, there's nothing that lonely secretary sitting at the bar would like better than for you to buy her a(nother) drink while she rambles on and on about what a jackass her boss—your target—is. That fantastic Colombian ambush scene in Harrison Ford's *Clear and Present Danger* (1994) was the result of an accomplished Mind Slayer getting in good (in more ways than one!) with a horny—*talkative*—secretary who just happened to work for a congressman.

Paparazzi are notorious for bribing doormen, maids, and ex-boyfriends in order to gain access to just the right spot at just the right time to get the right shot. A camera . . . a sniper rifle scope . . . both have lenses . . .

- **Inward spies**, a.k.a. "Internal spies," are similar to Local spies in that both are potential "*Fifth Columnists*." Inward spies are only a little further up the food chain than Local spies. Definitely not little people, Inward spies are people already embedded and entrenched, inside your targeted area of operation, occupying strategic locations, key positions. Such people can easily be convinced to provide all the information and logistic assistance you need simply by your promises—bribes or threats—of what will happen to them when you come to power. Think bureaucrats and politicians.
- **Converted spies**, a.k.a. "Double agents." Their spies become your spies: "The enemy's spies who have come to spy on us must be sought out, tempted with bribes, led away and comfortably housed. Thus they will become converted spies and available for our service." —XIII:20

Since so many spies are inherently mercenary at heart, when caught in the act, spies looking out for their own skin quickly "turn," becoming double agents. These agents in turn (no pun intended) will then help you attract additional spies to your cause:

> It is through the information brought by the converted spy that we are able to acquire and employ local and inward spies . . . The end and aim of spying in all its varieties is knowledge of the enemy; and this knowledge can only be derived, in the first instance, from the converted spy. Hence it is essential that the converted spy be treated with the utmost liberality. —XIII:21/23

Of course, any spymaster worth his official OO7 Fan Club decoder ring is always on the alert that his new double agent isn't actually a triple agent, an agent provocateur sent to sow distraction, disruption, and doubt. Recall from *The Godfather* (1972) how an ailing Don Corleone correctly foresaw that, after he was dead, the other crime families would move against Michael, the new head of the Corleone family. The Don cautioned his son—correctly, it turned out—that whichever Corleone lieutenant first came to Michael proposing that Michael meet to negotiate with the other families, that man would be a traitor setting Michael up to be assassinated.

- **Doomed spies**, a.k.a. "Expendable agents." Remember Cao Cao's ball of wax ploy? Cao Cao knew full well he was sending his spy to his death:

> It is owing to his information, again, that we can cause the doomed spy to carry false tidings to the enemy. —XIII:22

A classic "doomed spy" story comes from World War II where the spy used was literally doomed before he began . . . because he was *already dead!* In a brilliant disinformation plot the equal of Cao Cao's ball of wax, Allied intelligence dressed a corpse in a British officer's uniform and then dumped it into the Atlantic off of Spain where a passing German ship was certain to spot it. Handcuffed to the dead man's wrist was a briefcase filled with false documents containing disinformation about Allied troop strength and movement, and about where the inevitable Allied liberation beachhead was to occur. German intelligence, ironically the envy of the espionage world prior to World War I,[233] was completely taken in by the ruse.

In everyday use: you allow the local watercooler gossipmonger to "overhear" or otherwise "uncover"[234] slanderous information—true or false—that they'll soon be wallpapering the office with. By the time the falseness of the allegation comes to light (1) it should already be too late to save the reputation of the targeted person and (2) any and all blame for the spreading of the false information will land squarely in the lap of your doomed agent.

233. See the section on Japanese intelligence operations, pages 234–50.

234. Such people love playing detective so don't leave your information just lying around in too obvious a spot. Information too easy to come by is always suspect.

Ideally, you would arrange for someone you don't like to spread the false rumor, killing two birds with one stone.

- **Surviving spies**, a.k.a. "Living Spies," are your true James Bonds, highly trained, highly valued agents whose information is always timely and their killings always tasteful—shaken, not stirred. These are called surviving spies because (1) they have a knack for surviving, at least long enough to bring back vital information, and (2) because you want them to survive—as opposed to their being expendable.

Corporate whistle-blowers fall into this category, brave souls who step forward to right a wrong. Oskar Schindler would also qualify. Someone in the right place at the right time with access to timely intelligence. Valuable assets indeed, which must be protected. An obvious modern-day example of this would be the true story of FBI agent Frank Pistone who spent years undercover infiltrating the Mafia.[235]

According to Master Sun, a secret network composed of all five types of these agents, what he calls the "divine manipulation of the threads,"[236] is a sovereign's most precious asset:

> Hence it is only the enlightened ruler and the wise general who will use the highest intelligence of the army for purposes of spying, and thereby they achieve great results. Spies are a most important element in war, because on them depends an army's ability to move. —XIII:25

For Sun Tzu, spies occupy a special place in any army and should therefore be accorded special treatment, more leeway than more orthodox troops, and they should always be amply rewarded.

But as important as spies are, the spy handler—station chief, coordinator, us—is even more important. A spy handler must be both level-headed and shrewd (XIII:14), possess benevolence and straightforwardness (XIII:15), and, most important, possess what Sun Tzu calls "subtle ingenuity of mind,"

---

235. As portrayed in the 1996 movie *Donnie Brasco*.

236. In *The Seven Classics of Ancient China* (Basic Books, 1993) Ralph D. Sawyer translates this phrase as "spiritual methodology."

without which he'll be uncertain of the truth of spies' reports (XIII:16). And he will swiftly punish any breach of security:

> If a secret piece of news is divulged by a spy before the time is ripe, he must be put to death together with the man to whom the secret was told. —XIII:18

Three may keep a secret if two of them are dead.
—Ben Franklin

SIDNEY REILLY: RULES OF THE WHITE DRAGON

James Bond is someone I dreamed up in my imagination—he's not a Sidney Reilly.
—Ian Fleming

Sigmund Georgrivich Rosenblum, better known to the world as Sidney Reilly, born in Odessa, Russia, in 1874[237] to a well-to-do Polish-Jewish family, has been hailed as the twentieth century's first "superspy."[238]

Ironically, it would be another Pole, Felix Dzerzhinsky—patron saint of the dread KGB—who would bring this "Ace of Spies" down in the end. But between the time of his uneventful birth and his *apparent*—shrouded in mystery—death some fifty years later, Reilly wrote the rule book on spying. It's even been convincingly argued that he created the modern art of espionage—and not just as the real-life inspiration for Ian Fleming's 007.

In 1890, at the age of sixteen, Sidney (by then calling himself Sigmund) fell in love with his first cousin but this forbidden love was not to be.[239] The resulting heartbreak on young Sidney's part, not to mention the resultant family scandal, forced Sigmund-Sidney to leave home, eventually arriving in the east end of London.

Though earning a well-deserved reputation as a ladies' man (read:

---

237. "Reilly fabricated so many stories about his early life that no one is entirely certain of his real name or when and where he was actually born." ("006?" By Jerry D. Morelock, Ph.D. *Armchair General*, January 2010.)

238. Morelock, 2010: ibid.

239. Sidney reportedly carried a torch for his cousin for the rest of his life.

womanizer!) in later life, in 1898 at age twenty-four we find him "settling down" by marrying a well-off widow named Margeret Thomas.

Around this same time, in anticipation of Britain's increasing rivalry with Imperial Russia, the nascent British Special Intelligence Service (SIS) began deliberately recruiting Russian émigrés to act as spies—an example of Sun Tzu's "Local spies."

It took little convincing for Sigmund Rosenbaum to become Sidney Reilly SIS secret agent.[240]

The enemy of my enemy being my friend, as the twentieth century dawned, both Britain and Japan eyed Russian ambitions with suspicion. Japan's growing annoyance with Russia culminated in war.

The culmination of Imperial Japan's growing annoyance with Imperial Russia was by now an all but forgotten pissing contest called the Russo-Japanese War (1904–1905). Japan got the upper hand with a surprise attack on the Russian naval installation at Port Arthur (now Lu-shun, China), catching the Russian fleet napping and sent them to the bottom—a success the Japanese would repeat scene for scene some thirty-five years later at Pearl Harbor (including obtaining pre-attack intelligence from well-placed spies or, in this instance, one spy in particular—Sidney Reilly).

The story goes that Japanese Black Dragon[241] "ninja" operatives were having trouble obtaining detailed plans for Port Arthur since the Russians were especially alert for any Japanese "tourists" skulking in the area—could their British "friends" suggest an alternate course of action? The enemy of my enemy being my friend, the spy handlers at SIS knew just the man, a promising young operative with an eye for detail.

Reilly Rule #1: Dot the *I*'s

This was Reilly's favorite expression, by the way.[242] Another way of saying "Pay attention even to trifles."[243] Inherent within this marching mantra is

240. SIS later became MIIC and ultimately MI-6. Today, MI-5 (created in 1909) handles internal/domestic security and counterespionage (similar to the FBI), while MI-6 handles external/overseas security (think CIA).

241. The complete history and training methods of the Black Dragon secret society is covered in depth in the chapters that follow.

242. Kettle, 1983:123.

243. Adage from Miyamoto Musashi's *A Book of Five Rings*. See the "Musashi: Taste the Wind, Ride the Wave" chapter that follows.

the obvious double entendre of it sometimes being necessary to "Dot the *eyes*" (i.e., do a little violence to further a lot of peace). Sidney Reilly would prove a master of both.

SIS was correct in reasoning that a "fellow Russian" would draw less attention around Port Arthur. However, even Sidney found it difficult to obtain pertinent information about the makeup and maneuvers of the Russian fleet.

Reilly Rule #2: Think Outside the Box (or in This Instance, *Inside* a Box-Kite!)

Unable to successfully infiltrate the heavily guarded port facility in order to obtain accurate intelligence, Reilly hit upon the idea of sending a small boy (some versions say a dwarf) aloft in a large Chinese box kite. From this vantage point, hovering high above the port, Reilly's early version of a U2 pilot was able to accurately sketch the entire layout of the Russian fleet at Port Arthur. Reilly then passed this diagram along to the waiting Japanese fleet. The Japanese fleet promptly sank the Russian fleet.

Ecstatic of their Port Arthur victory, even the usually stoic (and xenophobic) Japanese tipped their hat to Sidney, dubbing him "The White Dragon" in grudging admiration of a *gaijin*[244] able to master Asian espionage techniques.[245] This dubious honor is somewhat ironic given the fact that, as we will see in the following chapter on Japanese spying techniques, some experts trace the emergence of modern Japanese espionage to their having learned the craft from Europeans—in this instance, Prussian (German) intelligence.

Reilly Rule #3: People Only Know What You Show Them

In other words, you are who you appear to be . . . until someone else shows up who knows different!

It wasn't enough for Sidney—whose mind always played somewhere between paranoia and profit margin—that the SIS provided their agents not only with cover stories while operating in the field but also saw to their living

---

244. Jp. "Foreigner," particularly a European.

245. The color white is, incidentally, also associated with death in many Asian locales. Something Reilly was also familiar—adept—with.

arrangements while in Britain (e.g., housing, education, and/or cover employment in various schools and crafts)—all of which helped further their overall knowledge,[246] making them even more useful in the field. Just to be on the safe side (paranoia), and in order to increase opportunity (profit margin), Sidney liked to craft his own "identity," keeping a spare or two in his emergency travel bag just in case!

Thus, at one time Reilly claimed to be a chemist, with a Ph.D. from Heidelburg University. You have to remember that this was slightly back before Al Gore invented the Internet, so it was a lot harder to research someone's education history.

Sidney Reilly's actual education took the following course.

In 1904, under the name Stanislaus George Reilly, Sidney attended Britain's Royal School of Mines in South Kensington, graduating with an electrical engineering degree in 1905. It's probable the SIS paid for his tuition, grooming him for bigger and better things by helping him acquire skills no budding spy should be caught dead without. Sidney then went on to attend Trinity College, Cambridge, from 1905 until 1908.

Leaving Britain again in 1908, presumably still in the employ of the SIS, Sidney returned to Russia, to St. Petersburg, where he immediately obtained a job with an armaments firm—Sun Tzu's "Inward spy," the perfect position from which to report on Russian military arms developments.

Irony was a recurrent theme in Reilly's life. No one in Russia suspected his involvement in the Port Arthur disaster, so now Sidney, the man most responsible for the destruction of the Russian fleet, landed the job of being a Russian procurement agent for a German firm that had contracts to rebuild the Russian fleet! A clear case of the fox watching the henhouse . . . after the fox has already helped burn down the henhouse![247] And, as if to prove the point, in 1910 Sidney was able to steal the latest German battleship designs intended for the Russians. These designs then ended up in the hands of his friends at the SIS.

---

246. "Know the ways of all professions." *A Book of Five Rings* by Miyamoto Musashi.

247. "Men have memories as short as the hangman's rope is long." *Dracula's Art of War* by Vlad Tepes.

Reilly Rule #4: Hide in Plain Sight

Despite the inherent covert nature of his vocation, Reilly was no shrinking violet. Often, even when on assignment, Sidney literally lived "the life of Reilly," maintaining lavish apartments in several major European cities, including Paris and Berlin, where he hosted grand high-society get-togethers for celebrities and social climbers, wining and dining foreign businessmen and military men, while bedding their lonely—always talkative—wives, sisters, and even mothers, always on the alert for what Sidney called a "champagne coup" (i.e., loose tongues loosened even more by a bit o' the bubbly!):

> The deliberate courting of attention was all part of the act. He indeed enjoyed the high life and was a great womanizer; but, underneath it all, as his professional reports made clear, he was a very shrewd man. Part thug, part chameleon, he was above all a skilled and ruthless manipulator of other people. He used women as easily as men, even in the most desperate of revolutionary conspiracies. There is no instance of any woman ever giving him away—some even went to their deaths in the terrible summer of 1918 rather than betray him. —Michael Kettle, *Sidney Reilly: The True Story of The World's Greatest Spy*, 1983

Reilly Rule #5: Money Is Only Good If You Can Get to It

Long before G. Gordon Liddy[248] and Oliver North, Sidney Reilly invented the rainy-day slush fund, always making certain to have plenty of "off-the-books" funds available to pay for (1) worthwhile information and (2) hiring good help.

Sidney also knew the importance of keeping money in several banks under several different names and in keeping a ready supply of easy to get to "dash cash" for those times when it's necessary to get out of Dodge (or in Sidney's case, St. Petersburg, Berlin, Paris, etc.).

Much of Reilly's early financing came from his SIS handlers but being on

248. *Will* by G. Gordon Liddy (St. Martin's Press, 1995). Required reading at the Black Science Institute.

an expense account—no matter how liberal—subject to prevailing political winds and whims was not dependable.

Realizing this early on, Sidney began investing wisely, buying antiques and Napoleonic art. As a result, within a relatively short time, he had amassed a small personal fortune. This allowed him exceptional leeway for a spy, since, rather than being at the mercy of whimsical bureaucratic purse strings, Sidney was in position (financially) to employ his own network of informants and bankroll his own operations with his personal money.[249] This personal fortune came in handy especially following the Bolshevik (Communist) takeover of Russia in 1918.

For example, on one occasion in 1918, Sidney bankrolled a rogue operation attempt to capture Lenin, his proposed successor Trotsky, and other members of the Bolshevik Central Committee.

Reilly Rule #6: The More People Know You . . . the Less People Know You

We seldom see ourselves as others see us. In many instances, that's a good thing. We want—need—others to see us differently than what we really are. We need that bully to see us as someone who can stick up for himself—even when we're scared to death on the inside. We want that babe at the bar to see us as suave and debonair—even when we're scared to death on the inside.

A show of hands: how many of us, arriving home from work, first hang up our coat and hat . . . and then hang up the *mask* we've been wearing all day? For some, it's even more than one mask. For most people, it gets awful tiring having to lug that "Yes, sir. Right away, Boss!" mask around all day.

For others, like the "Ace of Spies," it's just another day at the office.

Reilly realized early on that the more people compare impressions—especially *contradictory* impressions—the less real and reliable information there is. Police investigators will tell you that the only thing worse than no suspect is too many suspects. Likewise, the more B.S. you have to sift through, the less chance of arriving at the truth in a timely fashion—if at all!

---

249. Kettle, 1983:18.

Reilly Rule #7: People Only Know the Face You Show Them

Years later, when by his own admission he was "the most wanted man in Russia," on the run from Russia's dreaded CHEKA secret police, Reilly polished up his big brass pair, whipped out a fake identity of "Commissar Relinsky" (made up in advance for just such an emergency), and hid the one place he knew the CHEKA would never look . . . inside CHEKA headquarters!

Forced to flee to avoid "the terror" unleashed following Lenin's assassination, Sidney escaped Russia by first again disguising himself as Commissar Relinsky, then spending several nights hiding in a brothel (in the room of a girl in the last stages of syphilis), before finally assuming the identity of a German citizen named Herr Bergmann and talking his way into a luxurious railway car reserved for those evacuating the German embassy.

Some of Sidney's other expedient personas included (but were certainly not limited to):

- A British lieutenant captain
- A Ph.D. chemist known as "Mr. Constantine" (finally, some use for that questionable Ph.D. in chemistry from Heidelburg University!)
- Monsieur Massino, a mysterious "Oriental" (Turkish) merchant
- That fleet-of-foot German "Herr Bergmann"
- The aforementioned CHEKA officer Commissar Relinsky

And these are just the ones Reilly allowed us to find out about![250]

Reilly Rule #8: Loose Ends Are the Ones They Hang You With

Before his "strategic withdrawal" from Russia, Reilly made sure to leave in place a network of loyal agents who would serve him well in the coming years. And while on the subject of "tying up loose ends," there's an event that occurred shortly before Sidney's exit from Russia, noteworthy if only because Sidney was seen in the area at the time . . . and Sidney rarely played the bystander role.

---

250. This would be a good time to review "The Five Rules for Lying Successfully" in Section I.

The same day Lenin was shot, August 30, a certain Commissar Uritsky was likewise gunned down, albeit in a separate incident. Immediately following the shooting, rumors began spreading (with the help of leaks from the CHEKA?) that Uritsky had been assassinated on orders from the British. As a result, a mob of enraged Bolsheviks (led by a CHEKA officer?) stormed the British embassy. In the resulting melee, a known "former associate" of Sidney Reilly named Cromie, having sought safety in the Embassy, was killed by someone who witnesses described as "an excited man in an overcoat and soft hat, wielding 2 Browning pistols."

Others later recalled seeing our ol' friend Commisar Relinsky mingling with CHEKA guards outside . . .

Michael Kettle, in his excellent *Sidney Reilly: The True Story of the World's Greatest Spy* (1983), concludes that the British were somehow involved in Uritsky's murder but not in the attempt on Lenin's life.

Could Commisar Relinsky have been dotting the *I*s and tying up loose ends before leaving Russia, perhaps settling accounts with a double or even triple agent, or perhaps with someone he knew wouldn't be able to keep his mouth shut if caught by Soviet Intelligence—thus placing an entire network of agents and supporters at risk? Unacceptable risk. The first rule of being a spy handler: take care of your people and your people will take care of you.

By the way, Lenin was shot by a counterrevolutionary named Dora Kaplan, who then disappeared into a building opposite the old British Military Mission . . . Hmmm. Did anyone think to check for a *connecting* tunnel?

In November 1918, the Bolshevik revolutionary tribunal tried Sidney in absentia and sentenced him to death.

In the years following the Communist coup, Britain's political policy toward the emerging Communist state vacillated, with some English voices calling for an all-out invasion of Russia in order to prevent the spread of international Communism, while others called for official recognition (read: placating) of the fledgling Soviet state.

Reilly held no such confusion. While his SIS handlers were still waiting for the British powers-that-be to decide pro or con, the fervently anti-Bolshevik Reilly was already recruiting displaced and disaffected Czarists (a.k.a. White Russians) to help beat back the growing red menace. In the years that followed, Reilly spent considerable effort (and considerable sums of his own money) both lobbying his Western allies against Communism and actively helping ferment counterrevolution in the infant Soviet Union:

> Whatever the diversity of opinion may be about extending military and economic help to Russia, there can be only *one* opinion on the urgent necessity of world-wide propaganda against Bolshevism, as the greatest danger that has ever threatened civilization. —Sidney Reilly, 1918

History has since given Sidney Reilly his due, a little too little, a lot too late:

> The one person who emerged with enhanced reputation from the Russian Civil War was Sidney Reilly . . . If the Allies, and particularly the British, had been prepared to carry out his recommendations, then things might have gone differently.
> —Kettle, 1983

In the initial days of the Bolshevik power grab, Reilly worked with MIIC (later called MI-6) gathering intelligence, helping Czarist and White Russian "assets" successfully escape the clutches of the Communists until, finally, with a price on his own head and the hounds at his heels, Reilly himself was forced to flee Russia.

He would spend the rest of his life as an anti-Bolshevik plotter, backing first one, then another promising White Russian leader who looked like they had a chance of dislodging the increasingly entrenched Bolsheviks.

Britain's (and therefore British intelligence's) official position was to do naught but monitor the political situation in Russia sans interfering in the politics of a "sovereign nation" (even though the smoke hadn't yet cleared enough to figure out who exactly was running that sovereign nation!). Not surprisingly, Sidney and his handlers began bumping heads so far as where political intelligence gathering left off and political interference ("adventuring" they called it back in those quaint days!) began.

Ironically, at least so far as MI-6 was concerned, Sidney Reilly was technically a *military*, not a *political*, agent; hence, his operating parameters were rigidly limited to intelligence gathering that might be of concern to the military, as opposed to trying to influence Russian politics per se.

Wasn't it Clausewitz who observed that "War was just politics by other means"?

Thus, with all the plots and counterplots going on in Bolshevik Russia in summer 1918, political "observing" and military "affairs" (i.e., "adventuring") were inexorably entwined.[251]

Reilly initially backed White Russian warlord Deniken Kolchak, who had successfully taken the fight to the gates of Moscow . . . but by Christmas 1919, the Russian Civil War was over and Lenin's Bolsheviks firmly in power.

After the Russian Civil War, Reilly joined forces with Boris Savinkov, a novelist, who had been a war minister in Aleksandr Kerensky's White Russian Provisional Government until its collapse in 1917.

Reilly and Savinkov now became the de facto leaders of the anti-Bolshevik cause,[252] creating the League for the Defense of the Motherland and Liberty in an effort to coordinate disparate anti-Bolshevik elements.

During the Russo-Polish War, Reilly and Savinkov helped coordinate the Polish in their fight against the encroaching Red Army, until March 1921 when the Treaty of Riga ended the Russo-Polish War. Savinkov and Reilly then moved on to Prague where they helped organize and outfit the Green Guard, a Ukrainian anti-Bolshevik movement.

One thing that Reilly and Savinkov had going for them was that Winston Churchill was their biggest fan. A student of history, Churchill saw similarities between the French Revolution and the Bolshevik Revolution. Churchill believed that, as had happened with the French Revolution, after a period of initial chaos, a strong leader like Napoleon Bonaparte would finally arise, seize power, and restore order. Churchill believed Savinkov was just such a leader.[253]

It also helped that Churchill was also a major proponent of increasing Britain's espionage and intelligence gathering capability:

> With the world in its present condition of extreme unrest and changing friendships and antagonisms, and with our greatly reduced and weak military forces, it is more than ever vital to us to have good and timely information.
>
> —Winston Churchill, 1920

251. Kettle, 1983:48.

252. Ibid., 96.

253. Ibid., 103.

Unfortunately, so far as Churchill's career as a prophet was concerned, in spring 1922 a treaty was signed between Germany and Russia, effectively legitimizing the Soviet government and thereby effectively ending any realistic likelihood of Savinkov ever coming to power in Russia.

Determined to fight on against what they rightly saw as the birth of international Communism, Savinkov and Reilly continued to sponsor insurgent[254] activity in Russia, including plots to assassinate Bolshevik leaders. Green Guards continued anti-Bolshevik attacks from their Prague base throughout 1923, following Sidney Reilly's three-step blueprint designed to bring down the Soviet Union:

1. Destabilize and draw off resources through coordinated attacks originating outside the country
2. Incite dissent within the Soviet Union by encouraging and addressing the grievances of peasants and dissatisfied factions within the Red Army
3. Obtain financial backing for both operations from powerful European and American special interest groups and rich individuals, for example, oil magnates and millionaires like Henry Ford

This latter task of "working the room" was Reilly's specialty.

Reilly Rule #9: Credibility Is Better Than Cash

Build credibility to the point where people (1) will believe anything you say and (2) would never believe anything negative said about you. By 1924, Sidney Reilly was Britain's consummate spy. When he showed up at MI-6's door with a piece of information, it was considered gospel. Not surprising that with great credibility comes great temptation to trade on that credibility.

Ironically, Sidney Reilly pulled off his greatest intelligence coup not with good, solid information—like he had used to sink the Russian fleet at Port Arthur—but rather with *dis*information that would sink a powerful political party, permanently changing the British government, the West, and thereby the world!

Just prior to the anticipated signing of a treaty between England and

254. "Terrorist" is what the big army calls the little army.

the new Soviet Russia in 1924, British intelligence obtained a letter that, in turn, had reportedly been obtained from dissident anti-Bolshevik Russian sources. Allegedly written by Zinoviev, head of the Soviet Comitern parliament, the letter revealed that Britain's powerful Labor Party was already riddled with Communist agents armed with a secret plan for the infiltration and subversion of Britain's ruling Labor Party in preparation for a Bolshevik-Communist takeover of Britain!

Some sources say Reilly himself delivered the letter to MI-6, others that he "only" testified to its legitimacy . . . even though he knew it was a complete fabrication. *His* complete fabrication.

The truth of the matter is that Reilly had first stolen authentic paper from the Soviet embassy in Berlin before then employing a master forger to counterfeit Zinoviev's signature. In the end, this single forgery was enough to (1) wreck the signing of the Anglo-Soviet Treaty and (2) bring down Britain's Labor Party—late summer 1924.

Just for the record, at the time Britain's Labor Party government was trying to abolish the British Intelligence Services and had never been enthusiastic about allocating needed funds for increased intelligence gathering—leading some to suspect that Reilly wasn't the only MI-6 operative who didn't mind seeing the Labor Party removed from power.

Other sources maintain that the fake letter wasn't originally crafted by Reilly but that once he recognized its potential for disrupting the planned Anglo-Soviet treaty signing he decided to throw his considerable credibility behind its authenticity and this, coming from a man with Reilly's track record, was enough to convince his intelligence handlers, who in turn convinced those higher up, that the letter was genuine.[255]

The "Zinoviev Letter" as it became known was published by the *Daily Mail* newspaper on October 25, 1924, and Churchill and his Tories wasted no time in using it to bring down the Labor government on their way to taking power. Remember: Churchill was a big fan of funding espionage.

The Soviets issued strong denials as to the authenticity of the letter, but by then the damage was already done, souring Anglo-Russian relations. A new wave of paranoia about Communists infiltrating Western governments floated across the Atlantic, indefinitely postponing the United States's recognition of

---

255. See Kettle, 1983: 122.

the Soviet Union—heralding the beginning of sixty-five years of wall building and nuclear saber-rattling.

Amazing what one man with the right piece of paper—a *forged* piece of paper at that!—can accomplish.

According to Kettle, the Zinoviev Letter was the "high-water mark" of Reilly's career. Unfortunately for our Mr. Reilly:

> The Soviet Government had a shrewd idea who was behind it all. With Savinkov caught, still languishing in prison at the time, Reilly became the Soviet Union's principal target.[256]

The reference to Savinkov refers to his having been captured in Russia on June 20, 1924. The story of his capture requires that we digress to explain the brilliance of another master of subterfuge, one of Sidney's fellow Poles named Felix Dzerzhinsky, patron saint of the KGB and creator of the elaborate man-eating fly-trap known as "The Trust."

Officially known as MUCR (Monarchist Union of Central Russia), ironically nicknamed "The Trust," this organization was the brainchild of Felix Dzerzhinsky and Commissar Kiakowski (also a Pole), directors of the Soviet OGPU counterintelligence (successor to the CHEKA, predecessor to the KGB). These two master Mind Slayers devised a plan to create a bogus organization that would serve as a two-way pipeline (1) funneling the Soviet's self-serving disinformation out of Russia while (2) enticing expatriate dissidents, White Russian émigrés, and the occasional pro-Western spy back into Russia under the pretext of meeting and coordinating with the (supposed) anti-Bolshevik members of The Trust.

The Trust was a roaring success:

> Soon, all White Russian secret messages into Russia were passing through The Trust; messages sent from Paris or Berlin often received replies from Moscow with a week.[257]

The Trust supplied leaked "information" to known spies and to Western sympathizers who, in turn, passed these false facts and figures along to Western intelligence services. In return, The Trust received "considerable

256. Ibid., 130.
257. Ibid., 110.

amounts of money." Again with the irony: Western intelligence unknowingly funding Soviet intelligence!

How did cunning Hannibal phrase it in his Truth XXI?

> The wise feed off the foolish, but are all too soon hungry again.

The Trust's biggest coup came when the OGPU caught, tortured, and eventually turned a man named Pavlovsky, Savinkov's main agent in Russia.[258] Pavlovsky was persuaded[259] to send a message to Savinkov of an impending uprising against the Soviet government by the secret anti-Bolshevik "shadow government," convincing Savinkov to return to Russia.

Hook, line, and sinker, Savinkov was arrested by the OGPU in Minsk on June 20, 1924.

Dzerzhinsky promised to release Savinkov in exchange for a full confession and for help luring Sidney Reilly back to Russia. Savinkov languished in prison for nearly a year before finally committing suicide by throwing himself out a prison window in May 1925.[260]

Busy in America lobbying to make sure the Soviet government did not succeed in getting a bailout loan from Wall Street, upon hearing of Savinkov's capture, Reilly immediately returned to Paris. Sidney is knee-deep in elaborate scenarios for freeing Savinkov when word comes in May 1925 that Savinkov has committed suicide.

All eyes now look to Sidney as the leader of the anti-Bolshevik movement. Reilly soon receives word from White Russians (via The Trust) that the shadow government in Moscow and Petrograd want him to help them salvage the same "impending uprising" of anti-Bolshevik forces Savinkov had been lured back into Russia to lead.

The Trust ploy works. Traveling under the false identification of "Stern-

---

258. An example of Sun Tzu's "converted spies."

259. For a complete course on "expedient field interrogation," see *Theatre of Hell: Dr. Lung's Complete Guide to Torture* by Dr. Haha Lung and Christopher B. Prowant (Loompanics Unlimited, 2003).

260. Others sources have Dzerzhinsky, in an uncharacteristic fit of rage over Savinkov's lack of cooperation, throwing the would-be Russian Napoleon out the window himself. This seems unlikely given Dzerzhinsky's usual stoic demeanor . . . More than likely, Dzerzhinsky ordered one of his men to throw Savinkov out the window!

berg," Reilly arrives in Leningrad where he is immediately taken into custody by OGPU (Russian Army intelligence) agents.

Ironically, Felix Dzerzhinsky and The Trust had not initially intended to capture Reilly. Instead, they had arranged a faux meeting with Reilly designed to convince him that the anti-Bolshevik shadow government was a reality before then allowing Reilly to leave Russia unmolested. If The Trust had succeeded in pulling off this ruse (1) The Trust would not be exposed as a fraud, and (2) Reilly himself would then have (unknowingly) become a powerful recruiting force for The Trust as well as (3) a credible source for spreading The Trust's disinformation in the West.

However, once they learned that their most hated—and feared—enemy was within their grasp, an impatient Soviet Politbureau and a paranoid Stalin[261] ordered Reilly's immediate seizure.[262]

Details are sketchy but, in the best James Bond fashion, we can expect Sidney's treatment as Dzerzhinsky's guest to have been initially cordial, perhaps even jovial, before then turning increasingly Goldfinger-*esque*:

> "Do you expect me to talk?"
>
> "No, Mr. Bond. I expect you to die!" (Cue laser beam to the crotch!)

Finally, or so the legend goes, one morning while taking a supervised walk in the Lenin Hills, Sidney Riley, the "Ace of Spies," was shot in the back by a man named Ibrahim, the OGPU's crack marksman.

The Trust continued to operate for several more years.

As with all things Reilly, Sidney's death created its share of speculation. Many believed Reilly had suspected The Trust all along and in an effort to prove his suspicions purposely returned to Russia, sacrificing himself in order to expose them. However noble sounding, one would expect a man of Sidney's intellect to have come up with a more efficient—ultimately less painful—way of proving his point.

Of course, detractors of Sidney Reilly were quick to accuse him of having been a double (or was that triple?) agent, either working for Russian

---

261. Stalin's solution to most matters was: "No man, no problem!" For a complete history of master Mind Slayer Josef Stalin, see "Steel Lesson: What Would Stalin Do?" in *Ultimate Control* by Dr. Haha Lung and Christopher B. Prowant (Citadel, 2010).

262. Kettle, 1983:139.

intelligence all along or else turning traitor once captured in order to save his own skin, subsequently faking his death and living out the rest of his life in a comfortable dacha somewhere in Russia.

Still others keep the controversy of Sidney Reilly alive by claiming that information he gave up to the OGPU (either willingly or unwillingly) later helped the KGB recruit at his old alma mater Cambridge, leading to the creation of the infamous Philby spy ring.

> Politics indeed makes for strange bedfellows—and the bastards are always trying to hog the covers! —C.B. Black

SAKE AND SECRETS: THE JAPANESE ART OF SPYING

Pearl Harbor was the brilliant culmination of more than half a century of spying in Honolulu and was one of the greatest coups of a truly fantastic system of espionage. It is fantastic not only in the vastness of its organization but in the physical area of the globe's surface which it covered . . . the Japanese began serious espionage activities in the United States in 1927.

—Ronald Seth, *Secret Servants: A History of Japanese Espionage,* 1957

One persistent theory for the complete disappearance of aviation pioneer Amelia Earhart and her copilot maintains that, after surviving an emergency landing in the Pacific during a 1937 attempt to circumnavigate the globe, the two adventurers were captured and executed by the Japanese after inadvertently stumbling across secret Japanese naval operations. It has even been speculated that Earhart agreed to deliberately—secretly—alter her course across the Pacific in order to spy on suspected Japanese maneuvers at the personal request of President FDR.

In a case of art imitating life, in the 1945 movie *Blood on the Sun*, Jimmy Cagney plays a feisty American reporter stationed in Japan who becomes inadvertently caught up in uncovering Japanese espionage just prior to Japan's launching of World War II.[263] This movie doesn't miss the mark by much so

263. This movie is arguably the first American "martial arts" movie with James Cagney—a juijutsu blackbelt in real life—showing off his considerable fighting talent in several well-choreographed no-holds-barred fight scenes against Japanese agents. Also in the running for America's first "kick-flick," Randolf Scott's 1943 *Gung-ho*.

far as there being a massive surge in Japanese espionage just prior to World War II. In fact, both of these scenarios are plausible, given the fact that the United States was well aware of the threat posed by the build-up in Japanese espionage operations.

So if increased evidence of Japanese spying, particularly spying against the United States, was well known prior to World War II, why didn't we see Pearl Harbor coming? The fact of the matter is that although the FBI was sanctioned to deal with espionage within the borders of the United States, J. Edgar and his boys were hamstrung by (1) the uncooperative attitude of the State Department and (2) a lack of coordination between the various intelligence and counterespionage agencies. Luckily, by 9/11 all that had changed.[264]

Recall how during the Russo-Japanese War of 1904–1905, Japanese Black Dragon agents (with a little help from Sidney Reilly) succeeded in obtaining detailed plans of the Russian naval installation at Port Arthur, allowing the Japanese to surprise and sink the Russian fleet.

Learning an obvious lesson from Port Arthur: that it was more difficult for Japanese to infiltrate predominantly (possibly racist, definitely paranoid of "funny-lookin' little fur-rin-ners") Caucasian-dominated areas, Japanese intelligence made a concerted effort to recruit non-Japanese agents who could more readily blend into the West, Caucasians of various ilk and proclivity: the easily corruptible, those already corrupted, the greedy, someone with an ax to grind—all were potential agents the Japanese could entice into working for them. Prior to World War II at least one such Caucasian, a former U.S. Navy yeoman, was convicted of spying for the Japanese.[265]

Likewise, immediately following the attack on Pearl Harbor, a Caucasian doctor named Bernard Kuhn, his wife, and their teenage daughter were arrested in Hawaii and charged with aiding in the attack on Pearl Harbor on December 7, 1941, by passing vital information along to the Japanese.[266]

The Kuhns had been discovered—not by brilliant U.S. counterespionage—but rather by chance after someone noticed them using a signal mirror to flash information from their apartment to the Japanese consulate.

---

264. Seth, 210. Yeah, Dr. Lung loves the smell of sarcasm in the morning.

265. Ibid., 218.

266. Further investigation revealed that the Kuhns were actually working for *both* Japanese and German intelligence. Seth also points out that even before formally becoming allies, Germany and Japan were exchanging intelligence, and their agents were working together in Central America.

As part of their long-term American espionage plans, long before Pearl Harbor the Japanese had established an airstrip in Costa Rica (camouflaged as a plantation) as the first step in plans to destroy the Panama Canal, in order to cripple the movement of the U.S. Navy. They also established secret bases in San Gabriel Bay on the Baja (Mexico) peninsula, placing them within easy striking distance to the West Coast of the United States.

Seth (1957) estimates that, at one time, Japan had as many as ten thousand spies disguised as fishermen operating through Latin America and Mexico and up to the West Coast of the United States. More ominous still, the Japanese had plenty of agents operating inside the United States.

One of the best known—finally revealed—Japanese spies operating in the United States was a certain Dr. Takashi Furusawa, operating in Los Angeles as both a spy recruiter and handler. So successful was Furusawa that he even succeeded in recruiting silent-screen superstar Charlie Chaplain's former valet, a man named Torzichi Kono.

Nippon über Alles: The German Connection

The investigation following Pearl Harbor revealed that Dr. Kuhn and his family were actually working for both Japanese and German Intelligence. Seth (1957) points out that even before formally becoming Axis allies, Germany and Japan were exchanging intelligence, their agents working together in Central America, and that this collaboration continued throughout the war.

This pre-Axis alliance need not surprise us if we accept Seth's contention that modern Japanese espionage was an imitation of the nineteeth-century Prussian Green House system set up by (in)famous master strategist and spymaster Wilhelm Strieber.

Strieber's Green House was a carefully constructed brothel in Berlin that specialized in compromising secrets out of army officers, politicians, and other well-to-dos by indulging their every perversion.[267] According to Seth, no sooner did the Japanese learn of Strieber's intelligence gathering successes with his Green House than they went about investing in similar pleasure palaces all over Asia. However, Seth was evidently unaware that pleasure palaces had been a long-standing tradition throughout Asia, some sponsored by criminal secret societies promoting the world's oldest profession

267. "Lust" being one of mind manipulating Five Warning F.L.A.G.S.

and not averse to a little extortion on the side, while other pleasure palaces were designed solely to drain strategic and tactical military, political, and business secrets from clients.

Evidently Seth had never heard of the femme fatale Black Lotus Society,[268] nor of *kuniochi*—the female ninja of Japan.[269]

The Japanese reportedly approached Strieber because Prussian officers (at the time helping organize and train Japan's new modern army along Western lines) had bragged that Prussia had the finest, most up-to-date espionage system in the world.

Coming with hat in hand, heads respectfully bowed, the Japanese humbly lamented their own lack of effective espionage training. They realized they were a small nation with little hope of standing up against larger—especially Western—countries except—perhaps?—through organizing an espionage system of their own . . . and if they were to organize such a system, naturally it would be foolish of them not to model it after the best. Would honorable spymaster Strieber condescend to teach them his oh so wonderful system?[270]

The Prussians bought the "We're just humble, harmless little Orientals" act. For all their vaunted success in the field of strategy and espionage, obviously no one in Germany had yet read Sun Tzu's *Art of War*: "When strong appear weak."

Seth also apparently buys into this "humble" plea for help by the underdog Japanese. Patronizingly, he explains how it had become necessary for the Japanese to seek outside help in updating their outdated spying technique, borrowing from others and imitating as they had always done:

> They were not an inspired people. They had taken their language, their form of writing, their philosophy, even one of their religions; from the ancient civilized Chinese . . . Japan was entirely ignorant of espionage. Under the autocratic [Tokugawa] Shogunate it had been absolutely necessary to employ agents to keep an eye on would-be rebels. Though she had cut herself off from the outside world, she had not been so foolish as to keep herself in ignorance of what was happening in China and had sent a few agents there. But this

268. See *Mental Domination* by Dr. Haha Lung and Christopher B. Prowant (Citadel, 2009).
269. See *Nine Halls of Death* by Dr. Haha Lung and Eric Tucker (Citadel, 2007).
270. Seth, 41.

> espionage was something quite different from the form and scope which the German military instructors were advising.[271]

Doesn't anyone take the time to study history? By the time members of Japanese intelligence approached Strieber, the Japanese people already had a long history of espionage, if nothing else, having inherited (stolen!) thousands of years of successful Chinese *Lin Kuei* and *Moshuh Nanren* espionage tactics and techniques. And that's not even considering one thousand years of the Japanese ninja honing their arts of stealth, strategy, and skullduggery!

In fact, the Japanese had approached the Prussians humbly, with hat in hand, adopting what in Japan is called a *kohei* attitude (Jp. humble *junior* student before a superior *sempai* elder or master). This subservient attitude made it more likely the Germans would instruct them.

And when all this smoke in front of the mirror cleared, the Japanese now knew not only these ancient Eastern secrets of espionage they'd always known, but thanks to their new German "friends," they also knew the latest Western techniques of espionage as well. A clear case of "You taught me all you know, but you didn't teach me all I know":

> The Japanese in every other aspect of their development had been copyists entirely, though copyists *par excellence*. Wilhelm Strieber had been an inventor and innovator in the realm of espionage, up to this time without peer. Yet curiously enough, the Japanese were to introduce innovations into the art of spying which were to outclass some of Strieber's . . . The Japanese became obsessed by espionage, and if total war was an invention of their National Socialist German friends, the original concept of total espionage must certainly be conceded to the leaders of Japan.[272]

Samurai Spies and Secret Police

A unique and insightful report was completed for German military intelligence in the 1920s, in anticipation of an eventual alliance between Germany and Japan, by none other than the man who would eventually become

271. Ibid., 53.
272. Ibid., 54.

Hitler's right-hand man, Rudolf Hess.[273] In his report, Hess observed—perhaps somewhat politically incorrect—that espionage came as "second nature to the Japanese":

> Japanese leaders had always treated their people like children. Since the time of the [Tokugawa] Shogunate,[274] plain-clothes and voluntary or impressed informers had been widely employed, and this had developed in the Japanese nation a penchant for spying that was so ingrained that they pursued it whenever the opportunity offered, particularly when traveling abroad . . . This is not to say that every Japanese found outside the boundaries of his own country was a trained spy or an agent of the Japanese intelligence service. Nor did the Japanese travel so that they might have opportunities of spying, which in their intense patriotism they believed would acquire merit for them. Nevertheless, whenever Japanese saw a chance of spying, he spied, and passed on whatever information he gathered either to a Japanese consul or to the police when he returned home.

Nearly forty years later, Ronald Seth agreed with Hess, tracing the Japanese "proclivity and propensity" for espionage—both foreign and domestic—back to the era of the Tokugawa:

> Every Japanese when he goes abroad considers himself to be a spy; and when he is at home he takes upon himself the role of spy catcher. I suggest that this preoccupation with espionage[275] is ingrained in the Japanese, since for many years

273. Hess also became Hitler's right-hand "pen," acting as secretary and editor of Hitler's *Mein Kampf*, written while Hitler and Hess were sharing a prison cell following Hitler's disastrous first attempt to seize power.

274. The Tokugawa dynasty of Shoguns took power in 1598 and ruled for the next two hundred and fifty years.

275. Keep in mind that Seth was writing in 1957 and you will perhaps be a little more forgiving (if not understanding) of his decidedly chauvinistic, often condescending, "observations" and opinions, when speaking in generalities about Japanese culture as a whole. It also helps to keep in mind that Seth was writing about a people that, a scant twelve years earlier, had been his blood enemy.

> under the Shogunate a system of secret police was extensively active whose main task was to secure the Shoguns against plots on their lives and against their positions.

Indeed, soon after taking power, the Tokugawa shogun gave loyal samurai lord Munenori Yagyu, founder of the famed *Yagyu* school of kendo, the job of keeping an eye on potential enemies of the realm. The Yagyu would go on to become the Tokugawa's secret police, the dreaded Kempai Tai.[276]

For the next three hundred years, Yagyu agents honed their craft until, by the dawning of the twentieth century, Kempai Tai agents had become the Japanese military's new ninja. Handpicked volunteers from the army with at least six years of service before becoming eligible, their training regimen mirrored the traditional nine "training halls" of ninjutsu, including training in espionage and counterespionage (e.g., the art of disguise, the use of codes), *bujutsu* weapons training, and *taijutsu* unarmed combat, even studying the customs, law, and languages of countries they were assigned to infiltrate.[277]

In 1854, Commodore Matthew Perry effectively ended hundreds of years of Japanese isolationism by sailing into Tokyo Bay with heavily armed ships and demanding that Japan open its ports to Western trade. Not only did Perry succeed in his mission of opening Japan's ports, he also, inadvertently, ushered in a new age of Japanese espionage. It was then that even the staunchest and most stubborn of Japanese isolationists realized how important it was for Japan—if it intended to avoid the kind of foreign domination that had already befallen neighboring China—to keep abreast of international affairs and foreign intrigues. And this would require the Japanese government sending Japanese spies overseas.

Fortunately, so far as the Japanese government was concerned, some Japanese citizens had already taken it on themselves to do just that.

Black Dragons Swim in the Black Oceans

Long before the Japanese government realized the necessity for moving its intelligence gathering into the modern era, in order to keep pace with its

276. Also written as Kempetai.

277. With a regimen of training identical to the nine training "halls" of classic Japanese ninjutsu. See *The Nine Halls of Death: Complete Ninja Training* by Dr. Haha Lung and Eric Tucker (Citadel, 2007).

Western rivals, nationalist secret societies had already taken up the cloak and dagger, codebook and "poison pen"—useful for (1) spreading disinformation, (2) for actually carrying poison, and (3) when need be, for being a handy "environmental weapon" for stabbing out an eye or two!

In his 1920s report, Rudolf Hess took special notice of one especially sinister Japanese secret society known as the Black Dragon, noting the efficiency and effectiveness of its recruiting. For example, although Japan was a highly structured society, Black Dragon agents were chosen from every walk of life, with their best agents being recruited from ronin, out-of-work samurai.[278]

Hess notes that the Japanese military suffered from the same army-navy rivalry found in many Western nations. He pointed to a potential flaw in the fact that the Black Dragon worked closely with army intelligence (many of whose members also belonged to the Black Dragon) but that the Black Dragon didn't get along with nor did they share information with naval intelligence.

The minute that Perry's ships anchored in Tokyo Bay, ninja spies were sneaking on board, recording every detail of the ships and the *gaijin* manning them. These ninja spies had been contracted by a group of concerned samurai who saw the arrival of Western ships off shore as a wake-up, heralding the end of their samurai way of life.

In 1867, these and other alarmed samurai staged a coup, overthrowing the last of the Tokugawa—who they felt were appeasing the foreigners. They replaced the two-hundred-fifty-year-old lineage of shoguns with a stronger imperial rule they hoped would present a unified force against the foreigners. To no avail.

In 1877, after a decade of watching the imperial court give concession after concession to the Westerners—the last straw being the Emperor's announcement that the elite samurai warrior class was to be abolished in favor of the creation of a Western-style army made up of conscripted soldiers from all classes—in a futile attempt to bring back the rule of the shoguns, old-school samurai staged a full-scale revolt.

Samurai swords versus modern firearms . . . You do the math.[279] As a consequence, the samurai class was officially abolished.

Many of these displaced samurai, still hoping to someday regain their lost status, still loyal to the same Japan that had just kicked them to the curb, still

---

278. More on these "wave men" in the Musashi chapter that follows.

279. Or rent the DVD of Tom Cruise's surprisingly impressive *The Last Samurai* (2003).

vowing to protect their country from foreign control, either formed themselves into nationalist secret societies or else joined already existing secret societies. These nineteenth-century samurai secret societies recruited veteran ninja to do their dark bidding and/or else trained their own cadre of secret-agent ninjas willing and able to gather intelligence and carry out assassinations both inside Japan and overseas.

The more successful of these secret societies were bankrolled by rich and powerful samurai families who controlled Japan's growing military-industrial complex known as the Zaibatsu, which was closely allied with the Japanese military and thus with the military's intelligence bureau, the much feared Kempai Tai.

Kempai Tai operatives were ninja in the true and traditional sense of the word: carrying out intelligence gathering, assassination, and general skullduggery wherever Japanese interests—and *ambitions*—warranted. At one point, inside Japan and abroad, the Kempai Tai had an estimated seventy thousand operatives.[280]

Because their interests so overlapped, and perhaps simply to keep their enemies guessing, early twentieth-century Japanese nationalist secret societies were intricately intertwined, often operating under various names. For example, one man might belong to several different, yet interconnected, groups. For example, an influential *yakuza kuromaku* (Grandmaster, lit. "Black Curtain") might belong to the same nationalist secret society as the chief of police detectives assigned to investigate him! These two, in turn, shared sake and secrets and hobnobbed with general, and ranking members of the Kempai Tai—all united by varying degrees of nationalism, imperialism, and personal ambition. Some of these conspirators went so far as to feign hatred of one another when meeting in public and political circles, all the while plotting together behind closed doors.

Secret societies like the Black Ocean and its offshoot the Black Dragon not only practiced their schemes in the streets of Tokyo but also fielded agents and front operations abroad. Some of these overseas agents worked for the military, spying out potential military threats and probing for weaknesses in targeted territories and soon-to-be enemies. Other agents worked for more personal Zaibatsu concerns, infiltrating rival foreign companies and corporations, stealing industrial secrets, sabotaging rival businesses, and

---

280. Seth, 156.

helping Japanese companies get a leg up on the competition. Still other secret societies infiltrated agents into religious groups, student unions, and even martial arts clubs, both in Japan and abroad.

The granddaddy of all Japanese nationalist secret societies was *Genyoshakai*, The Black Ocean Society, founded in 1881 by wealthy Samurai-turned-businessman Kotaro Hiraoka. Originating in Kyushu province in Japan, this shadowy "Japan is destined to rule the world!" brotherhood first spread throughout Japan before expanding operations overseas where—following Sonshi's Chapter XIII espionage outline—they vigorously recruited turncoats in foreign countries to gather intelligence and carry out "acts of influence" (i.e., disinformation, sabotage, assassination) in China, Korea, Manchuria,[281] Russia, and Indochina, and later expanding to Western countries.

In short order, the Black Ocean became the supreme school for spies—unsurpassed in either East or West in gathering intelligence, manipulating human frailty, and fielding ruthlessly efficient agents. As a result the Black Ocean Society became the template for many of the twentieth century's spook organizations, including British MI-6, the Russian KGB, the American World War II Office of Strategic Services (OSS, forerunner of the CIA), and the National Security Agency (NSA, founded in 1948, the same year as the CIA).

In many ways foreshadowing a modern Al Qaeda terrorist network, the Black Ocean was the first truly effective *international terrorist* operation since the medieval Muslim Hashishin "Assassins" cult.[282]

Both inside Japan and abroad, Black Ocean operatives infiltrated religious groups, academic institutions, and other already-existing secret societies—for example, the Chinese triads "mafia."

Where easily infiltrated businesses and organizations were not already in place, Black Ocean operatives set up false front organizations and businesses designed not only to operate secretly behind enemy lines but also to recruit traitors, agents provocateur, and double agents from among the

281. Where, not coincidentally, Kotaro Hiraoka owned the mining rights to large tracts of land.

282. For a complete course in the murderous history and martial arts techniques of the Hashishin/Assassins, see *Assassin! Secrets of the Cult of the Assassins* by Dr. Haha Lung (Paladin Press, 1997) and *Asssassin!* (Citadel, 2004).

enemy population. Basic Sun Tzu Chapter XIII or, if you prefer, eighth Chinese strategist Li Ch'uan:

> When my foe sends spies to pry into my affairs, I bribe them with lavish gifts, turning them around and making them into agents of my will.

So successful was the Black Ocean Society that, by 1901, it had not only recruited an estimated ten thousand members but its success had also spawned numerous imitators and offshoots, for example, the *Daiagi-kai*, the Reawakening Greater Asia Society (founded in 1908 and dedicated to the conquest of mainland China) and its most (in)famous offshoot: *Kokurkykai*, the Black Dragon Society—formed after an international scandal in 1895 following the discovery of evidence linking Black Ocean ninja to the assassination of Queen Min of Korea.

The Black Dragon Society, also known as The Amur River Society,[283] was founded in 1901 to carry out intelligence gathering (and terrorism) operations inside Korea and China—both already targeted for conquest by Japanese militarists. Recall that it was Black Dragon operatives who "recruited" Sidney Reilly for help in taking down Port Arthur during the Russo-Japanese War.

The Black Dragon was founded by Rychei Uchida, the protégé of Black Ocean founder Kotaro Hiraoka. The Black Dragon's declared mission was to drive the Russians out of Manchuria and back across the Amur River, which marks Manchuria's northern border with Russia.

By 1927 the Japanese military—via its helpers in the Black Dragon—was carrying out what amounted to an unofficial terrorist war on the Amur River frontier, in Korea, Manchuria, Outer Mongolia and Inner Mongolia, and elsewhere, spreading their influence through such tried-and-true tactics and techniques as disinformation, disappearances, assassinations, and widespread bribery.

From its inception, and undoubtedly because it "co-opted" already in place Black Ocean operations, the Black Dragon Society grew at a phenomenal rate. In short order, it had taken over most operations of the Black Ocean to become the most powerful secret society in Japan.

Some Black Dragon supporters were well known and some—including

283. Named for the Amur (Ch. *Heilong*) River separating China from Russia.

politicians—quite vocal in their support of Black Dragon aims. Other wealthy and influential supporters were careful to insulate themselves from the Black Dragon, with a generous helping of "plausible deniability," at least in public. Since, as behooves a secret society, most of the Black Dragon's string-pulling *Kuromaku* "puppeteers" remained hidden, behind the black curtain.

Whereas the Black Ocean had had few qualms about recruiting thugs, criminals, and killers into its ranks—a policy that came back to bite them in the ass following the assassination of Queen Min—the Black Dragon made a show of recruiting young students with "clean slates" into its ranks—students who could be molded, students eager to sacrifice themselves as *Soshi* ("Brave Knights") of the Black Dragon.

The *true* leaders of Japan, the Zaibatsu who ran the military-industrial complex and secretly financed both Black Ocean and now Black Dragon operations, came from "the old school" of feudal internecine samurai politics and so knew the value of having a ninja in the right place at the right time.

Following their victory over the Russians, Japanese Zaibatsu, political, and military leaders—many secretly Black Dragon members—began openly encouraging nationalist groups like the Black Dragon by pouring money and manpower into their overseas espionage operations. By the 1930s, Black Dragon operations and sleeper cells were operating worldwide: from Manchuria to Indochina, from Hong Kong, Africa, and Turkey to the Caribbean and the United States.

In anticipation of World War II, the Black Dragon formed alliances of convenience with criminal, nationalist, and fascist subversive groups worldwide, including—but by no means limited to—the Hung triads of China and Hong Kong, the nationalist White Wolf Society of Turkey, as well as several occult-oriented secret societies in Italy and Germany, including the infamous Thule Society and the Aryan Vril, both of whose membership included prominent Nazis.[284] In another curious Nazi/Asian connection, Professor Haushofer of the University of Munich, said to have been initiated into one of the most important Buddhist secret societies during a stay in Japan, counseled Hitler on how to develop his powers as a "medium."[285]

284. Other prominent Nazi members have been linked to a mysterious Asian Buddhist secret society known as the Green Dragon, reportedly based in Tibet, where, curiously enough, the Nazis sent several expeditions prior to the outbreak of WW II.

285. Ostrander and Schroeder, 1970. See also *The Morning of the Magicians* by Louis Pauwels and Dr. Jacques Berger (Mayflower Books, 1971).

Back in Asia, Black Dragon operatives infiltrated religious groups, secret societies, and fringe political groups, from Singapore to Hong Kong to mainland China.

Black Dragons supported the overthrow of the Chinese Manchu Dynasty in 1911 and were instrumental in helping Sun-Yat Sen become the first—and only—president of China.

Black Dragons were looked at with suspicion when that same Sun-Yat Sen met an "untimely death" in 1925. However, one man's death can be another's open door. So while Sun-Yat Sen's death plunged China into a decades-long civil war, it *conveniently* weakened an already divided China even more, making the Chinese mainland easy pickings for the coming Japanese invasion.

By infiltrating Chinese tongs and triads prior to World War II, the Black Dragon was also able to establish a "fifth column" of secret supporters and subversives inside the British colony of Hong Kong in anticipation of Japan seizing that colony at the outbreak of hostilities.

Following this tried-and-true pattern, Black Dragon operatives likewise infiltrated governmental posts, disaffected political fringe groups, recognized religious groups, as well as extremist sects and cults, key social organizations, and already existing secret societies in dozens of other Asian countries, especially those controlled by European colonials and by American interests. So far as the success of such operations, one need only point out the fact that, like the Pearl Harbor disaster, the American Pacific fleet in the Dutch East Indies was defeated by espionage before the Japanese invasion.[286]

For example, in French-controlled Indochina (today Cambodia and Vietnam) not only did Japanese agents infiltrate already existing Vietnamese Hoi Kin (lit. "secret societies") prior to the invasion but also, where expedient, Japanese agents helped establish several Vietnamese secret societies and religious fringe groups, many of which would later prove influential in the development of Vietnamese politics long after the French "reclaimed" the area from the Japanese after World War II. Perhaps the best example of Black Dragon infiltration, inciting, and influence in Indochina is the evidence that Black Dragon operatives were influential (instrumental?) in helping establish the Cao Dai religion in Vietnam in the 1920s. The Cao Dai, in turn,

286. Seth, 269.

would be important players in the political landscape of Vietnam for the next fifty years.[287]

The Future of Spying? It Happened Yesterday!

At its height in 1944 the Black Dragon had *over ten thousand members* . . . that we *know* about! What happened to all ten thousand of these agents after World War II? Were they all rounded up and imprisoned by the Allies? No. Did they all go down like samurai, killed fighting or dying by *seppuku*[288] in the last days of the war? Or maybe they had all gathered for a company barbeque in Hiroshima or Nagasaki right before they dropped the big one . . . actually *two* big ones? Doubtful.

Or did all ten thousand of these highly trained, definitely deadly agents just throw up their hands and say, "Oh well, we lost. The Emperor isn't really all that divine. So we might as well just all go home and get honest jobs for a change. All *ten thousand* of us." Sure. That's probably the way it happened.

Following World War II, several members of the Japanese intelligence network in general, and several members of the Kempai Tai in particular, were hanged for war crimes. One of the conditions of Japan's unconditional surrender was that Japan was henceforth forbidden to operate a foreign secret service. Yeah, right:

> But the questions nag for an answer: can a people in whom the principles of espionage are so deeply ingrained ever be compelled to refrain from spying by an injunction placed upon them? —Ronald Seth, *Secret Servants*

In other words, you shouldn't ask—or expect—people to go against their nature.

Just as they'd successfully done in Germany (forgiving any spymaster and/or rocket scientist who agreed to come work for the West against Communism) and in Italy (where the Allies showed no qualms working with Lucky Luciano's mafia friends), so too in postwar Japan U.S. intelligence

---

287. See *Cao Dai Kung-fu* by Dr. Haha Lung (Loompanics Unlimited, 2002) and *Lost Fighting Arts of Vietnam* by Dr. Haha Lung (Citadel, 2006).

288. A.k.a. *hara-kiri*, ritual suicide.

agencies recruited former Japanese scientists guilty of experimenting with germ warfare, members of the feared Kempai Tai, former administrators and agents of Japan's infamous Tokko "Thought Control Police," even ruthless yakuza gangsters—all in the name of fighting Communism:

> Thought Control agents, purged and purged again, keep reappearing in positions of responsibility—often with American encouragement. —Kaplan & Dubro, *Yakuza*, 1986

Over the past fifty-plus years, Seth's cynicism has since been validated, as evidence of renewed spying by the Japanese continue to come to light, up to and including (paranoid?) allegations involving sinister Japanese advances as:

- Creating "hypnotic mind-control" by merging ancient *Shugendo*[289] meditation with modern "psychotronic" devices
- Attempts to create "psychic assassins" capable of influencing and even killing others over long distances
- and the curious involvement of a Japanese Mind Slayer cult leader in the assassination of an American president![290]

Keep in mind that, in a post–World War II world, one that has since learned how to use computers, we need not only concern ourselves with formal intelligence services within the paltry Japanese military, but also with private sector intelligence operations fielded by the still powerful Zaibutsu, by international yakuza criminal ventures, and more and more by increasingly bizarre religious groups—for example, the Aum Shinrikyu "death cult" that released poison gas into a Tokyo subway in March 1995, leaving a dozen dead and more than fifty-five hundred injured.

Think "psychic assassins" is pushing the envelope of credulity just a little? Think again. During the height of the Cold War, both Russia and the United States poured millions into serious research of everything from ESP

---

289. Jp. "Way of spiritual power," ancient rituals and practices of Japanese *Yamabushi* (mountain warrior monks).

290. For frightening evidence that Lee Harvey Oswald was under the influence of an adept Japanese Mind Slayer, read "Oswald and The Sleeping Tigers" in *Mind Penetration* by Dr. Haha Lung and Christopher B. Prowant (Citadel, 2007).

to shape-shifting to teleportation.[291] But it wasn't until 1995 that the U.S. government formally acknowledged the existence of a series of top-secret mind-experiment programs known by several names but finally settling on Project Stargate.[292] This CIA-sponsored group of psychic spies operated from the mid-1960s up through 1988.[293]

In one such "Gov-X" program, a secret unit of eight or more men was made up of recruits who had scored high on ESP tests. Taught to control their ESP ability through meditation, biofeedback, and specialized drugs, these psychics were initially employed to "remote view" (i.e., psychically perceive) enemy "soft targets," pinpointing the location of hostages and/or reading the minds of enemy leaders and scientists, in addition to locating "hard targets" (e.g., hidden military installations).

Project Stargate was eventually discontinued, but not before attempts were made to turn Stargate's psychic spies into psychic assassins capable of using ESP to kill with a psychic bolt from afar! At the time, Project Stargate and other such programs were considered legitimate military defense research once Western intelligence services discovered the Soviets were likewise pouring millions into the development of a similar program.

Evidently, despite that post–World War II ban on espionage, Japan, like everyone else, was (is?) also busy trying to take espionage to the next level. For example, during President George Bush Sr.'s trip to Japan, the president became ill enough to vomit during an important state dinner.

Needless to say, the American president hurling in public, reportedly

291. Yeah, pretty much everything they alluded to for years on *The X-Files* TV show and on the hit sci-fi show *Fringe* premiering in 2008. See footnote 292, below.

292. No relation to the 1994 Kurt Russell movie *Stargate* and its subsequent spin-off TV franchise *Stargate*, *Stargate Atlantis*, and *Stargate Universe*. Although, in conspiracy circles, the argument has been made that, by surreptitiously promoting the movie and TV series of the same name, government propagandists helped stifle any meaningful discussion of real Project Stargate experimentation. FYI: as if rubbing our noses in it, the TV show *Stargate* featured an episode where the government agency in charge of keeping the truth of Stargate technology secret from the public do so by underwriting a cheesy fictional TV adventure series called "Wormhole" that parodies the actual secret Stargate program to a *T*. A similar "hide-in-plain-sight" disinformation argument was made when the NSA's factual Echelon satellite array was figured prominently in Steven Segal's fictional 1995 movie *Under Siege 2: Dark Territory*.

293. As portrayed in the 2009 movie *The Men Who Stare at Goats*, based on the 2005 book of the same name by Jon Ronson (Simon & Schuster, 2005). See also *Psychic Warrior: Inside the CIA's Stargate Program* (St. Martin's Press, 1996).

even splattering the Japanese prime minister, caused Bush to lose face (i.e., honor and respect) in the eyes of all Asian people. This practically ensured that Bush would then feel obligated to give economic and political concessions to Japan in order to regain his lost face. According to at least one knowledgeable source, an accomplished Japanese psychic in the employ of Japanese intelligence (or, some maintain, a remnant of the Black Dragon Society) caused Bush to become ill by using an ancient ninja mind control influencing technique known as *ki-doll*.[294]

Accordingly, some experts believe that the future of espionage might just be ESP-inage!

WHY CAN'T I BE A SPY?

You can. You probably already are:

> The eye desires clarity. The ear desires keenness of pitch. The mind values wisdom most of all. If your eyes see All-under-Heaven with clarity, there is nothing that can escape your sight. If your ears hear with keenness, there is no sound in All-under-Heaven, that you will not hear. Reasoning with a mind in harmony with All-under-Heaven, there is nothing you can not know. When knowledge from all directions comes to you the way the spokes of a great wheel converge at the hub, then your clarity will know perfection . . . The secret of the Tao lies in what cannot be seen. The secret to managing a kingdom's affairs lies in listening to what cannot be heard. Victory lies in knowing what cannot be known. This is both a wondrous and yet subtle thing to comprehend!
>
> —The T'ai Kung

As the Bhagavad-Gita's Arjuna learned, no matter what walk of life we find ourselves participating in, we have no choice but to participate; like it or not we're in the game. At the very least, we have to choose to be either player or piece, the Mover or the moved. And if the Mover, then we must learn to see what others miss—dim distinctions at first, then glaring

294. *Strange Universe*. November 12, 1997.

discrepancies that, under direct and careful scrutiny, become *patterns of behavior* to be exploited:

> Collecting, reporting and filing are, of course, a feature of all intelligence work. It is the small, probably unimportant-seeming pieces on their own which, when collected together, form the essential, all important completed mosaic. But the individual agent must be trained to recognize until it becomes an instinct the correct interpretation of isolated minutiae. —Ronald Seth, *Secret Servants*

But even the best intelligence is useless unless it leads to timely action:

> If one sees good but is indolent in acting, when the time to fill the hand is upon you but your head is instead filled with doubt, then one is not yet doing the Will of Heaven.
>
> —The T'ai Kung

If we have not adequate intelligence of the first order (that being *innate* intelligence) to acquire in a timely fashion and apply in an even more efficient fashion intelligence of the second order (that of the *gathered* variety), then let us hope that we are *thrice* ignorant and will so be spared both the anxiety and the certainty of our pending downfall!

II.

The Slyness of Ssu-ma

Tactical advantage*[295] *requires being able to shift from big to small, from being overly strong to appearing weak, from using large numbers of soldiers to using but a handful to accomplish your purpose, to changing the* chi[296] *of the battlefield at will.

—Ssu-ma

IN THE ANCIENT Chinese classic *Ssu-ma fa* (Ssu-ma's Art of War), the author T'ian Jang-chü, better known today as Ssu-ma, laments the passing of more "chivalrous times"—when bold and honorable warriors met in one-on-one combat to decide issues political and personal, for the most part sparing the general populace unneeded bloodshed and hardship.

Indeed, Ssu-ma lived in an era that witnessed a dramatic transition between old and new ways of making war, with traditional and highly ritualized one-on-one chivalrous combat giving way to more contemporary—practical—battles employing huge armies of mostly conscripted soldiers.

As a Taoist, Ssu-ma naturally saw war as deplorable. But he was also a realist who understood that war was necessary and sometimes unavoidable. As such, when we have no other choice than to gird up our loins we should strive (1) to get it over with ASAP (2) with as little bloodshed as possible.

295. Ch. *Ch'üan*, lit "power" to decide the outcome of a situation.

296. Energy, vitality, flux.

Despite his streak of romanticism, Ssu-ma was no pie-in-the-sky Taoist monk; rather, he was a man of the field—the *battlefield* to be precise. And so we find Ssu-ma's insights into the motivations of men in general, and the behavior of men in wartime in particular, not only realistic for his day but perennial, also easily adaptable and applicable for use in our modern day-to-day battles.

In ancient China, "Ssu-ma" was a job description. It meant horse master, a title originally limited to an officer in charge of the care and training of military horses, in ancient China one of the most vital positions in the army. As a result of this crucial responsibility, down through the ages "Ssu-ma" also came to be used to identify a master of military matters in general. Thus, masters such as Sun Tzu might correctly be referred to as "Ssu-ma."

During his lifetime, T'ian Jang-chü's Ssu-ma skill became so renowned and universally respected that, in order to differentiate him from lesser ministers of war, he was called *Ta Ssu-ma*—"The Great" Ssu-ma, or the Accomplished War Minister.

Ssu-ma Jang-chü, a descendent of T'ien Wan Ch'en, served Duke Ching of the kingdom of Ch'i. Jang-chü was eventually awarded the surname[297] T'ien in recognition of his helping Duke Ching win battles.

One rags-to-riches version has a peasant boy named Jang-chü joining (or being drafted into) the army of Duke Ching. Exhibiting a natural affinity for working with horses, in short order the young man had earned the title of *Ssu-ma*, "Horse Master."

One day, overhearing a general complaining to Duke Huan how difficult it was to train new soldiers in a timely fashion, especially if those soldiers wouldn't even show up on time, Jang-chü ventured the idea that since men were subject to the same desires and fears as horses, it could not be that much more difficult to train a man as one would train a horse:[298]

> *Too much whip and they flinch away in fear. Too little discipline, and they run wild, Ssu-ma informed the Duke.*
>
> *Intrigued by this concept, Duke Ching called for an officer named Ku to be brought before them. "This officer is always tardy," the Duke*

297. Akin to being invited to join the royalty.

298. Yeah, Ssu-ma beat Pavlov out by at least twenty-five hundred years!

informed Ssu-ma. "Even his own men joke that he will one day be late for his own funeral. Since you claim men and horses can be trained alike, what is the first thing necessary for training a horse?"

"One must first get the horse's attention," Ssu-ma told the Duke, beheading Ku with a single sudden stroke of his sword. "Behead in order to instruct."[299]

"But, the man is dead! Surely he cannot take instruction well now?" Duke Ching exclaimed.

"One man walked into your tent, but ten thousand will see him carried out." Ssu-ma assured Duke Ching.

Thus the saying from ancient times: "Kill one to control ten thousand."

How Jang-chü went from being a simple peasant boy to such a decidedly *ruthless* commander isn't clearly spelled out but the facts of his life are that he started out a man of unremarkable (if not lowly) birth, becoming first Ssu-ma respected "master of the horse" before being elevated to General, and a "master of men."

Many Chinese *Ping-fa* texts trace themselves, if not physically then at least philosophically, to Chang Lu Shang, the first king of Ch'i, better known as "T'ai Kung," taking their inspiration (if not actual strategies and tactics) from the man most responsible for commanding the army of the emerging Chou[300] Dynasty when it overthrew the Shang Dynasty at the decisive Battle of *Mu-yeh* in 1045 B.C. Experts all agree it was the T'ai Kung's innovative strategy and tactics (including the liberal use of prewar propaganda,[301] spies, and the deployment of elite special forces) that carried the day.

Also known as "Lu Wang" and "T'ai Shih Shang-fu," the T'ai Kung had

---

299. A similar tale is told of a young Sun Tzu, who, having been challenged by a king to prove the viability of the unorthodox training methods Sun Tzu was proposing by instructing the king's giggling concubines in the art of war, unceremoniously beheaded the concubine giggling the loudest. In short order, Sun Tzu had trained the now *most attentive* concubines so well they became the king's bodyguard! FYI: Some point to this incident as the beginning of the all-female secret society known as "The Black Lotus." (See *Mental Dominance* by Dr. Haha Lung and Christopher B. Prowant [Citadel 2009]).

300. Often spelled "Zhou."

301. The T'ai Kung had spread the word long before the battle that the Chou people had nothing personal against the Shang people, only against their "evil" leaders. For a complete rendering of the T'ai Kung's Art of War, see *Mind Assassins* by Dr. Haha Lung and Christopher B. Prowant (Citadel, 2010).

originally served the Shang for many years, before defecting to the Chou where he loyally served first King Wen and then his successor, King Wu.

Sanctimonious Confucian scholars of later years vilified the T'ai Kung for being ruthless and for his "despicable machinations" that included his use of espionage, sex, and bribery to achieve victory. While true that the T'ai Kung was no stranger to using any and all available avenues to achieve victory, his willingness to use expedient manners and methods to resolve matters grew out of his ideal of (1) avoiding war whenever possible and (2) finishing a war as quickly as possible with as little loss of life as possible. Many who came after him, Sun Tzu, Sun Pin, and Ssu-ma, would also hold these as the highest of ideals.

The T'ai Kung's wisdom is preserved in his *Liu t'sao* ("The Six Secrets"), a *Ping-fa* completed shortly before his death.

For this service, the Chou Dynasty Emperor awarded the T'ai Kung rulership over the newly created state (kingdom) of Ch'i. The T'ai Kung's descendants in the state Ch'i encouraged the study of military science, making the *Liu t'sao* the basis for Ch'i military studies, which, in turn, went on to influence later Chinese strategists, such as K'ung Ming, Cao Cao, and of course Sun Tzu and his descendant Sun Pin, as well as strategists outside China, most notably in Japan.

Speaking of Sun Pin, there are indications Sun Pin may have directly contributed his pen (or quill as the case may be) to the final compilation of the *Ssu-ma fa*. This is hardly surprising, since some sources list both Sun Tzu and Sun Pin as relatives of Ssu-ma Jang-chü, all three being members of the T'ien clan. Our present version of the *Ssu-ma fa* dates from around 378–342 B.C. and was compiled from earlier versions by King Wei, himself also a descendant of the T'ien lineage and so, above and beyond merely preserving a valuable military treatise, had a vested interest in seeing a definitive work of his ancestor preserved.

Ssu-ma Jang-chü, while a great strategist in his own right, was undoubtedly influenced by the T'ai Kung's teachings,[302] though some experts maintain that the *Ssu-ma fa* also shows the influence of pre–Chou Dynasty military writings.

---

302. The T'ai Kung is still honored in China as "the first of Generals." So acclaimed was he that during the Tang Dynasty he was given his own temple and enshrined as the living incarnation of the God of War.

Postscript: Near the end of his long life, three ambitious high officials named Pao, Kao, and Kuo crafted lies against Ssu-ma T'ien Jang-chü. So trying were these lies that, for the sake of sparing his family disgrace, the elderly Jang-chü resigned from the court service and died soon after, without clearing his name.

After this, T'ien clan relatives, led by cousins T'ien Ch'i, T'ien Pao, and Ti'en Ch'ang, swore a blood feud and formed a secret society vowing to revenge themselves on T'ien Jang-chü's detractors. This blood feud lasted many years (by other accounting, many decades),[303] with the end result being the complete extermination of the Kao and Kuo clans by T'ien followers.

T'ien Ch'ang's great-grandson T'ien Ho would go on to become King Wei of Ch'i, gaining and securing his throne (reigning from 378 to 342 B.C.) by employing his great-grandfather Ssu-ma Jang-chü's insights and strategies. He is the same King Wei who later compiled the definitive version of the *Ssu-ma fa*, roughly around the same time both Sun-Tzu's and Sun Pin's works appeared, the latter of whom is believed to have had an actual hand in helping collect and revise this final version.

Throughout his writings, Ssu-ma exhibits a very Taoist attitude in recognizing the interconnectedness of all things. The Taoist ideal was/is to be in harmony with earthly nature and with the universal nature—the *T'ai Chi*.

To be in harmony was said to be in harmony with the Will of Heaven. Hopefully you recall the Will of Heaven from our previous study of Cao Cao's Nine Strategies in Section I.

To retain our natural—original—balance, we must give duty and due to both the workings of Heaven (things unseen) as well as maintaining a realistic assessment of earthly matters (things seen).

Thus, for men at war, a balance must be struck between what takes place on the battlefield and all influencing factors leading up to—supporting or detracting from—action on the battlefield. For example, down through the ages, how many great generals—Hannibal, for instance—have won on the battlefield only to be beaten at home in the senate or in the throne room? This is why part of the *Ssu-ma fa* is set aside to consider such things as changing laws, protests, and civil unrest at home, factors that cannot but impact—positively or negatively—on the men in the field, bolstering or undermining the morale and machinery of war, hampering a cause, perhaps even endan-

303. Still others say it continues to this day!

gering the soldier in the field. According to Ssu-ma, an able and good commander must thus take all such things into consideration before raising his war standard.

However, while directly affecting one another, matters in the field and matters at home must be kept in separate spheres—"compartmentalized" we would say today. Thus, Ssu-ma tells us that when the call to battle comes:

> On the very day a general receives the command to make war he immediately turns his face from his home and enters the army camp where he is the first to beat the drum for assembly.

In other words, the general must show the way, leading by example, or as Jesse Jackson once intoned: "Can't teach what you don't know. Can't lead where you don't go!"

Teaching and then leading come from training.

Well-trained men win battles. All great strategists agree: all things being equal, when armies of equal strength meet, the army who has devoted more time to training wins.

Ssu-ma, master trainer of horses, knew something about training stubborn animals suffering from collective attention deficit disorder so it behooves us to study his tried-and-true techniques for first adapting and then applying his knowledge of "breaking" wild horses to training more effective human beings.

To accomplish this, the *Ssu-ma fa* first reveals *why men fight*, before then teaching us (training us?) how to spot potential *fatal flaws in men,* giving us ways of *testing the types of men*—in order to weed out weaker stock.

Ssu-ma then goes on to stress The Seven Tenets of Training, including How to Motivate Others, The 13 Steps to War, and How to Wage War Successfully—providing us with tactics and techniques we can apply not just to the battlefield but to all our fields of endeavor.

WHY MEN FIGHT

According to the *Ssu-ma fa*, men fight for one of four reasons: glory, profit, shame, or death.

When we compare these with Hannibal,[304] we see that these two master

304. See the "Hannibal's Six Movers of Men" chapter previously, figure 12, in particular.

strategists' assessment of men's motivations are pretty much the same despite the fact that Ssu-ma and Hannibal Barca lived hundreds of years apart—and on different sides of the world from one another.

THE THIRTEEN FATAL FLAWS IN MEN

Ssu-ma realized early on in life that men, like horses, possessed flaws.

In order for a horse or a man to become *useful*, he must be pushed beyond his flaws by a firm hand. That firm hand in turn must be guided by an eye for detail.

In order for a man to become *exceptional,* however, he has to recognize those flaws in himself—preferably before his enemies do. That's something, so far as we know, our equine cousins are incapable of doing.

The thirteen "fatal flaws" observed by Ssu-ma are to be spied out and avoided when picking your horse and when choosing men to fight beside you. Conversely, these flaws—vulnerabilities—are to be fully and ruthlessly exploited when you observe them being exhibited by your enemy.

How does the commander train such flaws out of his men? First and foremost *by example*. Ssu-ma instructs us:

"Acting from without, control what is within."

At the very least, this means the man (or woman) in charge needs to project an *authentic* air of confidence. Confidence can be more infectious than an HIV/H1N1 cocktail.

Recall from our earlier discussion in the chapter on the power of persuasion how the person who speaks up first is often (and sometimes *falsely*!) thought to be the smartest guy (or gal) in the room. All human beings have a soft spot for such "take charge" people—that soft spot is called their *brain*!

Whereas con men and other unscrupulous Mind Slayers routinely "pad the bill" to make themselves look more confident and in charge than they really are, in a life-or-death battlefield situation, a commander can't afford to pad the bill and lie to his men. Yet at the same time, that commander has a responsibility to assuage any doubt that might prevent his men from performing at peak efficiency. More on Ssu-ma's method for alleviating doubt and other paralyzing emotions in a minute.

An important part of a leader projecting confidence and awe is the ability and willingness to dole out both rewards and punishments in swift, equitable, and consistent fashion. Just as discipline dispels doubt, so too consistency breeds respect.

So "acting from without, control what is within" means that not only does the commander project a disciplined, awe-inspiring example for his men to follow, this adage also points out how by literally moving men "on the outside" we can effect inner change.

Nietzsche says, "Do the thing and you have the power."

In the same vein, the first rule of brainwashing is: what we do we become. In other words, get a POW to "go along just a little" by agreeing to do some small favor for his captors (e.g., just come to the "re-education" meeting tonight) and, in short order, he'll not only be spilling his own guts, he'll also be convincing his fellow POWs to do the same.[305]

Early on, Ssu-ma realized that the best way to get a horse used to a bridle and saddle was to put a bridle and saddle on the horse. Likewise, in order to break men's fatal flaws, you simply move them in the opposite direction from those flaws, causing them to *perform actions* in direct contradiction to their character flaw.

Twenty-five hundred years after Ssu-ma figured this out, a psychologist named Robert Ellis came up with something he called "Rational Emotive Therapy," which said pretty much the same thing: Get up and get moving! And you'll probably find out your problems aren't nearly as bad as you think.

A practical illustration of how the body has a mind of its own:

> You're sitting in a room feeling depressed, perhaps even suicidal when suddenly the door bursts open and a wild-eyed maniac runs into the room swinging around an already bloody machete screaming how he's gonna kill every "lyin' MFer" in the room! Suddenly all that depression vanishes, all your thoughts of suicide are gone in an instant as—without conscious thought—your body is scrambling out the nearest window intent on surviving!

---

305. For a complete course in POW interrogation and brainwashing techniques, see *Theatre of Hell: Dr. Lung's Complete Guide to Torture* by Dr. Haha Lung and Christopher B. Prowant (Loompanics Unlimited, 2003).

So the next time you're thrust into a position of command, first discern which one(s) of these fatal flaws is standing in the way of your soldier giving you one hundred percent[306] effort, performing at one hundred percent efficiency, and then point them in the *opposite direction.* Put them to work as far from their flaws—from their *excuses*—as possible. For your enemy, on the other hand, you of course want to *encourage* these thirteen fatal flaws as much as possible.

- **Arrogance:** This type doesn't like to follow orders. They do not respect the command structure. Overconfident, they endanger both themselves and others.

*Over*estimating one's self is as potentially dangerous as *under*estimating an opponent. Like a beautiful stallion that would make the finest of mounts, you have to first break this type to the bridle and saddle (i.e., get them used to following commands), and do so without breaking their fiery spirit, which would be a powerful addition to your stable.

Instead of hobbling this type, stifling their natural energy, employ the "judo principle," assigning them tasks deliberately designed to (1) challenge their overestimation of themselves and (2) burn off their excess energy. Send them on autonomous missions that require little supervision, allowing them to shine without the possibility of their compromising the larger mission.

Arrogance is forgivable in the young—no wild colt takes to the bridle and saddle on its own volition. If, however, you have an old warhorse fighting your commands all the way, still refusing to follow orders, that man endangers others and should be removed in such a way as to serve as an example to others.

- **Paranoia:** This type of horse shies away, flinching, and is easily startled. And it's impossible to train either a horse or a man if you can't get close to them. Having been struck before by a heavy hand, they are understandably fearful of being struck again. Many young soldiers lack trust in authority figures—either because they've been

306. Don't you just hate those numbnuts who talk about giving one hundred and ten percent, as if invoking that imaginary ten percent makes them look more enthusiastic . . . as opposed to just more math dyslexic!

disappointed or outright abused by authority figures (from parents to priest) in their past. This type of fear is hard to pin down because it's more intangible than the kind of fear that focuses on an actual physical object or situation, a coming battle for instance. That type of fear we'll discuss in a minute.

This paranoia type of fear lacks trust and so manifests constant suspicion. According to Ssu-ma: "Benevolence attracts people. But benevolence without trust defeats itself." Thus, your initial benevolent overtures designed to draw this type of person closer to you are apt to be viewed with suspicion. Therefore, training this type of horse (or man) takes special effort and extra time . . . and success is by no means a given. This type routinely exhausts resources and patience and comes dangerously close to invoking the old adage that it is better to have an animal with too much fire (one that will initially fight you) than to be burdened with a beast whose spark of life has burned out. The former is a challenge. The latter, a waste.

- **Disruptiveness:** To "disrupt" is to make noise, to deliberately break routine or test tradition. This is first and foremost attention-getting behavior. All animals exhibit this type of behavior so why should men be any different? The child who cries the loudest gets fed first; the squeaky wheel gets the grease. Disruptive people only remain disruptive so long as they get the attention they crave.

A disruptive person is easily corralled by putting them in charge where the success of a venture falls squarely on their shoulders. They will now find themselves in a position where they will have to police the disruptiveness of others. A disruptive horse placed among docile beasts will calm down. Whereas one bad apple might spoil the whole bunch, in this instance, calmness rubs off, at least in animals.

- **Laziness:** This is a relative term. People are generally lazy when assigned to do things they really don't feel like doing—like work. Ask a teenaged slack-jawed sagger how many stars are on the American flag and he'll look at you like you just asked him for the formula for rocket fuel. Now ask that same kid about his favorite basketball team and you'll not be able to shut him up while he spouts off statistic after statistic, point spreads on tonight's game, and gives you the square root of all the jock straps on the team! That's because passing a GED is work, whereas following every move your favorite team makes is fun. In other words, give a person an assignment that involves work they really enjoy doing and they will not only do the job right the first time, they'll do it in record time. This is why Ssu-ma cautions us to always hitch the right horse to the right cart. As much as possible, we must pair the person with an assignment that engages their attention and respects their abilities. That way, both the soldier and the army benefit.

- **Weariness:** There's a big difference between being tired and being lazy. Reward your best workers with vacation time. Constantly re-inspire and re-invigorate your troops. Don't use up your best workers. That's what Sun Tzu's "expendable agents" are for.
- **Doubt:** Doubt is dispelled by confidence. When confidence is not innate in the men, it must be exuded by those in command. Example: Patton, Hannibal, Alexander, all the greats.

According to Ssu-ma: "Timely decisions fortify the mind." Even when a general is doubtful, he must hide this fact from his men. Study the St. Crispin's Day speech Shakespeare puts in Henry V's mouth. Henry doesn't insult the intelligence of his men by hiding the fact that the situation is dire. But his courage fortifies the men. Think Churchill during the Battle of Britain, Colonel Travis at the Alamo, Lionidas's speech to his three hundred.

Doubt and low self-esteem are a self-destructive ouroborus, parasitically feeding on itself—venomous head devouring poisonous tail.

Men doubt because they do not see clearly today the possibilities of tomorrow. So how does a leader combat low self-esteem and dispel doubt in his men?

> Men treated as men behave as men. When meeting the upright remain upright, speak calmly and employ anger[307] sparingly. —Ssu-ma

Doubt in an enemy's eyes, on the other hand, is a welcome sight. Encourage your enemy's doubt—keep him guessing as to your actions and

307. Also translated as "fire."

agenda—by employing your men with confidence and deploying your forces sans hesitation:

> When doubt does not hamper our movement, the enemy thinks we are without plans. —Ssu-ma

- **Fearful:** This is not the same as the paranoid discussed above. Genuine fear is our friend. Fear is what's kept us alive this long. Fear is our friend so long as fear points out the *real* things (and people) in life we need to watch out for. Fear that has a factual, actual focus is genuine fear—and genuine fear is our friend.

  Vague and unsubstantiated fears, on the other hand, are often fears stemming from some drama, trauma, or mama incident in the past that harmed us (or at least scared the bejesus out of us!), make us hesitate in the present, and make us fear the future. Ultimately, these vague fears spring from doubt. And, as already mentioned, doubt is dispelled by discipline. Thus, the commander allows his men to suckle off his reserve of courage:

  > Actions well-executed, in accord with the ancient ways, will be fruitful under Heaven. Goals clearly spoken drown out all noise of ill omen and men will be strong. —Ssu-ma

  See the section "How to Motivate Others" that follows.
- **Shirking:** This type avoids responsibility as much as possible, not necessarily because they are lazy, but because they fear—often with good reason—that the reach required of them will exceed their grasp and they will fall flat on their face.

For some shirkers this is merely a *fear of failure* that is easily remedied by showing them they can succeed—again, a case of your simply *doing the thing* (action) and taking away your unfounded fear (thought) of not being able to actually do the thing.

Ironically, you may discover that this type of person may be an excellent worker and only shirks responsibility when actual responsibility is thrust upon him. He is a prime example of what is called the Peter Principle—simply put, promoting someone beyond their level of comfortable capability.

Again, we are reminded of Ssu-ma's admonitions to "hitch the right horse to the right cart."

- **Cowering:** The same horse that shies away from being yoked to a carriage and forced to prance through public might prove to be the most dependable of long-distance runners when given the job of carrying you swiftly across wide-open plains. As with horses so with men.

In many ways, cowering is similar to shirking in that the person is not necessarily useless, only that they are trying to keep a low profile and not draw attention (i.e., unwanted responsibility) to themselves. This is the little kid who tries scrunching lower at his school desk so as not to be called on by his teacher.

Don't confuse "cower" with "coward." Like the shirker, the cowering type most often only needs galvanizing, needs his true worth recognized and put to work. Find him a comfortable niche to call his own and he will prove the most loyal of soldiers.

- **Complaining:** In the same way some people are disruptive in order to gain attention, complainers also seek attention first and foremost. Through complaining (the adult form of bawling your eyes out) complainers hope to bring attention to the fact that they are smart and insightful (for "obviously" being the only one smart enough to point out whatever's wrong).

Chronic complainers may also suffer from what's known as a martyr complex (where they see themselves sacrificing themselves for an ungrateful world, sublimating their own needs so others can be happy).

Chronic complainers must be kept from contaminating the enthusiasm of the rest of the troops—in the same way a sick horse must be separated from healthy animals. Complainers are easily manipulated by simply commiserating with them, agreeing how they are "oh-so-smart" and how the rest of the world doesn't recognize their "obvious" genius.

- **Unruly:** Unrestrained, lacks a focus and a proper venue for releasing his considerable energies, a thoroughbred trapped in too small a pen. And for this prize animal, *any* pen is going to be too small. Your basic

James Dean. Give this rebel a cause he can believe in and, all on his own, he will focus his unruliness to a keen edge—a keen edge you can draw across your enemy's throat whenever you choose!

- **Regretful:** This type is motivated by either guilt for things he's done in the past, or else he pines for dreams and fantasies he's never gotten a chance to realize. The former makes him a prime candidate for blackmail (when the sin he committed in the past isn't common knowledge and he wants to keep it that way). Perhaps he made a mistake in the past and desperately wants to rectify it, seeking redemption and wanting to make restitution.

The latter, the road not taken, the touchdown never attempted, gives a wily Mind Slayer an opening with which to bond and entice his regretful mark simply by offering to give the mark a chance to finally realize his dream. A variation of this is the person who wants to reclaim and relive his "glory days;" show him how to achieve this and his front door and wallet will both swing wide open for you.

- **Slackness:** Any trainer of animals will tell you they'd rather find themselves tasked with training a beast who has "fire in the belly," one that has enough spunk to defy you initially, than to attempt training a timid, perhaps previously beaten-down beast, one who simply cowers in the corner. The former has an innate fire that the right hand can master and put to good use. But it is nigh impossible to build up a blaze where there is no fuel to begin with.

Often it is the most disruptive, unruly horses that, ultimately, under the guidance, firm hand, and judicious whip of the right trainer, turn out to be champions.

THE SEVEN TENETS OF TRAINING

A horse, a horse! My kingdom for a horse!
—Shakespeare, *Richard III*

Ssu-ma's first rule: take care of your horses (and your men) and they will take care of you. It's not surprising then that he was known for personally seeing to the needs of both his horses and his men—making certain rations were divided evenly, seeing to the ill, even asking after families.

And the most important way Ssu-ma took care of both his horses and his men was to see that they were both properly trained.

Natural talent and the occasional "rain man" idiot savant aside, the more you train in your particular field of endeavor, the better your chances of (1) maintaining your cool in the face of the unexpected and (2) obtaining your goals in the face of obstacles and obstinate asses to the contrary.

As with the training of horses, the proper training of men is paramount, as evidenced by Ssu-ma's following Seven Tenets of Training:

1. **Prior training wins out:** How well men are trained prior to battle is the best indicator (though no guarantee) of their performance in battle.
2. **Even the finest of horses can be startled into bolting:** No matter how well you train, there's always the unexpected. Chance—and adversity—favor the prepared mind.
3. **Train men and horses toward what they will face:** *Realistic* training is the key. Plan (train) for every eventuality . . . knowing full well you can never plan for every eventuality! Temperament tells. Ssu-ma took into consideration that men from different areas of a kingdom might think differently, that they might have different temperaments and loyalties.

> Ways differ from region to region. Each of the four corners has its own nature. Through teaching of the Tao customs come to agreement. —Ssu-ma

The consummate horse master, Ssu-ma knew that stallions shouldn't be yoked to pack mules, that you train your horses and your men according to their promise and assign them according to their performance. Today, this would be called being "politically incorrect."

4. **Know your ground:** Like all great commanders, Ssu-ma was conversant in the Three Knows: know yourself, know your enemy, and know your environment. Knowing your environment means knowing the area in which you'll be operating. Sun Tzu devotes a whole chapter to recognizing the various types of physical terrain (ground) a commander is likely to encounter during a campaign. But "ground" is not only a physical area; it also refers to additional (background) factors that need to be considered before engaging in any campaign

(e.g., logistics and resources available, the political atmosphere, the psychology of both your forces and those of your opponent).

Knowing your ground helps you pair the right man (or horse) to the terrain: pack animals versus war mounts; strong, long-legged stallions good on the long run and stout, short-legged ponies for the uphill climb.

5. **Hitch the right horse to the right cart:** When you need a team of Clydesdales to pull your Bud wagon, My Little Pony isn't gonna do! Taken literally, this reminds us it was the T'ai Kung's unexpected and unorthodox (*ch'i*) use of horse-drawn chariots that allowed the Chou to beat the Shang at the decisive Battle of Mu-yeh in 1045 B.C.[308] These were horses trained long and hard specifically to pull a chariot. Had the Ta'i Kung hitched free-running stallions or even heavier, slower horses more accustomed to pulling heavy-laden supply carts, the Shang might still be running China!

Use the right man—or horse—for the job and the job gets done. Try to skimp and save money by hiring and/or half-ass training less-than-adequate workers, and don't be surprised if you end up with less-than-adequate results.

> Employ men to their capacities. —Ssu-ma

6. **Not all bridles fit all horses:** See to your equipment. You always train your troops to "think on their feet," and a good commander always knows how to improvise when need be. Yet even the best of warriors have been defeated by simple logistics—by not having the right tools in the right place at the right time to turn the tide of battle. In any war, bread is always more important than bullets.

THE TAO OF TRAINING BOTH HORSES AND MEN

Problem Solving 101 consists of four steps:

1. **Define** the problem
2. **Brainstorm** possible solutions—rejecting no idea no matter how far-fetched

308. *Chariot* by Arthur Cotterell (Overlook Press, 2005).

3. **Prioritize** those possible solutions as to feasibility—given time constraints, available resources, etc.
4. **Apply** those prioritized solutions until you solve the problem

More than twenty-five hundred years ago, Ssu-ma came up with a similar, albeit more detailed, six-step methodology for solving the problem of how to train both horses and men by first testing them:

- First, name the action you wish them to perform.
- Then show them the action you wish them to perform by performing it correctly yourself. Remember: can't teach what you don't know; can't lead where you don't go.
- Assign them the action you want them to perform. If more than one person (or horse) is involved, be certain to clearly explain the part each must play.
- If they perform the action correctly, reward them. Then have them repeat the action again, rewarding them first each time, then every other time, and finally every time in four.
- If they perform the action incorrectly, determine if they failed to perform correctly because of (1) *your* lack of instruction or (2) their lack of attention.

  If the former: the fault lies with you and you must modify your demonstration, better honing your teaching skills, or bring in other experts to display proper technique.

  If the latter: the fault being their inattention to your instruction, punish them swiftly before allowing them to perform the action again and again, interspaced with corresponding punishment until—ultimately—they perform the action correctly.

  If they remain steadfast in their inattention to learning, punish them severely, using their punishment as an incentive for others to try harder.

  It has been pointed out that "Some men are beautiful centaurs; others are simply the horse's ass."[309] In other words, not all men (like not all horses) are trainable to the point of usefulness, yet even

309. Vlad Tepes, *Dracula's Art of War*.

the most useless of men and horses can still be made to benefit others—the former's punishment serving as an example to other men; the latter ensuring the employ of those who work the glue factory!
- Assign each man according to his tested attitude and aptitude.[310]

Not every horse breaking from the gate reaches into the home stretch . . . let alone crosses the finish line. Many pull up short, without ever getting close to the finish line. Sometimes you cross the finish line . . . Sometimes the finish line crosses you!

HOW TO MOTIVATE OTHERS

Manipulate their spirit. Push them according to their gravest fears, pull them according to their greatest desires.
—Ssu-ma

Ah! The ol' "carrot and the stick," the Taoist yin-yang. Or as Vlad Tepes so succinctly—so *ruthlessly!*—put it in *Dracula's Art of War:*

> In all ages, to move men is as simple as holding bread in one hand and a bludgeon in the other.

Men rush toward what they want and war against what they hate—and fear. Says Ssu-ma:

> A man with his mind set on victory sees only the enemy before him. A man whose mind is filled with fear, sees all manner of fear to come.

But here's the key: *fear never arrives*. What we fear is always in the future. Even when faced with a current enemy, we fear what he's capable of doing—in the future. That future might be next week, it might be tomorrow, or we might be fearing the punch he's about to throw any minute. But no matter how imminent, even if only a few seconds in the future, there is still time for us to respond—to do *something*! And if we've taken the time to train ourselves for just such an eventuality or, in the case of a commander, to train our

310. That is, temperament.

men (or our horses) to face such possibilities, then our chances of surviving any future threat just doubled.

We defeat fear by living in "the now," by putting full effort into training today and by keeping the minds of our troops and fellows focused on today's toil, on the task at hand.

> Wars are won by winning battles. Battles are lost by worrying about winning the war.[311]

Thoughts of the future must serve to galvanize, never paralyze. On the march, the commander's thoughts must be three hundred and sixty degrees; the thoughts of his men, only to the fore.

Ssu-ma makes it clear that a clearly established system of swift reward and swifter punishment helps focus men's attention *and* ambition:

> When they are too terrified of the enemy, it is useless to threaten men with punishments no matter how severe and with execution . . . Remind them instead what they have to live for and demonstrate clearly to them the part they must play in securing victory. —Ssu-ma

Or as God avatar Krishna in the Bhagavad-Gita corrected the great warrior Arjuna that what he thought was a hopeless lose-lose situation was really a win-win:

"Die in battle and you win heaven. Conquer and you enjoy Earth."

If you correct men's doubts and delusions, they can be made to submit to orders, can be led, and can be encouraged to accomplish great deeds. Men must be encouraged—either through promise of pleasure or threat of pain—to take a chance, to risk all.

Ssu-ma observes that we "Achieve victory by being endangered." This means not only (1) that the prize goes to those who first dare put themselves in harm's way but also (2) that human beings tend to do their best work while under pressure.

Or as another (in)famous commander once put it:

---

311. Vlad Tepes, *Dracula's Art of War.*

> The sword in the scabbard remains safe—knowing neither break nor breakthrough. —Vlad Tepes

The craft of convincing others to go to bat for us, to join us on a campaign from which, in all likelihood, they'll not return unscathed, takes talent.

In the classic 1956 Western *The King and Four Queens*, a nosey bartender asks newly arrived in town debonair con man Clark Gable what he does for a living, to which Gable responds, "I sell things."

"What kind of things?" the bartender wonders aloud.

"*Notions*," says Mr. Gable with a smile.

Thus Ssu-ma observes:

> The Commander saves the people because of his benevolence. He wins battles because he is upright. He makes correct decisions because of his wisdom.

THE THIRTEEN STEPS TO WAR

Three things are vital for victory: The Will of Heaven, material resources, and excellence of intent.

—Ssu-ma

Thirteen might be considered unlucky in the West, but for Ssu-ma, thirteen was the number of contemplative and practical preparatory steps to take *before* embarking on war. Note that, with a little imagination and an eye to detail, these steps can work on any endeavor on which we choose to embark:

Use Things to Their Proper Nature, in Their Proper Place, and to Their Fullest Capacity

Ssu-ma applied this rule to both horses and men. Determine each person's part to play and assign appropriate rank and position. Remember Ssu-ma's admonition to fit the right horse to the right cart.

Bring All Resources to Bear

Utilize all the men and material at your disposal.

Seek Out Specialists in Their Field

Where they don't occur naturally, train them to meet your need. Recruit present and former experts in the pending field of endeavor. Learn from those who have "been there, done that." Learn not only from those who have been successful but from those who failed as well. Make public all past accomplishments of both your staff and your organization, as this is your best recruiting tool. Also use this stage to make public any indiscretions committed by you or your troops that an enemy might try to use for blackmail.

Relay Commands Clearly and Succinctly, in Simple Language

If people don't know, they'll guess. And if history has proven anything it's that, nine out of ten times, when people are left on their own to guess . . . you guessed it, *they guess wrong!* It's human nature to try and fill in the blanks. Leave no blanks for others to fill in. Talk to your audience in a language they'll understand. Keep them updated in a timely fashion.

Keep Abreast of Trends and Sympathies; Listen to the People

In the same way you keep your troops updated, in order to keep them from guessing and inevitably guessing wrong, you have to keep yourself abreast of anything and everything that can either aid or trip up your mission.

Influence[312] People's Hatred

Hate is a great source of focus and not necessarily always a bad thing. We should hate evil, right? And isn't our enemy du jour usually evil? If not, how difficult is it to make it appear so?

Dispel All Doubt

First in yourself, then in those you and your mission depend on. Doubt leads to hesitation and hesitation leads to, at best, *failure*. Worst-case scenario:

312. That is, change, manipulate, direct. Mind Slayer 101.

you're out of all your scenarios because you're *dead*! Never jump the gun, never allow your enemy to force (or entice) you to move until you're truly ready. But when you are ready . . . no holding back! No holds barred! From the Bad Poet's Department: *Better the body stiff, than the mind "What if?"*

Maintain Systematic Planning

ABC might seem boring to some folks, but this kind of thinking, along with crossing the *T*s and dotting all the *I*s,[313] not only ensures a smooth operation but also helps instill confidence in your troops. Familiarize your people with *your* way of doing business and then stick to it. It's not about "my way or the highway"; it's about finding a way that gets the job done. It doesn't matter who your date dances with, so long as they go home with you.

Refute Weakness; Nourish Strength

We nourish strength by adopting a zero-tolerance policy on negativity. Punish negativity, in yourself as well as in others. The old adage holds true (and not just about people but about all things in life): if you can't say something positive—*shut the fuck up!* People need to learn the difference between constructive criticism and bitching. The difference is that the former is encouraged while the latter just drew his last paycheck!

Make the Foundations Solid and the Formations Firm

Build from the ground up. A house built on shifting sands is doomed from the onset. Do your homework. Know the battlefield beforehand. Research the market to ascertain the viability of introducing your new product now. That's right, the Three Knows again.

Train Constantly; Gather Strength

Cao Cao gets the credit for: the more you sweat today, the less you bleed tomorrow. This Ssu-ma rule is basic Nietzsche: you never have enough because you never know when you'll need more. Gather all the people and

313. "Ace of Spies" Sidney Reilly's favorite phrase, remember?

resources you'll need to accomplish your goal . . . and then gather them *a second time* (this is called Plan B, *B* for backup).

One wily medieval Japanese Mind Slayer—unbeknownst to anyone—was actually the grandmaster of two *rival* ninjutsu clans that were constantly at war with one another. This Mind Slayer's thinking—correct, it turned out—was that the menace and machinations of each kept the other on their toes.

Perceiving the True Nature of Things

Miyamoto Musashi admonished his students (those who survived his training!) to "Perceive those things which cannot be seen." Or as we say in the West, the devil is in the details. Notice the little things. Ssu-ma said it this way: "To control strategy, preserve the subtle."

Respond Appropriately to Circumstance and Flux

In life in general, and on the battlefields of life in particular, circumstances remain in constant flux. Permanency is an illusion. We get comfortable, falling into predictable—potentially deadly!—routines and we resist change. To even attempt to resist change is to try standing against the very nature of the universe, or as the Taoist phrase it, going against "The Will of Heaven." The key—again for life in general, but for the commander of men in particular—is to *anticipate change*. Better still, to *initiate change* ourselves.

At our disposal, we have both orthodox (*cheng*) and unorthodox (*ch'i*) forces. This means, in all our endeavors, no matter how dark and dire the circumstance might at first appear, we always have at our disposal the choice to use either (or both in concert) *cheng* or *ch'i* to influence the flux:

> The large is *cheng*, the small *ch'i*. When your cheng force is well-disciplined and arranged according to proper use, and your *ch'i* force set in place and determined, victory is assured. *Cheng* force divides to become *ch'i*. *Ch'i* coagulates to mimic *cheng*. Observe the enemy with both *cheng* and *ch'i* in mind.[314] Plot his movement forward and back. Test his readiness and resolve in many places at once. Touch his mind, troubling

314. Some sources prefer: "Observe enemy forces by using both *cheng* and *ch'i* forces."

him at many points at once. Startle him to know his fears and discipline. —Ssu-ma

THE TAO OF WAGING WAR

Having correctly assessed your enemy's acumen and prowess, you can then match him. This is called weighing. The Art of War is first and foremost the weighing of strengths. Combat is first and foremost the weighing of courage. Deploy your force with skill. Employ men to their capacities. Force your enemy to deploy his men in haste and ignorance. Force his men beyond their capacity. Therein is victory.

—Ssu-ma

The setting for the Hindu holy book Bhagavad-Gita is a battlefield at the onset of a great civil war between the ruling houses of India. India's greatest warrior at the time, Arjuna, has been given the honored (albeit dubious) task of sounding the trumpet that will signal the beginning of battle.

However, since this is a true civil war, Arjuna recognizes friends and even relatives on both sides of the battle lines. Suddenly, a wave of despair and futility washes over him and—uncharacteristically—he throws down his bow and announces "I will not fight!" Fortunately, Arjuna's chariot driver Krishna (who, unbeknownst to Arjuna, just happens to be the God Vishnu come to earth) then takes time to explain to Arjuna why he must fight: first, because he is warrior-bred and thus it is his duty (dharma) and, second, because some wars have to be fought, whether for righteousness' sake or simply for survival's sake.

Though we have no way of knowing if Ssu-ma ever heard the tale of Arjuna, it's obvious our Chinese Master of the Horse holds pretty much the same view: war is sometimes necessary.

According to the *Ssu-ma fa*, warfare is vital to the state because (1) warfare can be used to bring order to a disorderly realm, (2) warfare is the means for punishing evil, and (3) warfare allows the righteous to free the oppressed.

Keep in mind that Ssu-ma romanticized the days of antiquity when chivalrous knights met in ritualized combat to settle scores, where the outcome of a campaign was sometimes decided by single combat between the best warriors chosen from each side, similar to the ancient Greek-Trojan tradition, David and Goliath, the Samurai of Japan, and the knights of Arthurian legend.

However, by Ssu-ma's time, constant internecine warfare, leading to the conscripting of ever-larger Chinese armies, had disenfranchised many members of the nobility, creating a class of stateless wanderers—vagabond knights—in many ways similar to Japanese ronin samurai of Musashi's era. Though displaced, these vagabond knights[315] still strove to exemplify the ideal of "The Six Taoist Standards":[316]

1. **Sympathy**[317] for the sick and wounded.
2. **Benevolence** for noncombatants caught in the crossfire. Also respect for property, especially that of the farmers. In olden times, "benevolence" also referred to the tradition of one commander chivalrously waiting until his enemy counterpart was fully prepared for battle. A surprise—*sucker punch!*—being out of the question. This can be seen as similar to the Cheyenne Indian tradition of "counting coup" by striking an enemy (with a "coup-stick" or with their bare hand). Meant not so much to humiliate a foe as it was a show of one's own courage.
3. **Good faith:** The observance of tradition and the keeping of treaty, which would have included acts of benevolence between commanders.
4. **Righteousness:** A synonym for "certainty of purpose." In other words, a "Man of Tao" did not act until certain of the rightness of his cause. This applied not only to making war but also to the equitable dolling out of reward and punishment—war sometimes being seen as an extension of the latter:

> When Virtue is absent, deceptive and evil rush to fill the void. Those lacking understanding of the Tao have no honor even though they may employ men of honor. Those lacking understanding of the Tao fail to reward those who obey commands, instead encouraging those who fail to obey commands. Instead

315. Some sources translate this "mendicant knights."

316. Ch. *li*, civilian conduct, often rendered "proper manners" or "proper conduct." This is distinct from *fa*, conduct expected of one in the military.

317. Keep in mind that "sympathy" is one of the Five Warning F.L.A.G.S. emotions to which we are all susceptible.

> they reward violent actions while ignoring actions that avoid violence. In this way the people lose faith. —Ssu-ma

Or, as noted centuries later by a ruthless European prince, one with a reputation for being especially conversant in the dispensing of punishment:

> When the highest receive adequate reward and the lowest receive just punishment, right and wrong need not contend with one another. —Vlad Tepes

5. **Courage**

> The high-minded are attracted to courage. Low men flee from courage. —Vlad Tepes

6. **Wisdom:** The proof of wisdom isn't always in the winning; oft times it's in being smart enough to avoid the fight in the first place. Sun Tzu's ideal. Ssu-ma's ideal.

Ssu-ma's Taoist rules of conduct can be applied to any campaign, be that campaign military, political, financial, or personal—as in relationships.

Whatever the mission, whatever the ultimate objective of your campaign—winning a kingdom or simply winning someone's heart—whatever the mission, according to Ssu-ma all actions we take to accomplish our goals:

1. We should be in accord with the Will of Heaven.
2. We should make use of all resources available to us.
3. We should make all resources available to those who can best utilize those materials for the greater good.[318]
4. Our actions should promote progress and prosperity—and not just for ourselves.
5. We should use force sparingly, not as a cure-all.

Ssu-ma accepted that war was sometimes necessary to eradicate evil, reasoning that "If men, for a reason, kill men, killing them is permissible."

Like the T'ai Kung, Ssu-ma was utilitarian in his outlook: whatever works to accomplish the mission with the least loss of life.

---

318. Jeremy Bentham called this "utilitarianism"; that is, actions should accomplish the greatest good for the greatest number.

As already mentioned, the ritualized, highly stylized, one-on-one combat in the early Chou era eventually gave way to the more realistic and practical larger-scale warring states type of warfare. Whereas before, Chou-era commanders would wait courteously for their enemy counterpart to fully assemble his forces in place, the two commanders often exchanging complimentary wine casks to show their mutual admiration and their agreement to "play by the rules" (i.e., observe *li* and *fa*), in the more realistic strategists of later days, men like Ssu-ma, Sun Tzu, Sin Pin, Cao Cao, and Kung Ming knew that to catch your enemy napping spared lives in the long run.

Therefore, like all well-rounded treatises of war, the *Ssu-ma fa* accepts the necessity for a certain amount of subterfuge and skullduggery:

> My enemy's confusion bodes well for me. I seize the advantage, arriving where he is hesitant, striking where he is doubtful.

Confusion in our enemy—whether found there naturally or confusion we put there—is a godsend . . . one we can surely use to bedevil him:

> Attack your enemy's confusion, doubling his confusion, cut your own chances of losing by half. —Vlad Tepes

Having reluctantly accepted that there are times when waging war becomes necessary, Ssu-ma gives us advice both philosophical as well as practical on how to effectively wage war:

- **Employ spies for matters distant. Observe matters near:** Intelligence, first and foremost.
- **Observe the seasons. Observe the passing of the sun and the coming of the moon:** Test the times. In other words, "know your environment," one of the "Three Knows."
- **With the people in mind, calculate hardship:** Wars should relieve the people, not trouble them further.
- **Instructions to the people should be thorough:** Keep the people well-informed of whose job it is to keep you well-supplied. Let each man know his part to play.
- **Create good faith:** Generosity and compassion create good faith.

- **Quietness is the basis of order:** Observes Ssu-ma: "Secrecy, silence, and strength of internal things, herein are formations solidly formed."
- **With the people in harmony, the army is in rapport.**
- **Destroy all doubt. Assure your troops of the rightness of your cause:**

> When the commander's mind is focused, the minds of those under him are focused as well. The commander in accord with Heaven is likewise in accord with his men. Having set[319] their hearts, their strength is his to command. Victory he freely shares with them. In defeat he alone is to blame. —Ssu-ma

- **Reward the army, encourage courage.**
- **Blades define the battlefield. Words define the court:** According to the *Ssu-ma fa*, a sharp delineation between military matters and civilian matters should be maintained at all time, because their interests and goals are often diametrically opposed to one another. The closer these two spheres of influence can be aligned, the safer the realm. Within the state display cooperation; within the army display uprightness; in battle display good faith. When first observing the enemy, remain still.
- **When the enemy appears confused, measure him twice:** It may be a trick. The sword drawn—cuts! Hesitation equals death. Having decided on a course of action, act quickly, before your plans are discovered.
- **Allow the enemy to feed your troops:** Says Ssu-ma:

> When the army is in need, seize what is needed from the enemy. Pulling when an enemy pushes, thus you seize hold of all he loves. —Ssu-ma

---

319. Or "settled."

HOW TO RULE

Authority does not come from being in harmony with others; rather it stems from your ability to make warfare. To kill one man to vouchsafe peace for many men does not disturb the Will of Heaven. To embark on war out of love for the people does not disturb Heaven. Begin war so as to end war so as not to disturb Heaven.

—Ssu-ma

Conquest is easy; control is not. To rule requires what has been called "the conscious exploitation of force." Here, then, we find the source of Mao's insistence that "All political power comes out the barrel of a gun."

Familiarity may breed contempt, but fear most certainly breeds *attention*. Having conquered, we now rule by awe. "Awe" is the happy medium between admiration . . . *and abject terror.* Here we have Machiavelli's most (in)famous observation: that it is better for a prince to rely on fear to secure his rule than for him to rely on the capricious love of the people.[320]

Ssu-ma is very clear (as are other ancient treatises on war) that the worst of scenarios is where a king tries to command what takes place on the battlefield. Today, we call this "micromanaging"—that is, your boss gives you a job to do and then wants to keep looking over your shoulder to make sure you're "doing it right." The need to micromanage is eliminated if you're smart enough to assign the right person to the job.

Sun Tzu, among others, also railed against a commander in the field being micromanaged and second-guessed from the throne.[321] Sun Tzu even went so far as to proclaim that there were times when the commander in the field must disobey (or at the very least ignore) orders from the court. Winning a battle, winning a *war*, has a way of smoothing over the ruffled feathers of a king who is correct in believing that orders issued from the throne aren't being followed in the field.

Just as important, and just as potentially harmful in the long run,

---

320. Once you get to know Machiavelli a little better, you'll find that his *ideal* was that a ruler should have a correct balance of both fear and love but that, forced to choose between the two, fear is more dependable.

321. See *Sun Tzu's Ping fa*, Chapter III, verses 12–15.

according to Ssu-ma, is the military dabbling in—or Heaven forbid!—controlling politics:

> In ancient times, when the military was allowed to rule the Court, the realm was seen to decline. When the Court was seen to rule the battlefield, similar decline was observed. With either the Court or the military in decline, the virtue of the people was seen to wane. At Court words are much cultivated and so respect and courtesy carry the day. Without being summoned to the Court, one does not appear unannounced. At Court it is easy to withdraw, but difficult to advance. On the battlefield, words mean little where action carries the day. One need not observe traditions and rites of propriety in order to succeed by following military protocols.

The ancient Romans also understood the need for keeping political matters and military matters separate. It is for this reason that their professional military legions were ruled over by consuls pro tem, each of which were appointed by the Senate to command for only one year—regardless of any prior military service or, in most cases, lack thereof. Predictably, this lack of a qualified command corps led to all manner of unprofessionalism. This was a major factor weighing heavily in Hannibal's favor during his campaigning in Italy.

While these two spheres—the political and the military—were ideally to remain separate, Ssu-ma was quick to point out that there are similarities connecting the commander in the field to the king on his throne, as well as similarities between the basic actions that must be undertaken if both are to rule effectively:

- **Both the king on the throne and the commander in the field must unify and solidify:** For the king, the people must be of one accord. As the mind of the commander in the field is of one accord, so do his troops move of one accord.
- **Both the king on the throne and the commander in the field must balance gain with loss:** For both the king as for the commander, gain and loss must be balanced against life and death. Neither political projects nor military campaigns should be undertaken

when potential loss outweighs potential gain. Campaigns should never be launched purely for personal gain.[322]

- **Both the king on the throne and the commander in the field must promote the upright and instill shame.**[323]
- **Both the king on the throne and the commander in the field must show, through swiftness, that reward and punishment are held in equal esteem:** In other words:

  > Execute minor offenders swiftly and you will never be troubled with major offenders. —Ssu-ma

- **Both the king on the throne and the commander in the field must impose order over chaos:** Like water, both discipline and order flow downhill. And all must be drenched equally. An illustration:

  > *Once a haughty courtier bearing a message from the king had his ornate carriage driven wildly into Ssu-ma's camp. Holding his anger in check, in the courtier's presence Ssu-ma asked a young soldier what the penalty was for recklessly racing into camp.*[324] *"Beheading!" answered the soldier without hesitation.*
  >
  > *"Do you see that even my most novice soldier knows the rules of my camp?" Ssu-ma calmly informed the now cowering courtier as he slowly advanced towards the man with sword in hand . . . But Ssu-ma was no fool. He knew he couldn't kill the courtier—a man well-connected at court—and get away with it. So Ssu-ma calmly beheaded first the courtier's driver and then one of the courtier's horses!*

To rule correctly and consistently one must balance control and chaos. To those who have never tasted battle, war appears chaotic. Indeed:

> War is controlled chaos . . . the more we can control the chaos, the better we war! —Vlad Tepes

---

322. (1) Revenge and (2) the regaining of honor being the only possible exceptions.

323. That is, a sense of honor.

324. Lest it startle the horses and/or panic the troops into thinking they were being attacked.

But how much more chaotic does battle appear to the untrained and uninitiated than the first time you saw trading being done on the floor of the New York Stock Exchange?

During wartime, the more chaos and confusion in your enemy's mind, the better—whether weeds of doubt and inadequacy growing out of his own lack of self-esteem, or else entangling vines of confusion *you* purposely planted there.

But whereas confusion in enemy court, camp, and corps is a blessing, chaos and confusion in our own house, our own kingdom, or in the ranks of our own men is a curse. The wise leader of any sort—the king on the throne, the commander in the field—must impose order on top of chaos, quickly quelling any confusion swelling in the minds of those under him. According to Ssu-ma, to do so requires the liberal use of:

- **Benevolence** to counter selfishness and self-interest, thus preventing scarcity.
- **Credibility** to counter disinformation, including morale-sapping slander, innuendo, and rumor, all of which engender and encourage distrust.
- **Straightforwardness** to counter dishonesty and doubt.
- **Unity** to counter disunity. When the mind of the king is of one accord, the mind of the people will be of one accord. When the mind of the commander is of one accord, the movement of the troops will be of one accord.
- **Righteousness** to counter deviousness and conspiracy.
- **The "authority of necessity"** to counter those who would benefit from multiplying the kingdom's troubles.[325]
- **Centralized order** to counter disorder:

> When people cannot lead themselves then they must be led, if not by virtue then by law. If virtue does not spur them to work together, unify them by laws. Law inspires the indolent. Law removes the doubt of the doubtful. Declare the law loudly once, then implement it with certainty. —Ssu-ma

325. That is, Occam's razor.

To stave off *unwanted* chaos, king and commander must learn to spot "The Nine Types of Forbidden Men" that must, in turn, be *ruthlessly* eliminated—by any means necessary![326]—before they can do harm, to society in general and to military operations in particular.

Of course, each of us would also benefit by learning to spot and then eliminate—right: *by any means necessary!*—these nine types of Mind Slayers from our lives:

Bullies who prey upon the weak, whether individuals or countries. Saddam Hussein and Kuwait ring a bell?

Murderers who use war to settle personal enmities.

Brutes who take what they want with force simply because they can.

Spoilers whose lives have been ruined and now want nothing more than to ruin the lives of others.

Those born to advantage (i.e., hedonists and egotists),[327] born with a silver spoon in their mouth who believe the rules don't apply to them.

Those who commit fratricide. If your own family can't trust you![328]

Those who commit regicide. He who turns on his ruler offends the Will of Heaven.

Those who rebel without cause and would cause others to do so as well.

Those who ferment[329] chaos simply for the sake of chaos.

The Mind Slayers' Silver Rule:[330] the only permissible chaos is *your* C.H.A.O.S.—the hurtles, hardships, and hazards it's sometimes necessary and expeditious for you to create in order to better your lot in life, to further your cause and feather your nest.

The ancient observation that men could be trained like horses should in

---

326. Jp. Masakatsu!

327. Or, in today's shrink lingo, self-centered sociopaths.

328. "He who turns on his own blood, turns his back to the world."—Vlad Tepes, *Dracula's Art of War*.

329. Some sources translate this "worship" chaos.

330. Mind Slayers' Golden Rule: Whoever has the gold . . . rules!

no way be seen as somehow demeaning to human beings. If anyone has the right to be insulted by the comparison, it would surely be our equine cousins.

Horses, when at their best, are proud creatures, useful and brave, wild of spirit but easily focused to the task at hand. Whether best suited as the extension of the warrior they carry—horse and rider merging into one unconquerable centaur!—or whether more humbly harnessed to tasks designed to deliver sustenance to the famished or yet more bricks toward the building of man's ever-taller edifices, still the horse maintains his dignity and his pride of purpose.

Man would do well to learn from the horse . . . If only for the sole reason that our own diligent acquisition of the horse's admirable attitude might help keep us as individuals—Nay! The whole of our race—one step further away from *the glue-factory!*

12.

Musashi: Taste the Wind, Ride the Wave

Ride your horse along the edge of the sword,
Hide yourself in the middle of the flames,
Blossoms of the fruit tree will bloom in the fire,
The sunrise is in the evening.
—Zen koan riddle

BY THE TIME of his death, Miyamoto Musashi (1594–1645) was universally acknowledged as *Kensei*, "Sword Saint," the greatest swordsman who had ever lived in Japan. That Musashi should ultimately succumb to, of all things, natural causes is perhaps the single most amazing aspect of his amazing—and amazingly violent—life. But like many warriors, Musashi was not so much violent by nature as he was a man nurtured by violent times. As such, he did not so much contribute to the violence of his era as he did help refine it.

Born Ben No Soke, during his life, Musashi is known to have killed well over a thousand men—sixty during personal duels, the rest while fighting in six different wars over the years. Thus, the best testimony to his skills of survival in general and his mastery of Japanese bujutsu martial arts in particular is the fact that despite so many life-or-death encounters, Musashi died of old age.

Fortunately for us, two years before his death, Musashi took the time to write his thoughts, tactics, and techniques down in his *Go Rin No Sho* (*A Book of Five Rings*). Though written four hundred years ago, *A Book of Five Rings* remains one of the greatest classics on warfare ever written, often mentioned alongside Sun Tzu's *Ping-fa*.[331]

Far from being an outdated manual on medieval Japanese kenjutsu sword fighting, Musashi's *A Book of Five Rings* gives us an appreciation of Musashi's battlefield insights and his tried-and-true (as opposed to tried-and-*died*!) strategies, all easily applicable to other areas of endeavor. Modern-day Japanese—from businessmen to policemen to yakuza men—consult their always-within-arm's-reach copy of the *Go Rin No Sho* on a daily basis.

Though considered the consummate samurai warrior and, like all samurai, dedicated to serving his daimyo (lord) and to observing the code of bushido,[332] Musashi lived much of his life as a ronin,[333] a masterless samurai.

Whenever a samurai daimyo was killed, or otherwise lost his lands (for choosing the wrong side in the many civil wars that plagued Japan's medieval era), the samurai serving him were left with the option of either committing seppuku or else become ronin in the hopes that another samurai lord would give them tenure. For Musashi, this was often the result of his backing the wrong side in the constant wars taking place between various samurai factions.

The way of the ronin is to "taste the wind" and "ride the wave."

"Taste the wind" means to always stay alert to which way the wind is blowing—be those winds likely to affect you personally, politically, militarily, or financially—or all four. This means learning to spot Mr. Trend and Mr. Trouble *before* they come barreling around the corner with blood in the eye! If we can train ourselves to spot trouble coming soon enough, trouble might not catch us barricading (and booby-trapping!) the front door, or else spot us ducking out the backdoor.

The latter, the "better part of valor," echoes Sun Tzu's ideal that, if our

---

331. For more on the life and philosophy of Miyamoto Musashi, see "No-sword, No-fear" in Dr. Haha Lung and Christopher B. Prowant's *Mind Control* (Citadel, 2006) and the section "Musashi Crosses at the Ford" in *Mind Penetration* (Citadel, 2007).

332. Jp. lit. "Way of the Warrior," a chivalrous code similar to that followed by medieval European knights. "Bushi" literally means "warrior" and is made up of the syllables "bu" (which can mean both "sword" and "writing brush," implying that a Samurai should also be a man of letters) and "shi" which means "death."

333. Jp. lit. "wave man," a man who moved from place to place, as if being tossed about on ocean waves.

legs aren't long enough to *outrun* trouble, then we at least need to become practiced in tripping trouble up at the starting gate—preferably before he ever hears the starter pistol!

Ever imagine you can smell rain coming? You can. But what you really smell is called gibberellin, an oily secretion plants give off to protect themselves from rain. Also, ever notice how, walking toward the ocean, you smell the salt air long before you crest that final dune to actually look out over the water?

In the same way, veteran sailors can smell (probably more "feel" on their skin) subtle changes in air pressure, and previous experience tells them that "Aye, 'tis a foul blow a'brewin'! Time to batten down the hatches, mates!"

On a personal scale, we observe others' *normal* body language and their normal day-to-day comings and goings—so we can more quickly spot when something is "out of the ordinary," indicating they're up to something—probably no good. And we listen carefully to their "shadow language" (Freudian slips, *tell*ing lies, and especially what they're *not* saying) so we can spot Mr. Trouble before he decides to pitch a tent on our front porch.

On a larger scale, it's vital that the general, the businessman, and the wily Mind Slayer keep abreast of real-time intelligence so as to instantly and consistently adjust their battle plans to the shifting winds of circumstance and flux.

"Ride the wave" means to go with the flow. There's a time for fight and a time for flight. Why? Because mother nature says so, that's why.

When the other guy's army is bigger than your army—and you're fresh out of Hannibals and Pattons!—it's time to go guerrilla on his ass: melt into the background, bind up your wounds, collect and conserve ammunition, aim small to miss small. Try his patience while tempering your own. You bob and weave, maybe throw in a little Ali "rope-a-dope" to keep him guessing.

This is the same way an accomplished sailor sways with movement of the ship—riding the waves—his feet remain firmly rooted to the deck.

As with the sailor, so with the ronin.

Curiously, while the samurai *ideal* was two equally trained, equally armed warriors fighting toe-to-toe, the *reality* of history shows how, time and again, samurai—like any savvy warrior cadre who survived long enough for history to make note of them—were always looking for an edge over their enemies.

That's why Musashi went out of his way—figuratively and literally, traveling the length and breadth of Japan—in a lifelong quest dedicated to mastering both conventional and unconventional styles of fighting. You may recall that this is what the Chinese masters called *cheng* and *ch'i*, direct and indirect methods.

Make no bones about it, Musashi could, if he chose, go *cheng* toe-to-toe with the best swordsmen in Japan. But Musashi was also master of the indirect, *ch'i*. This is why, ironically Miyamoto Musashi—the most universally acknowledged master of the samurai sword who ever lived—defeated his greatest opponents not with his blade but with his brain.

Ever on the alert for that one special trick[334] that would give him the edge, Musashi first mastered the traditional samurai long sword (*taishi-katana*) before going on to develop a style of fighting using *two* katana.

Still not satisfied, Musashi continued to perfect his martial arts skills by mastering all the traditional samurai weapons—the bow, the spear, the *jutte*,[335] and so on. He then went on to study "forbidden" ninja weapons: the *manriki* fighting chain, the *kusauri* sickle, and *Kakushi-jutsu*—the ninja art of fighting with small, easily concealed weapons (e.g., *shuriken* throwing stars).[336] By the end of his bloody career, Musashi successfully killed opponents with every conventional samurai weapon of his day, quite a few ninja weapons, and even by using unconventional "environmental weapons"—an empty scabbard, a tree limb, even a kitchen ladle!

Still, no matter what the tool in his hand, Musashi defeated his foes first and foremost using *yuku mireba*—his power to "see" into the heart of his enemy—and then play on their emotional weaknesses: their bravado, confusion, and their susceptibility to the Five Warning F.L.A.G.S.

Yuku mireba was how Musashi learned to "taste the wind."

Having "tasted the wind," Musashi could then "ride the wave," choosing the path of least resistance—swimming *with* instead of *against* the current—using any tactic and any available weapon—conventional or unconventional . . . *Masakatsu!*—to win.

As with the ronin Musashi, so with us!

---

334. According to martial arts maestro Peter Gilbert, tricks well-mastered are called "techniques." Techniques half-learned are merely "tricks."

335. Iron baton affixed with a hook on the side designed for locking onto and disabling samurai swords.

336. See *Classical Budo* by Donn F. Draeger (Weatherhall Press, 1973).

IAIDO: SECRET OF THE "FAST DRAW"

Samurai are to Japan what gunslingers are to America's Wild West. Many people are unaware that the classic 1960 Western *The Magnificent Seven* (and its less than magnificent sequels—ad nauseum!) were inspired by an equally classic 1954 Japanese film called *The Seven Samurai*.

Every ten-gallon-hat aficionado knows any gunslinger worth his six gun was required not only to be able to clear leather in the blink of an eye but be able to instinctively draw a bead on that third button down on his opponent's vest. "Instinctively" being just another name for (1) paying better attention and (2) training harder than the fellow next to you—that fellow the bear just caught up with![337]

As with the gunslinger, so with the samurai.

In Japan, they call it *Iaido*—the Secret of the Fast Draw—slipping that three feet of stainless steel from its scabbard before your opponent even suspects you've wrapped your fist firmly around that sharkskin grip. *Iaido,* just one more thing Musashi took the time to master.

For Musashi, *Iaido* meant getting your weapon to the party before your opponent was *cheng*—direct and to the point, literally. First sword to clear the scabbard meant first cut. First cut, best cut—*only* cut! Last cut.

Iaido-justsu, the art of fast-drawing the sword, is divided into four distinct skills that must be mastered: *nuki tsuke* (draw the sword and making the initial strike all in a single movement), *kiri tsuke* (the "finishing cut," what Westerners call the coup de grace), *chiburi* ("cleaning the blade"), and *noto* (replacing the blade, in preparation for the next encounter).

As with all things Musashi, we can use this Iaido outline for both problem solving and conflict resolution in many endeavors both on and beyond the physical battlefield.

Nuki tsuke: Draw and Strike in One Fluid Motion

What was it Ssu-ma taught us?

> The sword drawn—cuts! Hesitation equals death. Having decided on a course of action, act quickly, before your plans are discovered.

---

337. First hiker tells second hiker, "Look. A grizzly! We gotta outrun him!" "No," the second hiker informs first hiker. "I only have to outrun *you*!"

For samurai, to draw the blade was to use the blade.

To draw a blade quickly can be accomplished by any swift hand. But the Iaido ideal requires not only clearing leather but putting the shot where it's intended. Whether slapping leather or clearing your scabbard, hitting your target with a bullet or blade requires either luck or focus. Since luck is often arbitrary, we do better to trust our fortune and our future to focus. *Luck* can never be practiced, but *focus* can be perfected.

Martial artist or portrait artist, focus is ever the key.

The tale is told of an elder Pablo Picasso repaying the attentiveness of a café waitress by quickly—masterfully—sketching her picture on a napkin.

"Humph. How long did it take you to draw *that*?" snickered an older woman sitting nearby, turning down her nose at Picasso's simple—flawless—portraiture.

"Why, thirty years, madam. *Thirty years,*" Picasso replied calmly—coldly.

So, too, we may watch the master martial artist strike flawlessly, whether with the sword *in* his hand or the sword *of* his hand, but still we do not see the many years he has had to practice and perfect his mind-set, his stance, his grip, and his draw, all in order to finally achieve the flawless arc of his impeccable strike.

Kiri tsuke: The Follow-Through

All great athletes will remind you of the importance of "the follow-through," in effect, the importance of finishing what you start, of not suddenly pulling up short just as the finish line is in sight.

What was that famous warning whispered in George W. Bush's ear just prior to the invasion of Iraq: "You break it . . . you fix it!" In Iaido, first cut generally equals death, but that doesn't mean you drop your guard, or that you relax. A wounded enemy—even a dying enemy—can still have enough life left in him to kill you on his way out the door.

To put it in terms Westerners might better identify with: Don't you just love it when someone pulls off a fourth down with seconds on the clock and a Hail Mary come-from-behind to win one for the Gipper? It's an American tradition to root for the underdog, to praise the big come back—especially one leading to the big payback!

It's human nature to love these kind of come-back stories. In Japan, they tell stories about Yoshitsune Minimoto (who, after his clan was decimated, survived and spent years secretly studying with *tengu* ninja, learning the forbidden skills that years later allowed his clan to return and overthrow their enemies), the forty-seven ronin (who willingly suffered years of humiliation falsely branded as cowards while waiting for just the right moment to get revenge for the death of their beloved daimyo); and "The Lone Wolf" Ito Ogami (who, after his family was massacred, spent years wandering Japan with his infant son in tow, both hounded by ruthless assassins).

Yoshitsune, the forty-seven ronin, Lone Wolf and Cub, all share one thing in common beyond the fact that they all eventually returned to get their revenge: had their respective enemies took the time to finish the job, we would never have heard of any of these underdogs making heroic comebacks.

Machiavelli referred to these as "The Sons of Brutus" (a term first coined by the Romans), meaning simply—realistically, *ruthlessly*—if you kill the father, you had better follow through and kill the sons as well, lest twenty years down the road, they return, *literally with a vengeance!* According to the Romans (and Machiavelli), prudence calls for this element to be completely eliminated. Or to quote a more contemporary military genius:

> Strike an enemy once and for all. Let him cease to exist as a tribe or he will live to fly at your throat again.
>
> —Shaka Zulu, 1811[338]

Throughout history, down through the present day, we've seen this happen time and again. For example, in 1995 when Serbia invaded Bosnia-Herzegovina and reportedly massacred eight thousand Muslim men and boys in Srebrenica, all those well-meaning but history-dyslexic people and politicians started shaking their heads in disbelief . . . when all they had to do was think back forty years to remember how during World War II the Bosnians had then sided with Hitler, helping him massacre Serbs. Forty-odd years later, Serbian sons of Brutus were taking their revenge.[339]

Following through applies to all elements (primarily people) left over after an operation (e.g., palace coup, hostile corporate takeover) that may prove troubling. These can include disgruntled ex-employees you had to let

---

338. See *Shaka Zulu* by E.A. Ritter, 1955.

339. For all the gory details, see *Theatre of Hell: Dr. Lung's Complete Guide to Torture* by Dr. Haha Lung and Christopher B. Prowant (Loompanics Unlimited, 2003).

go because of the recent "downsizing" or that psycho ex-girlfriend with the tire-slashing fetish.

To tone it down just a little (in case all this talk of whacking the Sons of Brutus before they can come back to whack you is making you uncomfortable . . . and possibly liable in a court of law!), following through is simply a reminder for us to dot all the *I*s (Sidney Reilly's favorite line again!) and cross all the *T*s, finishing what we start. If nothing else, the aforementioned examples should serve as a warning to us to follow through, not to leave any loose ends lying around—loose ends someone could conceivably use to tie us up and/or strangle the life out of us!

Using this definition, following through can run the gamut from making sure your financial books (both sets of them!) are kept up-to-date, to making sure you really do follow through and destroy that sex video you and your girlfriend or boyfriend . . . or both(!) . . . made just for fun.

The devil may be in the details, but peace of mind is certainly in the follow-through.

Chiburi: Cleaning Your Blade

Having struck the fatal blow, the master samurai swordsman flicks his blade, snapping the blade with a flourish in such a way that any drop of blood still clinging to it falls from the blade. An Iaido master always performs *chiburi* before replacing the blade in its scabbard.

Cleaning your blade—metaphorically—may remind some Westerners (and some Easterners as well) of the New Testament admonishment to "shake the dust from your feet" when leaving a place where you've not been welcomed with open arms. Likewise, Easterners (and some Westerners as well) may note a similarity with the Buddhist metaphor of the human mind being like a perfect mirror obscured by dust (symbolic of our ignorance). To "see" our true self, we need only wipe the dust from the mirror.

In the course of accomplishing our goal, depending on the severity and immediacy of the situation, coupled with our own enthusiasm and ruthlessness—end justifies means?—to accomplish our goal, there's a likelihood we may get a little dirty (or even bloody) along the way, that we're liable to step on a few toes, even make a few enemies.

At the end of any war, having conquered your enemy's lands, you have a choice of repatriating all your enemy's POWs or else slaughtering them all—potential Sons of Brutus that they are. When you're the winner, you can get away with things like that. In other words, you can be a gracious winner or an all-out asshole, rubbing your victory in the loser's face. You can start building walls, or you can start repairing bridges. You can decide to stand fast with the past, or take a chance on the future. The past is usually safer, the future more scary and uncertain. No mystery which one people tend to cling to.

But there are times, even in the heat of battle, during a protracted campaign, during an all-night game of Texas Hold 'em, when it's time to cut your losses and walk away. Yeah, Kenny Rogers knew what he was talking about.

It takes both hands to grab onto the future. So, unless you're that four-armed Shiva the Destroyer god of the Hindu, sooner or later you're gonna have to let go of the past.

Remember that first-grade blackboard on which Mrs. McGillicutty taught you your ABCs? You don't still carry that blackboard around with you do you? Of course not. You learned what you needed to know—your ABCs—and then you moved on, taking the knowledge with you . . . but leaving behind all the excess baggage . . . or, in this case, that blackboard.

Having successfully delivered the master-stroke to his target, the swordsman flicks his blade, literally and figuratively cleaning away the blood (the past).

The past is prologue. Clean your blade.

Noto: Replace Your Blade

Having accomplished your goal . . . resist the temptation to pat yourself on the back and go on vacation. Instead, start rebuilding any bridges you burned on your way to the top. Smooth over some of those feathers you've ruffled on your way to becoming cock of the walk.

Be a gracious winner. Or as Hannibal instructs: "Shame your enemies with your mercy" (Truth XLV).

After a brief celebration (a way of showing appreciation for those who helped you succeed),[340] call a meeting to debrief your people, listening

---

340. Remember, take care of your people and they'll take care of you.

to their feedback on how to improve performance even more on *the next project*.

SENKI: DEVELOPING YOUR "WAR SPIRIT"

Musashi was one of the original "think outside the box" guys. Few are born with this skill and, unfortunately, just as few take the time to develop it. Compounding this perennial lack of imagination and enthusiasm is the fact that, even when effort is made, *appreciation* does not automatically lead to *application*.

Look at it this way: you might have a true appreciation for Shakespeare's writings and Leonardo da Vinci's art, but that doesn't mean you can apply that appreciation and write like ol' Will or do all that cool art and inventing stuff Leonardo did.

Thus, while many may *appreciate* Musashi, just as many run into the problem of how to practically *apply* the teachings of Japan's greatest swordsman to their everyday–modern and all too often mundane—battles.

But if we learn nothing else from Musashi, we must remember his cardinal observation that whether on the battlefield, in the board room, or even in the bedroom:

"All battles are first won in the mind."

One of Musashi's nine major rules was "Learn the ways[341] of all professions." By this, Kensei meant not only should we learn to respect the various craftsmen for their unique skills but we should also learn to see the world through their eyes.

For example, in what is perhaps his most (in)famous duel, Musashi carried the day by using a boat oar to kill his opponent. Had Musashi suffered from "object fixedness"—the tendency to see only one use for an object or tool—and not been able to perceive[342] the possibility of using the oar as a weapon—it is doubtful we would know the name Musashi today.

Musashi instructs us that in order to develop such *yuku mireba* perception and insight, our overall attitude (i.e., our strategy for life in general and

341. Jp. Dō, lit. "way," "path," "discipline," "skills and crafts."

342. Yuku mireba.

enthusiasm for special endeavors in particular) must begin with our first concentrating on developing what he calls *senki*, our "war spirit."

Senki includes but is not confined to:

1. ***Focus:*** Where we look.
2. ***Concentration:*** How (i.e., in what manner) we look.
3. ***Determination:*** What we are looking for.

Thus, whatever the task at hand is, we must focus on it with the same intensity as we would if facing a samurai in a life-or-death confrontation. As on the battlefield, so in the boardroom, so in the bedroom.

First and foremost this means (1) getting our opponent off-balance and (2) keeping them off-balance. This rule applies whether our opponent is a deadly enemy we're facing across a battlefield, a corporate lawyer we're facing across a boardroom negotiating table, or else that fine filly across the room we're just trying to get some face time with.

Every general comes to the battlefield with a plan—we need to unbalance that plan. Likewise, that slick corporate lawyer comes to the table with his every move planned out in advance. Our job is to unbalance him, the same way we'd sweep the legs out from under an opponent during a karate match. And how are these any different from the plans that fine babe at the bar has for tonight? She could use a little "unbalancing" too.[343]

In martial arts, nothing is more important than maintaining your balance. This refers not only to your physical balance but also to your *mental equilibrium*. This is why we say a mentally disturbed person is "unbalanced."

Before we can unbalance our opponent, we must first learn to understand his inner nature: what drives him; not only the "mask" he projects to the world, but his inner nature—the inner beast he tries so desperately to keep caged. *Yuku mireba* means seeing him the way he really is, deep down.

Musashi gives us five ways of unbalancing an opponent by moving his "spirit" (i.e., manipulating his emotions):

- **Attack where his spirit is lax:** In other words, where he lacks focus. Exploit any laziness, sloth, and/or hesitation you perceive in

343. For a complete course in how to "unbalance" the opposite sex (or the same sex for that matter!), see *Mental Domination* by Dr. Haha Lung and Christopher B. Prowant (Citadel, 2009).

your enemy. Where a condition of laxity does not exist naturally in an opponent, the Mind Slayer creates it.

- **Throw him into chaos and confusion:** Where a condition of chaos and confusion does not occur naturally, the mesmerizing Mind Slayer creates it.[344]
- **Frustrate and anger him:** Where a condition of frustration and anger does not occur naturally, the crafty Mind Slayer creates it.
- **Terrify him:** Fear, the first of the deadly Warning F.L.A.G.S. Go out of your way to create this condition. Remember Machiavelli's advice that it is better (safer!) for a prince to be *feared* than *loved*. Where a condition of fear does not occur naturally, the wily Mind Slayer creates it.
- **Take advantage of the enemy's disrupted rhythm:** When he is unsettled and "thrown off his game" and "out of kilter," he is more vulnerable to both physical and mental attack. Where such a condition of disruption does not occur naturally, the industrious Mind Slayer creates it.

344. C.H.A.O.S. Theory ("Create hazards/hurdles/hardships and offer solutions").

13.

By the Blade and by the Book: Omar in Command

Brothers, it has come to my attention that people fear me. They saw that when the Prophet Muhammad was alive, Omar was harsh and that during the Caliphate of Abu Bakr,[345] Omar was also hard and stern. Now that he has become Caliph himself, God knows how hard Omar will be!

—Omar's speech upon becoming supreme leader of Islam

AS IS SO often the case, it is not always the man with the dream but the man who continues that dream, carrying it to the next town over, that makes that dream worthy of history's notice. If not for Plato, would the name Socrates have survived? If not for Saul's being struck blind on the road to Damascus, would the Nazarene carpenter's message of peace ever have made it out of Palestine?

So, too, the message of the illiterate Arabian camel driver Muhammad might have long since been covered over by the relentless sands of the desert, never having been heard outside of the Arabian peninsula were it not for

345. Omar's predecessor.

gifted orator, crafty tactician, and, when expedient—or just when necessary to get people's attention—*utterly ruthless* Caliph Omar[346] ibn al-Khattab.

While Islam remained confined to the Arabian peninsula during Muhammad's lifetime, during Omar's rule the frontiers of the Islamic empire expanded greatly, with Omar conquering the Persian empire, vast areas of Roman territory, and bringing the whole of Egypt under Islamic rule.

Omar ibn al-Khattab was only twenty-six years old at the time a new prophet named Muhammad arose to challenge the powerful Koresh,[347] the tribe who ruled the main Arabic city-state of Mecca and extorted pagan pilgrims wishing access to the ancient holy site within the city called the Kaaba.

The polytheistic Koresh were content to let this former camel driver rant and rave all he wanted about "cleansing the Kaaba" in order to replace the three hundred and sixty idols presently housed there with his one god Allah, that is until Muhammad's ramblings began to scare off the Koresh's *paying* customers.

In short order, the Koresh had put a price on Muhammad's head, forcing him and his handful of followers to flee to neighboring Medina—where his cult continued to grow.

Omar was himself a Koresh, the son of an ardent pagan named Khattab Al-fa Ruq whose name means "One who distinguishes right from wrong." Whether his father ever actually got around to teaching his son Omar the difference between right and wrong[348] we don't know, but by all accounts:

> Umar was a chip off the old block and while others urged caution, with typical Qurayshi cunning, Umar was ready for violent actions. —Karen Armstrong[349]

What Armstrong refers to as "Qurayshi cunning" was well-known back in Muhammad's time:

> In a campaign that combined trickery and force, the Quraysh managed to take control of Mecca . . . Cultivating a shrewd

346. Variously spelled "Umar" and " 'Umar."

347. Variously spelled "Quarayshi" and "Quarish."

348. Keep in mind there's a pretty good chance our modern idea of right and wrong differs considerably from what was considered right and wrong in sixth-century Arabia.

349. *Muhammad: A Biography of the Prophet* (HarperSanFrancisco, 1992:120).

> statesmanship known as *hilm*, the Quaraysh had become the greatest power in Arabia during the sixth century.[350]

Reportedly, Omar passionately shared his father's *hilm* as well as his father's love of the old pagan faith.[351] Still, Omar eventually converted to Muhammad's cult after his sister Fatima and her husband Sa'id converted.

The most common tale told of Omar's first encounter with Muhammad has Omar drunk and stumbling around the Kaaba when he ran into Muhammad reciting the Koran.[352] Omar's first thought was to kill the irritating Muhammad but he was dissuaded from doing so by the soothing words Muhammad read from the Koran. On the spot, Omar converted to Islam, pledging his life to Muhammad.

Not so fast: some *Western* scholars argue that the traditional tale of Omar being the faithful lieutenant to Muhammad is later Islamic revisionism when in fact it seems that Muhammad first appeared as the prophetic herald of the original Hagarene (as Muslims were first called) "messiah" Omar.[353]

Today, accepted Muslim tradition tells how once he became a Muslim, Omar refused to keep a low profile—as prudent as this would have been given the persecuted minority status Muhammad's cult enjoyed at the time. Instead of doing his mandatory *salat* prayers in private, Omar boldly did his in front of everyone at the Kaaba. Was Omar deliberately trying to pick a fight with his former friends and family still in the Koresh?

There's always a certain smidgen of suspicion accompanying sudden conversions of conviction—be they religious, political, or a wedded web thereof—as to whether or not the abrupt about-face was prompted by a sincere desire for change or by the sincere desire for additional change in one's purse.

Whether Omar was a sincere true believer, or only an astute opportunist-cum-meteorologist—who could see which way the political and religious winds were blowing!—who decided to hitch his camel to Muhammad's rising star, one thing's for certain: Omar was never Muhammad's yes-man.

---

350. Ibid., 66–67.

351. Ibid., 71.

352. Variously spelled "Coran" and "Qu'ran." This tale is unlikely, by the way, given the fact that the Muslim holy book—a mishmash of sayings God, through the Angel Gabriel, supposedly gave to Muhammad—wasn't compiled into finished form until many years after Muhammad's death. (*Why I Am Not a Muslim* by Ibn Warraq. [Prometheus Press, 2003]).

353. Robert M. Price's "*Of Myth and Men*." *Free Inquiry*, Winter 1999/00 Vol. 20, No. 1.

For example, in 628 Muhammad and Omar clashed over the former agreeing to sign "The Hudaibiya Agreement," a ten-year peace treaty with the Koresh, this after Muhammad and all his followers had already been run out of Mecca.

Omar was furious that, in order to placate the Koresh, Muhammad had agreed to the Koresh demand that he remove his title as "Messenger of Allah" from beneath his signature, and that he proclaim the Koresh's three patron goddesses to be equals to Allah.[354]

Again, was it "Omar the true believer" who saw the obvious shame in a true "Prophet of God" humbling himself before pagans, or was it "Omar the opportunist" keenly aware that your cause never grows strong by showing weakness before an enemy?

Either way, Omar's disappointment and disgust were somewhat assuaged when, just two years after signing the peace treaty, having spent the interval of peace wisely training and arming their own army, Muhammad's forces infiltrated and conquered Mecca, slaughtering all the members of the Koresh, in direct violation of the the Hudaibiya Agreement.[355]

Since then in Islam "Hudaibiya" has come to mean entering into negotiations and/or signing a peace treaty only in order to gain time, temporary peace, and tactical advantage. In other words, a ruse used to buy time until you're strong enough and your blade sharp enough to stab your unsuspecting enemy in the back!

Prior to this treacherous attack on Mecca, Omar had protested, pointing out that the treaty was still in effect. Muhammad reportedly shrugged and said, "Warfare is deception."[356]

---

354. After Muhammad's final victory over the Koresh, Muhammad removed all verses praising these goddesses of the Koresh from the Koran, claiming Satan had tricked him into putting them in the Koran by pretending to be the Angel Gabriel. These verses have since become known as "The Satanic Verses," something Muslims never speak of openly, as Muslim author Salman Rushdie learned the hard way when a *fatwa* was issued against him by the Ayatollah Khomeini for publishing a novel titled *The Satanic Verses*. Other scholars maintain it was Omar who finally removed these verses from the final version of the Koran published during his Caliphate.

355. Muhammad personally oversaw the beheading of seven hundred Koresh men and one woman who were then buried in a mass grave. The remaining Koresh women and children were sold into slavery. (Armstrong, 1992)

356. Quoted in Al-Muttaqi' Al-Hindi Hadith. "Hadith," reputed to be actual sayings of the Prophet Muhammad, are second only to the Koran as scriptural and legal authority in Islam.

Omar never forgot this lesson.

With the death of Muhammad, one of his lieutenants named Abu Bakr became "Caliph," ruling for a mere two years before dying of natural causes, to be succeeded by Omar.

Under Omar's leadership the Muslims of Arabia began raiding their neighbors.

Did Omar do so simply because he was greedy? No. He did so for two very good reasons:

- He knew his people better than they knew themselves. Without an outside focus, they would turn their madness inward, and go back to factional fighting.
- Second, Persia had something Omar wanted . . . *an empire!*

Conquest is easy, control is not. Omar's methodology for control was simple. Always give people a clear choice: the "carrot or the stick," or in this case, "the Book or the blade."

Religion-wise the Persians were pagan Zoroastrians, not protected "People of the Book" (i.e., Muslims, Christians, Jews). As such, under Muhammad's Islamic law, they could be *forcibly* converted to Islam. Not surprising, given a choice between accepting "The Book" (the Koran; i.e., conversion to Islam) or else "the blade" (being beheaded on the spot!), most Persians chose the former.

By 637, Omar had conquered the Persian empire, having soundly defeated the Persian army the year before at the battle of Qadisayah where, facing an army of 120,000 Persians, Omar had rallied his much smaller Muslim force with the battle cry:

"Paradise is under the shadow of our swords forward!"

By the way, a lot has been made down through the years of all the advances of "Muslim art and science" brought *with them* into the lands they conquered, specifically when they conquered Spain. However, a quick glance at history will show that "Muslim science" was really *Persian* science:

> But the cultural heritage of the Persians was far weightier than the Arabs and their role in the development of Muslim civilization was immense. They brought to it theologians, philoso-

> phers, mystics, poets, artists, scientists, mathematicians, a great architectural style, geographers, and great ruling dynasties. —Swartz, 2002:30

Triumph over the Persians was followed by the conquest of Syria and then Egypt—both Roman Christian lands.

Within a year of the fall of Persia, Omar had taken Jerusalem. As Omar's army surrounded the city, in an effort to spare the city from destruction—or, at the very least, save the lives of the Christians—Jerusalem's Christian Patriarch asked to meet with Omar. Omar agreed, arriving in coarse, humble desert clothing in deliberate and stark contrast to the Patriarch's splendid expensive robes.

After listening patiently to the long-winded, self-serving platitudes and attempted placations of the Patriarch, Omar explained the new facts of life to the Patriarch of Jerusalem:

> Submit and be spared. Resist . . . and your God will have his hands full till the next Ramadan moon sorting out which heads and which limbs go with which torsos!

The Patriarch wisely chose the former.

Omar then addressed himself to the terrified citizens of Jerusalem:

> All men are equal. Do not flatter those in authority. Do not seek favors from others. By such acts you demean yourselves . . . God has for a time made me your ruler. But I am one of you. No special privileges belong to rulers.

Shortly following the capture of Jerusalem, Omar ordered construction to begin on what was to become, after the Kaaba, Islam's holiest shrine: the Mosque of Omar, deliberately built on what Jews believe(d) to be the former site of King Solomon's temple. Muslims on the other hand maintain that this is (also) the spot where Muhammad tied his magical horse al-Burak before ascending into heaven, an event still celebrated in Muslim mythology as "The Night Journey."

Like most politicians, and all dictators, the power of symbolism was not lost on Omar. After all, to this day his grand edifice in Jerusalem is known as "The Mosque of *Omar*" not the "Mosque of Muhammad's Night Journey."

That Omar recognized the need for a strong, singular *supreme* authority isn't in doubt. Neither is the fact that—if nothing else than for convenience sake—Omar decided *Islam* was to be that supreme singular authority. To hasten the day when all the world would bow toward Mecca, Omar instituted many new rules, including:

- Establishment of the Islamic calendar.
- Imposing of the *dhimma* (a poll tax on Christians and Jews).
- He barred the construction of any new non-Muslim religious structures in Muslim-held territory (except new mosques, of course).
- Public expressions of non-Islamic religions restricted. Crosses could not be displayed openly.
- Restrictions on tempting Muslims to convert to another faith (death for a Muslim to do so).
- Christians and Jews were forbidden from preventing their family members from converting to Islam.
- Non-Muslims could not be buried in close proximity to Muslims.
- Jews and Christians were required to show respect by standing in the presence of Muslims.
- Jews and Christians could not ride horses, carry arms, or raise their arms in a manner threatening to a Muslim.

Christians and Jews were forbidden to sell alcohol. Forbidden to use Arabic calligraphy on their seals and to build houses higher than those of Muslims. Nor could they employ Muslims as servants.

Though still constrained by Muhammad's rule forbidding the "forced" conversion of Jews and Christians, by placing such harsh restrictions on them, Omar wielded both the carrot and the stick as adroitly as he did a scimitar: showing Jews and Christians (1) the carrot, the advantages of converting to Islam, and (2) the stick, his pressure tactics ensuring that only the most fervent of *infidels* held out against the message of Muhammad. As a result, many Jews and Christians converted to Islam for purely economic reasons; others so they could marry Muslim women. Still others did so because, well, after a while you do get tired of being beaten with the stick and, trust me, you don't want to know where they stick the carrot!

Omar's restrictions on conquered people were not done arbitrarily.

Omar knew that (for men like him at least) *conquest* was easy. *Control*, on the other hand, is not.[357] So while Omar's laws were no doubt onerous to those living under the dhimma, these restrictions proved a wise long-time move on Omar's part. And, to Omar's lasting tribute, all these laws are still in strict effect in Islamic countries under Muslim Shariah law.

Having survived dozens of bloody battles, having conquered a goodly portion of the known world, and having set Islam well on the path toward world domination, ironically Omar was killed not while fighting but while performing his mandatory[358] morning prayer.

Stabbed six times, he died three days later, murdered by a Persian non-Muslim, angered because Omar had ruled against him in a tax dispute.

Before his death, Omar appointed a six-man committee to elect his successor Caliph. They ultimately chose Uthman ibn Affan (a.k.a. Othmann). But without Omar's strong hand to guide them, factions long-suppressed under Omar's rule reemerged and internecine fighting broke out. Those opposing Othmann believed leadership should have gone to Muhammad's son-in-law, Ali), and this infighting eventually led to Islam breaking up into the two perpetually warring sects—the Sunni (backing Othmann) and the Shia (backers of Ali)—that comprise Islam to this day.

Omar had ruled for only ten years, six months, and four days before being assassinated. Yet during that relatively short decade, he had succeeded in changing not only the world at the time, but in unleashing religious and political forces that would—and still to this day!—ravage the planet.

As with many great and ruthless leaders, it's hard to separate the man from the myth from the monster. Omar's political and religious conquests are solidly carved into the hard headstone of history, and so are not in dispute. Still we are left only to ponder the same question that lesser men always ask at the passing of greater men: Was he a product of his times—seizing opportunity where he found it? Or was he instead the driving architect of those times—clearing the chaff from a too-long-neglected field, planting the seditious seeds of a bold new crop, and then patiently waiting—unafraid!—till it was time to harvest the whirlwind!

Inevitably, all that we're left with in the wake of the passing of any great man is that man's philosophy—hopefully, the actual philosophy that drove

357. Modern-day lesson: Iraq and Afghanistan.

358. A *predictable* enemy is truly a godsend.

the man to dare greatness and then vouchsafed his claim to same—as opposed to some tepid, watered-down idealization of that man's thoughts, adulterated and amended in later times to fit the self-serving needs of those that, had they lived in his day, would not have been fit to ride beside him yet, in our day, ride on his name.

OMAR'S TWELVE RULES

Do Not Be Misled by Someone's Reputation

Hannibal's Truth XXIX proclaims:

> "Fear spills less blood. A single scare is worth a thousand spears."

Or to paraphrase, reputation spills less blood:

> The more fear you put into an enemy's heart, the less the chance he'll ever put a sword in his hand. —Vlad Tepes

Omar undoubtedly knew of Hannibal, who, next to Alexander the Great and Julius Caesar, was heralded as the grandest of strategists. Omar would have also heard of Old Testament[359] warriors like Joshua and Gideon and, more recent to his time, the guerrilla tactics and triumphs of the brothers Maccabaeus. But even if completely ignorant of the lives of all these great leaders, Omar's own upbringing on the harsh sands of Arabia—tribes beset by constant internecine warfare—must have taught him early on the value of maintaining a good reputation—and of how easily such a reputation can become inflated. Remember that *under*estimating an enemy is the only thing worse than *over*estimating his potential. At least the latter makes you overtrain and overprepare.

A person's reputation not only tells us a lot about that person, but it can tell us even more about the person(s) who bring that reputation to our attention.

Your own reputation is both your armor and your American Express Gold Card.

---

359. Tracing themselves back to Father Abraham, Muslims accept most of the stories in the Old Testament as true.

As a young ne'er do well, Francois Eugene Vidocq, the eighteenth-century ex-convict turned police spy turned head of the French Surete secret police, relied on his reputation as a tough character to move safely among his fellow cutthroat criminals—both on the mean streets of Paris and while imprisoned. Later in life, when he went to work on the right side of the law, using various disguises and nom de guerre to further infiltrate criminal enterprises, Vidocq knew what people *believe* is often more important than the truth, and he continued to pass himself off as a dangerous character—one always more criminal than the criminals he was stalking.

> With such scoundrels it is always an advantage to be considered the most thorough rascal and the most ingenious one; this was my well-established reputation. —Vidocq, 1857

Still, we would do well to remember Ssu-ma's sober caution that "Reputation and reality must balance."

Do Not Judge a Person Only by Outward Performance;[360] Rather Look Inward to His Truthfulness and Wisdom

An extension of closely examining a person's reputation. Curiously, this brings to mind the fact that, as mentioned earlier, even during the early days of persecution when Muhammad's followers were still in the minority and surrounded by Koresh enemies in Mecca, neophyte convert Omar insisted on making a show of doing his prayers out in the open at the Kaaba, setting an example—and creating a reputation for himself—of both dedication and fearlessness.

One Who Seeks His Secrets Controls His Affairs

Like any able commander, and Omar was so much more than simply able, he knew the importance of gathering intelligence from your enemy, but also—if not more important—keeping your own plans from the enemy. Or as Count de Marencnes[361] so succinctly put it: "Precision personal intelligence can be more critical than precision-guided munitions."

When it comes to understanding—and exploiting—the nature of those

360. For example, in their performance of ritual *salat* prayers and *sawm* fasting.

361. Former Chief of French Intelligence.

secret things, Omar shares the same attitude with another great conqueror:

> Do not fear those things you can see, do not be troubled by rumors and loud noises you hear. Fear instead those things you neither see nor hear but that lurk in your enemy's breast! Secrets bleed like blood.[362] Mysteries call out to be understood. Every lock longs for a key, every empty cup thirsts for wine. A mystery begins where light ends. For every mystery laid to rest, another mystery rises. Better the mystery familiar. For every enemy laid to rest, another enemy rises. Better the enemy familiar! What I know today, my enemy knows tomorrow. What my enemy knows tomorrow is what I teach him today! A secret is useless unless someone knows it. The darkest secrets bury themselves. —*The 99 Truths: Hannibal's Black Art of War*

> A slip on the pavement is better than a slip of the tongue. —Jesus, son of Sirach

Fear the Person Whom You Hate

A good righteous hate gives you a certain amount of focus. But, for the most part, hate makes us act irrationally. That's because, more often than not, so much of our hate is born out of irrational thinking in the first place. Thus Hannibal warns:

> What a man loves, what he hates, what he needs, what he desires: These are the four pillars that support his house.
>
> —Truth IV

Who we hate and what we hate often reveals more about *us* than it does about who we hate and what we hate.

Prudent Is He Who Can Assess His Actions

Perhaps Omar had heard of Socrates's saying that "The unexamined life isn't worth living." Perhaps, like most of us, he just figured it out the hard

362. François Eugéne Vidocq agrees: "I had known for a long time that the best-guarded secret is one entrusted to no one . . ."—1857

way. This goes hand in hand with the former rule of how hate—or any strong emotion—can distract us and throw us off-kilter.

Do Not Defer Your Work for Tomorrow

Procrastination is something you shouldn't put off looking into.

> Today's small seed, tomorrow's tree blocking your way.
> —Vlad Tepes

He Who Has No Idea of Evil Can Easily Fall into Its Trap

Of course, "evil" is a relative term. One man's terrorist is another man's martyr and freedom fighter. Perhaps the more important point Omar is making here is that, unless we suspect something—or someone—is a danger to us, there's a good chance we'll never see 'em coming!

As the corny bumpersticker reads: "Be ALERT . . . the world needs more LERTS!"

> We prepare only for the storms we see coming. That is why my enemies are always wet! —Vlad Tepes

Judge a Man's Intelligence by the Questions He Asks

Or as the modern proverb puts it: better to remain silent and be thought a fool, than speak and remove all doubt.[363]

Less Concern for Material Well-Being Enables One to Lead a Free Life

The more things you have, the more things have you . . . and the more things your enemies have to choose from when attempting to rock your world. This harkens back to Miyamoto Musashi's "Cutting-at-the-Edges" ploy, where, when unable to attack an enemy directly, we instead attack at the periphery—in physical combat, attacking his extremities, when attacking on

---

363. What's the chance this saying is another Ben Franklin*ism*?

a Mind Slayer psychological level, targeting the things and people he loves. The ruthlessness of Hannibal's first Truth bears repeating:

> Enemy! When you look at me don't see something you hate . . . see the very thing you love the most. For that is what I will surely rip from you if you ever rise against me!

It Is Easier Not to Indulge in Sins Than to Repent

There are several modern-day aphorisms testifying to the universality of this sentiment, including "It's easier to apologize than get permission"; "Don't do the crime if you can't do the time"; and "It's easier to stay out than it is to get out."

Evidently, the human race as a whole hasn't gotten any better at resisting temptation than they were in Omar's day.

Mind Slayers *count on this*.

Contentment and Gratitude Are Two Great Virtues; You Should Not Care Which One You Are Gaining

Experience is what you get when you didn't get what you wanted.

Be Grateful to Him Who Points Out Your Defects

> A warrior is known by his enemies, even as a fat man is known by his appetites, a lean man by his fears. I give thanks for my enemy. Were it not for my enemy I would sleep past dawn, I would eat too much, I would become loud and overproud, and both my arm and eye would grow lax. My enemy determines when I rise, when and where I sleep tonight, what I eat and when, and whether I will ever see my home again. I thank my enemy for making me strong and look forward to repaying him in kind! —Hannibal the Conqueror, Truth VI

Four things come back not: the spoken word; the sped arrow; time past; and neglected opportunity.

—Omar Ibn al-Khattab, Caliph 581–644 A.D.

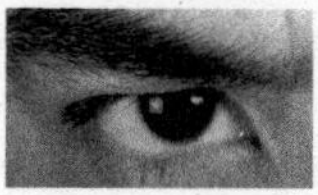

CONCLUSION:

"Why You Need to *Rock* Your World"

Where there is no strife there is decay: the mixture that is not shaken decomposes.
—Heraclitus[364]

EVOLUTION DOESN'T JUST HAPPEN because mother nature gets bored scarfing down DNA bon-bons while watching her soaps. Evolution occurs *because of* mother nature's "soaps"—because of all the mama (that would be her again), drama, and resultant trauma that seduces or startles or otherwise stimulates us just enough to make us get up off our lazy asses, thereby making us better human beings in spite of ourselves.

Tropical fish placed in a barren bowl remain lethargic. That is, until you place a simple rock in the bottom of their bowl. Then our finny little cousins will swim around and around that rock until their little flippers fall off.

And how do you expect all the little birdies to ever learn to fly if they are not first flung forth from the nest?

We humans are a lot like that.

Mythologist Joseph Campbell (1904–1987) succinctly outlined the

364. Greek alchemist and philosopher circa sixth and fifth century B.C.

universal "Hero's Journey," the various stages of life all of us pass through—regardless of the times we live in, regardless of our respective culture—on our way to personal revelation, empowerment, transformation, and finally self-actualization.[365]

The initial necessary step on this Hero's Journey most often comes about not because we suddenly—miraculously—grow ourselves a big brass pair, pull ourselves up by our bootstraps, and set off in search of a demon, dragon—or a Death Star—to slay, but rather because of some trauma or tragedy shocking us out of our comfortable malaise.

The Ice Age, the Fall of Rome, the Black Plague, Pearl Harbor, 9/11 . . . maybe if we could become better "self-starters," then Mama Nature wouldn't feel the parental responsibility to so violently shove us from the nest on a regular basis.

Don't fret. Just flap your arms harder . . . *harder!*

Struggle is our friend, though we seldom recognize his face as that of a friend while he's busy slapping us around. Yeah, it is a toxic relationship. But it sure beats the hell out of the alternative—*stagnation* . . . and death in an unmarked—unremarkable—grave.

Only by pushing against his walls does the prisoner grow stronger—and stay relatively sane in the process. At least until freedom once more becomes a possibility to him.

Of course, you might be one of those, like psychologist Erich Fromm (1900–1980), who maintains that freedom is highly overrated—or is that *undervalued*?

According to Fromm, it's human nature to want to "escape from *too much* freedom," that most of us are willing to give up that freedom every time some slick-talking Mind Slayer comes along asking us to.[366]

Of course, atheist Friedrich Nietzsche would have dismissed this *passive* Frommian assessment as blasphemy, knowing full well that we human beings *need* struggle to help challenge our innate "Will to Power"—an instinctual drive, fueled by our dissatisfaction with the status quo, spurring us to strive, to succeed, to conquer, to be all that we can be . . . despite all the legislative legerdemain crafted by oh-so-politically-correct genteel society at large to breed and browbeat this survival instinct out of us.

---

365. Maslow, remember? See Figure 4 previously.

366. *Escape From Freedom* by Erich Fromm (1941).

The good news is that our least resistance to any compromise to, dallying with or attempted diluting of our basic survival mechanism—our Will to Power—constitutes legitimate *struggle*.

Resistance is struggle. Struggle is life. Only the dead (so far as we know) are free from struggle. And that kind of "freedom" . . . well, you're welcome to it.

And, at least according to Nietzsche and Mother Nature (two authorities on the subject if ever there were!), *struggle is necessary*—necessary, that is, so long as you're still interested in seeing what's over the next hill and still interested in your DNA outlasting your enemy's DNA?

So every morning when you wake up (if only because you probably wouldn't like the alternative), thank the gods, thank Mother Nature, your selfish and xenophobic DNA, and even Nietzsche for tossing a few rocks into your fishbowl!

GLOSSARY

3-D: What propaganda does to an enemy: (1) demeans, (2) dehumanizes, and (3) demonizes—all in order to demoralize and ultimately defeat your foe.

Aces'-n'-Eights: A two-pair poker hand superstitiously believed to bring bad luck. Generically used to indicate that a Mind Slayer scheme has gone horribly wrong.

Amettori-jutsu: (Jp.) Literally, "a man of straw." Encompasses all tactics and techniques of deception. The name comes from the ploy of dressing up a scarecrow to make an enemy think it is a real sentry or soldier.

ASP: "Additional sensory perception." The full use of our five senses that give the impression to others we possess a "sixth sense," i.e., ESP.

Assassins: Medieval Middle Eastern secret society noted for its terror, treachery, and mind-manipulation techniques.

Atari-kokoro: Japanese mind-mastery techniques. (*See* Kiai-shin-jutsu)

Autogenic: Self-generated therapies (e.g., biofeedback, self-hypnosis, meditation, autosuggestion), coined by Anthony Zafutto, 1974.

Awfulizing: Imagining the worst that can happen, making mountains out of molehills. Chronic worry. Hint: this is something you *want* your enemies doing!

"Banking": Holding back valuable and/or damaging information (indiscretions, faux pas, etc.) you've discovered about a person for use in blackmailing and/or disgracing them at a later, more opportune time.

Big Brother: Oppressive government, always watching. Coined by George Orwell in his 1948 novel *1984*. (*See* Orwellian)

Biometrics: System of scientific measurement of body parts and actions designed to give insight into intent. (*See* Tells)

Bio-Resources: People whose talents you can utilize to accomplish your goals.

Black Curtain, the: (Jp.) *Kuromaku*, lit. "string-puller." Generic: the veil of secrecy and skullduggery sinister cadres hide behind. Synonym for "smoke screen." Specific: the head of a Japanese yakuza crime family. (*See* Ilumi-nati, Synarchy.)

Black Science, the: Generic: any strategy, tactic, or technique used to undermine a person's ability to reason and respond for themselves. Coined by researcher C.B. Black. Generic: synonym for mind control and manipulation.

Bloodtie: Dangerous and damaging information we hold over another. (*See* The Killer "B"s)

C.H.A.O.S. Principle, the: "Create hurdles (hazards, hardships, etc.) and offer solutions," i.e., profiting from difficulties and "crisis" you have secretly created.

Ching and Chi: Chinese, direct and indirect (i.e., sneaky) actions. Also spelled "Zhing" and "Qi."

Cock-Blockin': Generic: deliberate, or inadvertent interference in the plans of another. Specific: interfering with the seduction plans of another person.

Cogniceuticals: Drugs designed to enhance or entrance the mind.

Cognitive Dissonance: Mental anxiety created when a person must reconcile their contradictory ideas and/or actions.

Cult-Speak: Special passwords and coded phrases cults and cliques use to identify one another while marginalizing "outsiders."

"Cutting-at-the-Edges": Coined by Miyamoto Musashi (1594–1645). When a powerful enemy cannot be attacked directly, undermine his confidence and ability to fight by attacking and otherwise eroding his comfort zone and support network (e.g., family, friends, and financial resources).

Dead Dog Ploy: Giving up superfluous information in order to keep more important information hidden.

Dim-mak: (Ch.) Death touch.

"Dropping Lugs" (a.k.a. Lyin' by Implyin'): Using innuendo and rumor to plant doubt and seed suspicion, especially intended to undermine another's credibility.

Dyshemism: Words used as weapons. (*See* Word Slavery)

Ekkyo: (Jp.) Divination methods that allow us to determine a victim's birth order and examine their interactions with others, especially close relatives.

ESP*ionage*: Research and/or application of "extra sensory perception" to gather intelligence, e.g., when spying (a.k.a. *Psi*-War, not to be confused with *PSYWAR*, synonym for psychological warfare in general).

Fakir: Hindu mystic. (*See* Siddhas) Also used generically to mean a swindler or charlatan.

False Flaggin': Pretending affiliation to a group to which you do not belong. (*See* Fard)

False Humility: To demur to another or pass up an opportunity to advance ourselves only because society and good manners say we should.

Fard: Literally, "to paint the face with cosmetics." Generic: to wear a false face; to assume a false identity, a.k.a. "False Flaggin'" (*See* Nation of Islam, *also see* Bloodties and The Killer "B"s in Section V).

Fifth Columnists: Individuals within an invaded country who (secretly) sympathize and provide assistance to foreign invaders and hostile foreign elements.

Finders: Nickname for The Ancient and Exalted Brotherhood of International Finders, a European secret society, reportedly founded in Paris 1776, linked to everyone from Benjamin Franklin to the Freemasons to the Illuminati.

Five Warning F.L.A.G.S., the: The five Gojo-goyoku weaknesses: fear, lust, anger, greed, and sympathy.

Gojo-goyoku: (Jp.) "Five Element Theory." Derived from the Chinese pseudo-science of wu-hsing, which teaches that all reality (including actions and attitudes) is composed of five basic forces: earth, air, fire, water, and void. In all things and all times, one of these elements is dominant. Each element has a corresponding element in opposition to it. (*See* the Five Warning F.L.A.G.S.)

Good Cop/Bad Cop: Interrogation ploy where one interrogator pretends to be your friend while the other verbally and/or physically assaults you.

Gov-Speak: The Capitol Hill run-around, a.k.a., spin.

GreyTalk: Words and phrases deliberately crafted to confuse the listener.

Half-Assin': Hesitation and second-guessing. Exactly what we want our enemy doing!

Hiracarrah: East Indian secret society of professional spies, agent provocateurs, and assassins. Influential on the development of European espionage techniques.

HUTA: Slang, "Head up their ass." Someone who doesn't want to know the truth and/or is too lazy or corrupt to seek out the truth; such slugs are sometimes referred to as "belonging to the HUTA tribe."

Hyori: (Jp.) Deception.

Illuminati, the: Generic: the ultimate secret society bugaboo and boogeyman. Whispered about for centuries, the Illuminati reportedly controls the world economy and pulls the strings of world politics from behind the "Black Curtain." Specific: secret society in Bavaria circa 1776. (*See* "Nine Unknown Men")

In-yo-jutsu: (Jp.) Tactics designed to unbalance an opponent, to sow doubt and distrust in his mind.

Isaacs: Synonymous with the psychological term "patriarchal castration," e.g., authority stifles creativity. Anyone who follows orders/authority without question. Term coined in 1930s by Eric Neumann, a student of Carl Jung, named for Issac, unquestionably obedient son of the Biblical patriarch Abraham.

Jodomon: (Jp.) "The way of the cat." Individuals who take this approach depend on tariki ("another's power"). (*See* Shodomon)

Jomon-jutsu: (Jp.) Use of special words and phrases designed to affect an individual's emotional stability, e.g., words evoking fear, lust, or patriotism.

Judo Principle, the: Objects in motion tend to stay in motion. In a physical confrontation, your opponent pushes, you pull (and sidestep), sprawling him face forward onto the floor. He pulls, instead of resisting simultaneously, you step forward and push, shoving him back and to the ground. In both instances, you add his strength to your own. Psychologically: someone attempts to bully you into agreeing with them. You at first appear to do so, switching to your own (true) agenda at the last instant (after they have already committed themselves and their money, etc.).

Jujushin: (Jp.) Identifies "10 Minds," or ten levels of understanding and functioning into which human beings can be categorized.

Junishi-do-jutsu: (Jp.) Employing the ancient art of Chinese astrology to determine a person's overall temperament as well as his weakest time of the day, when he is most susceptible to physical attack and mental manipulation.

Kami: (Jp.) Evil spirits.

Kiai-shin-jutsu: (Jp.) Tactics and techniques that directly attack the intended victim psychologically by "shouting" into his mind. (*See* Atari-kokoro)

Ki-dol: (Jp.) The ability to wield *ki* (Ch. *Chi*) force to influence and overpower another, e.g., especially through hypnosis.

Killer "B"s, the: Techniques for infiltrating an enemy's mind: blind, bribery, and blackmail, bloodties, brainwashing, bully, and bury.

Koan: (Jp.) Riddles used in Zen Buddhism designed to "short-circuit" a student's rational mind in order to bring it to an insightful breakthrough. Often used as a synonym for an unanswerable riddle.

Kuniochi: (Jp.) A female ninja.

Kuroi-kiri: (Jp.) "The Black Mist," confusion in general. The Mind Slayer's art.

Kuro-kakure: (Jp.) Skullduggery in general, a dark and hidden agenda.

Kuromaku: (Jp.) Lit " a string-puller," originally from Kabuki. (1) A yakuza chief. (2) *See* The Black Curtain.

Kyonin-no-jutsu: (Jp.) Using an enemy's superstitions against him.

Long-con: Involved and intricate confidence scheme, big risk being directly proportionate to big payoff. (*See* Short-con).

"Make your bones": To prove worth by accomplishing a difficult task. Primarily criminal usage.

Makoto: (Jp.) "The stainless mind." Makoto is a balanced state of mind allowing us to remain calm even in the most trying of circumstance. The development of makoto consists of the active cultivation and practice of two skills: *haragei* (awareness) and *rinkioken* (adaptability).

Mama, drama, and trauma: Slang term for the "nurture" influences in a person's life (as opposed to the "nature" influences).

Mark, the: The victim/target of a confidence scheme.

Masakatsu!: (Jp.) "By any means necessary." Strategy that allows for the use of any tactic or technique in order to achieve your goal (i.e., the end justifies the means). (*See* W.I.T.)

Meat Space: Real space-time, as opposed to Cyberspace, virtual computer reality, and interaction.

Mekura: Japanese, the "inner eye" (i.e., insight and intuition).

Mind Control: Deliberate domination of another's thoughts. (*See* Black Science)

Mind Manipulation: Exercising influence over another mind, either deliberately or inadvertently. (*See* Black Science)

Mind-dancing: Psychological warfare.

MindWar: Preemptive measures (propaganda, etc.) used to attack an enemy's mind, intended to sap his will to fight *before* physical war becomes necessary. Sun Tzu's ideal.

MK: Spook-speak for "mind control." Coincidentally, these same initials are used to identify the MERCK pharmaceutical company rumored to be responsible for helping government agencies develop cogniceuticals. (*See* Spook-speak)

Mushroom Treatment, the: Overall strategy for dealing with enemies (i.e., "Keep 'em in the dark and feed 'em plenty of bullshit!"), that is, (1) deny them access to true information, while you (2) feed them disinformation.

Nightside: (1) The subconscious "dark side" of your personality. What Freud called the id. (2) The secrets you bury and the ones your enemies dig up. (3) Slang for Indonesian criminal underworld.

Nine Unknown Men, the: (1) Used as a euphemism for the Illuminati, (2) multicultural myth-legend of nine enlightened "masters" who walk the earth at any given time. When one dies, another takes his (or her) place. In some versions, these nine rule the Illuminati.

Ninja: (Jp.) "To steal in." Assassin-spies originating in medieval Japan known for their stealth and skullduggery. Generic (small *n*): anyone who employs stealth and secrecy to accomplish their ends.

Occam's Razor: Rule of thumb that warns not to make a problem more complicated than necessary. The simplest explanation is usually the best explanation. The straightest path gets you there the fastest. Named for English scholar and philosopher William of Occam (also spelled "Ockham"), 1285–1349.

One-Eyed Snake: This strategy was composed of tactics and techniques intended to give outsiders the illusion the ninja possessed true magical powers, e.g., the power to strike down a foe from afar using ESP, kill with a single touch without so much as a mark left on the victim (*Dim mak*), and control others with mystical hypnosis. (*See* Yugen-shin-jutsu)

Orwellian: Totalitarian, intrusive invasion of privacy by Big Brother. From George Orwell's 1948 novel *1984*.

Ottimati: Archaic, Lt. "Men of Substance," "The Big Ones" (Lt. Grandi), those pulling the strings behind the scenes. (*See* Black Curtain)

Pakua: (Ch.) The "Eight Trigrams." Pakua are eight symbols, consisting of three lines each. Each symbol represents one of eight basic relationships and interactions of life. Sometimes spelled "Baqua."

Plausible Deniability: Spook-speak for being somewhere else when the fecal matter collides with the oscillating rotor. (*See* Spook-speak)

Propaganda: Rumor's big brother, or Big Brother's rumor.

Propheteering: The cult game. Generic, hiding behind religion for deceitful and devious purposes.

Psychotronics: Any electronic device used to enhance or entrance the mind. In 1970s Czechoslovakia, psychotronics was used as a synonym for parapsychology. (Ostrander & Schroeder, 1970)

Ronin: (Jp.) A masterless samurai. Generic: a rogue

Satsujin: (1) (Jp.) "Insight" (*See* tells). (2) One of four divisions of yakuza crime strategy, meting out "murder."

Satsujin-jutsu: (Jp.) Insights into the minds or natures of men.

Seishinshugi: (Jp.) Literally "mind over matter."

Sennin: (Jp.) Mind masters, Mind Assassins.

Seppuku: (Jp.) Ritual suicide.

Shadow-talk: Akin to Freudian Slips. (*See* Tells)

Shadow-walk: "Tells" and other body language itching and twitching that help expose a liar.

Shinjiraren!: (Jp.) "It boggles the mind!" Exclamation used when amazed and/or confused by something. Generically, techniques designed to amaze and confuse.

Shodomon: (Jp.) "The way of the monkey," depends on jiriki ("one's own strength"). Individuals with this approach to life are independent; journeying alone, finding their own way; keeping their own counsel; and binding their own wounds—both physically and psychically. On the one extreme, these kinds of people are rugged individualists. At the opposite extreme, they are stubborn isolationists and control freaks, unable to take another's counsel. (*See* Jodomon)

Short-con: Simple confidence schemes quickly executed. Small risk = small gain. (*See* Long-con)

Shuhari: (Jp.) "Circle." Your circle of family and friends and acquaintances.

Siddhas: (Skt. "powers") Enhanced powers of mind and body claimed by Hindu yoga mystics and fakirs. Sometimes used as the name for such masters themselves.

"Sons of Brutus," the: Those elements (primarily people) left over after an operation (e.g., palace coup, hostile corporate takeover) that may prove "troubling" (i.e., seek revenge!) at some future date. According to the

Romans (and Machiavelli), prudence calls for this element to be completely eliminated.

Spook-speak: Euphemism and code words used by intelligence agencies.

Suggestology: The science/art of suggestion. Includes and/or touches on hypnotism, the power of persuasion, propaganda, etc. Coined by Dr. Gregori Lozanov, Bulgaria. (*See* Ostrander and Schroeder, 1970)

Synarchy: Rule by secret societies, pulling the strings from behind the scenes.

Tantric: (Skt. "forbidden") Taboo mystical practices (drugs, sex, nigromancy, etc.) used by Hindu mystics as a shortcut to enlightenment and siddhas. Also spelled "Tantrik."

Tells: Body language and speech faux pas that inadvertently reveal what a person is *really* thinking and/or may reveal a person's unconscious desires and fears. Also known as Shadow-talk and Shadow-walk.

Tengu: (Jp.) "Demons": either black or red in color, they are master shapeshifters. When appearing in human form, they appear as little men wearing short cloaks (made of feathers, leaves, or straw) and wearing large black hats. Tengu were great swordsmen and possessed powers of magic and invisibility. Shinobi ninja convinced their superstitious enemies that they were descended from the tengu.

10 Minds, the: Buddhists use each of the "10 Minds" (jujushin) as stepping stones to enlightenment. For ninja, on the other hand, the jujushin was just another stumbling block to place in the path of a foe. These ten minds are: Goat's Mind, Fool's Mind, Child's Mind, Dead Man's Mind, No-Karma Mind, Compassionate Mind, Unborn Mind; Single-Truth Mind, No-Self Mind, and Secret Mind. Each of the ten minds contains the seed of the others.

Thought Reform: Brainwashing by any other name.

Wa: (Jp.) Your spirit, presence, or intention.

Warning Flags, the: The five weaknesses: fear, lust, anger, greed, and sympathy.

Wet Wear: The physical brain.

Wet Work: Spook-speak for "bloody" business.

W.I.T.: "Whatever it takes." (*See* Masakatsu!)

Word Slavery: The deliberate use of words and language to control and/or otherwise influence another human being. Includes the use of subliminals, culturally taboo words, slur words (insults), and purr words (lulling and soothing words).

Wu-hsing: (Ch.) "The Five Movers." This concept maintains that all reality is made up of five basic elements: earth (chi), air (fu), fire (la), water (sui), and void (ku).

X: Spook-speak/gov-speak for experiment.

Yakuza: Japanese Mafia.

Yugen-shin-jutsu: (Jp.) Literally "mysterious mind," uses various methods of hypnotism and subliminal suggestion to influence and control the minds of others.

Zen-zone: That level of functioning where stainless mental awareness (makoto) and physical awareness merge, allowing us to instantly and effortlessly adapt to rapidly shifting circumstance.

Zetsutjin: (Jp.) "Offspring of a talkative tongue"; an accomplished talker and manipulator. Generic: a mastermind, *a Mind Slayer!*

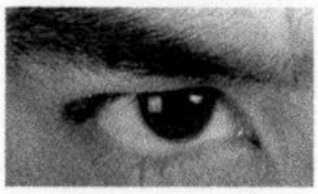

TABLE OF AUTHORITIES

Armstrong, Karen. *Muhammad: A Biography of the Prophet*. (HarperSanFrancisco, 1992).

Bhagavad-Gita (The Song of God). Misc. translations.

Baughman, Robert D., and Black, C. B. *666 Devilish Secrets of Islam* (Publication pending).

Corsi, Jerome, Ph.D. *The Obama Nation: Leftist Politics and the Cult of Personality*. (Simon & Schuster, 2008).

Cotterell, Arthur. *Chariot.* (Overlook Press, 2005).

Elgin, Suzette Haden, Ph.D. *Success with the Gentle Art of Verbal Self-Defense*. (Prentice Hall, 1989).

Ford, Charles V., M.D. *Lies! Lies! Lies! The Psychology of Deceit*. (American Psychiatric Press, Inc., 1996)

Hucker, Charles. *China's Imperial Past*. (Stanford University Press, 1975)

Humes, James C. *The Wit and Wisdom of Benjamin Franklin*. (Gramercy Books, 1995).

I-Ching (The Book of Changes). Misc. translations.

Kaplan, David E., and Dubro, Alec. *Yakuza.* (Addison-Wesley Publishing Co. Inc., 1986).

Kettle, Michael. *Sidney Reilly: The True Story of the World's Greatest Spy*. (St. Martin's Press, 1983).

King, Anthony. *Roman Gaul and Germany*. (University of California Press, 1990).

Ledeen, Michael A. *Machiavelli on Modern Leadership*. (Truman Talley Books/St. Martins, 1995).

Lepp, Ignace. *The Art of Being an Intellectual*. Trans. Bernard Murchiand. (McMillian & Co, 1968).

Lung, Haha, Dr. *The Ancient Art of Strangulation*. (Paladin Press, 1995).

———. *Ninja Craft*. (Alpha Publications of Ohio, 1997).

———. *Assassin! Secrets of the Cult of the Assassins.* (Paladin Press, 1997).

———. *Knights of Darkness: Secrets of the World's Deadliest Night-fighters.* (Paladin Press, 1998).
———. *Cao Dai Kung-fu.* (Loompanics Unlimited, 2002).
———. *Assassin!* (Citadel, 2004).
———. *Lost Fighting Arts of Vietnam.* (Citadel, 2006).
———. *The 99 Truths: Hannibal's Black Art of War.* (Publication pending).
Lung, Haha, Dr., and Prowant, Christopher B. *Black Science: Ancient and Modern Techniques of Ninja Mind Manipulation.* (Paladin Press, 2001).
———. *Shadowhand: Secrets of Ninja Taisavaki.* (Paladin Press, 2002).
———. *Mind Manipulation.* (Citadel, 2002).
———. *Theatre of Hell: Dr. Lung's Complete Guide to Torture.* (Loompanics Unlimited, 2003).
———. *Ninja Shadowhand: The Art of Invisibility.* (Citadel, 2004).
———. *Knights of Darkness.* (Citadel, 2004).
———. *Mind Control.* (Citadel, 2006).
———. *Mind Penetration.* (Citadel, 2007).
———. *Mind Fist.* (Citadel, 2008).
———. *Mental Domination.* (Citadel, 2009).
———. *Ultimate Control.* (Publication pending by Citadel, 2010).
———. *Mind Assassins.* (Publication pending by Citadel, 2010).
Lung, Haha, Dr., and Tucker, Eric. *Nine Halls of Death: Ninja Secrets of Mind Mastery.* (Citadel, 2007).
Lyman, Stanford M., and Scott, Marvin B. *A Sociology of the Absurd* (2nd ed.) (General Hall, Inc., 1989).
Machiavelli, Niccolo. *The Discourses.* Original translation Leslie J. Walker. (Penguin Books, ed 1998).
———. *The Prince.* 1513. Misc. translation
Mahabharata. Misc. translations.
Musashi, Miyamoto. *Go Rin No Sho (A Book of Five Rings)* (1645). Misc. translations.
Mead, Frank S. *Handbook of Denominations in the United States.* (Abingdon Press, 1975).
Natl. Geographic Society. *Greece & Rome*, 1968 et.al.
Newsweek, "Mind Reading Is Now Possible," 1.21.08:22.
Omar, Ralf Dean. "Ninja Death Touch: The Fact and the Fiction," *Black Belt*, September, 1989.
———. *Death on Your Doorstep: 101 Weapons in the Home.* (Alpha Publications of Ohio, 1995).
Only, Joshua. *Wormwood: The Terrible Truth about Islam.* (The Only Mission, 2009).

Ostrander, Shela, and Schroeder, Lynn. *Psychic Discoveries behind the Iron Curtain*. (Prentice Hall, Inc., 1970).

Paul, Annie Murphy. "Mind Reading," *Psychology Today*, Sept./Oct 2007:72–79).

Price, Robert M. "Of Myth and Men." *Free Inquiry,* Winter, 1999.

Reilly, Sidney. *The Adventures of Sidney Reilly*. (London, 1931).

Ringer, Robert J. *Looking Out for #1*. 1977.

———. *Winning Through Intimidation*. (Crest/Fawcett, 1993).

Ronson, Jon. *The Men Who Stare at Goats*. (Simon & Schuster, 2005).

Sawyer, Ralph D. *The Seven Classics of Ancient China*. (Basic Books, 1993).

Skinner, Dirk. *Street Ninja: Ancient Secrets for Surviving Today's Mean Streets*. (Barricade Books, 1995).

Stine, Jean Marie. *Double Your Brain Power.* 1997

Sun Bin. *Ping-fa (The Lost Art of War)*. Misc. translations, c. 200 B.C.

Sun Tzu. *Ping-fa (The Art of War)*. Misc. translations, c. 500 B.C.

Schwartz, Stephen. *The Two Faces of Islam: The House of Sa'ud from Tradition to Terror*. (Doubleday, 2002).

Seth, Ronald. *Secret Servants: A History of Japanese Espionage*. (Farrar, Straus and Cudahy, 1957).

Tepes, Vlad. *Dracula's Art of War*. Misc. translations.

Than, Ker. "Step by Step, Your Brain Mimics His Moves," *Psychology Today*, July/August 2005.

Tokitsu, Kenji. *Miyamoto Musashi: His Life and Writings*. (Shambhala, 2004).

Upanishads. Misc. translations.

Victorian, Dr. Armen. *Mind Controllers*. (Vision Books/Satin Pub. Ltd., 1999; Lewis International, 2000).

Vidocq, François Eugéne. *Memoirs of Vidocq: Master of Crime*. (AK Press/Nabat edition, 2003).

Voltaire. *Philosophical Dictionary*, Misc. translations. (1976).

Wang, Sam, and Aamodt, Sander. "Your Brain Lies to You," *Cleveland Plain Dealer, 6.29.08:G3*.

Webster, Nesta. *Secret Societies and Subversive Movements*. (1924).

Wilson, Colin. *Rogue Messiahs*. (2000).

Whitlock, Chuck. *Chuck Whitlock's Scam School*. (Macmillan, 1997).

Yuan and Xiao. *Tales of Emperor Qin Shihuag*. (Foreign Language Press, 1997).

Zaffuto, Dr. Anthony. Alphagenics: How to Use Your Brainwaves to Improve Your Life. (1974).

Zen and Shinto: The Story of Japanese Philosophy. (Greenwood Press, 1959).

GREAT BOOKS, GREAT SAVINGS!

When You Visit Our Website:

www.kensingtonbooks.com

You Can Save 30% Off The Retail Price
Of Any Book You Purchase!

- **All Your Favorite Kensington Authors**
- **New Releases & Timeless Classics**
- **Overnight Shipping Available**
- **All Major Credit Cards Accepted**

Visit Us Today To Start Saving!

www.kensingtonbooks.com

All Orders Are Subject To Availability.
Shipping and Handling Charges Apply.